SUPERHUMAN

AWAKEN.
TRANSFORM.
SAVE THE #$%*ING WORLD.

KATE GANCI

BlastOff Publishing LLC.
Powered by H.A.B.I.T

Copyright © 2019 by Kate Ganci
ISBN: 978-0-578-60251-6

All rights reserved. No part of this publication may be reproduced, stored in a retrieval system or transmitted in any form or by any means without the prior written permission of the author or publisher.
*Most names have been changed for the protection and privacy of the individuals.

*The information provided throughout this book reflects my own opinions, my own theories, and my own knowledge. It is for informational purposes only, not intended as a substitute or replacement for health care, psychiatric care, or the medical advice of physicians. Health care should not be substituted or neglected without proper management or approval by a doctor.

SUPERHUMAN is not meant to lure you into a fad, a cult, or a belief system. No one is trying to financially gain from you by selling you a dream. You have your own dreams, and I want to empower you to reach them. One person living their dream influences those around them and MY DREAM is for love-of-life to spread like wildfire; ego and greed are not welcome here. This is an opportunity for enlightenment which leads to a happy, fulfilling life. My first and main intention is to help people, to help animals, to help this world; to help anyone and anything that I can. I can't make something happen simply by writing a book, but *you* can by reading it and putting it to use. A book is only words on paper. Words are not powerful until they resonate, until they give you that little sign that you're meant to do something with that knowledge. The knowledge that I give you can lead you to self-exploration. Allow yourself to open to the truth within; allow for the unveiling of *real truths* as they are, and as they could be. Life is not as we see it when we are profoundly asleep.

I was once told by a beautiful, enlightened soul that there are three types of people: asleep people, drowsy people, and awake people. People who are asleep are, well, asleep. Drowsy people are either awakening, want to awaken, or are just not ready to awaken. It's no one else's job to nudge them. They must wake themselves up and allow those who are sleeping to decide whether they're going to wake up as well or pull the wool—I mean the sheet—over their eyes and fall back to sleep.

I don't know which of the three applies to you, but since you're reading this, you're probably not sleeping…

For my Benevolent One

ACKNOWLEDGEMENTS

Publishing a book has always been a dream of mine. Since elementary school, I've been creating little books. This book was my biggest project, and by far the most draining yet healing thing I've ever done. I want to thank all who helped hurt me and helped heal me—you contributed to my growth as a writer and most importantly, as a human being.

Mom, thank you for modeling the most compassionate, beautiful heart. You remain loving and caring no matter what, and I'm grateful that you're my mom; I got to see how to be a good person through you. You're the epitome of class and the kind of pure soul we need to see more of on this earth. Thank you for always letting me be who I am.

Dad, thank you for your strength, your stubbornness, your no-nonsense attitude, and your unconditional love. Your proverbs and words of wisdom have never gone unheard. You taught me a lot by just being who you are. You're a strong soul, and I'm grateful for you.

Sal, thank you, for in your life and in your death, teaching me the depth and power of forgiveness. You gave me one of my greatest life lessons.

Jay Cristopher, thank you for all your love and support. Your perseverance through life has always been both impressive and inspiring to me. Thank you for always believing in me.

Janet Paradine, thank you for this memory: In fifth grade, you looked fiercely and proudly into my eyes and said, "Kate, you are going to be an author,"…and I never forgot it or believed otherwise. Thank you for being a real teacher.

Frank Nicoletti, thank you for your help with editing in the early stages of this book. I am so grateful for all your personal time, knowledge, and insight.

Sarah Hynes, my editor, thank you for your hard work and kind words. You are appreciated.

Lisa DeSpain, my editor and project manager, thank you for your hard work, thorough attention to detail, and for making these final steps go smoothly. You have been of great help.

Kurtis Lee Thomas, thank you for all of your insight and for guiding me through every step of the publication process. It has been a breeze thanks to you. You and your team are greatly appreciated.

Rivenis, thank you for your incredible artwork which far exceeded my expectations and vision for the cover. Much respect.

Dear Human,

I have a question for you…

Do you ever feel that you might have an important role to play on this earth? Deep down you *know* that you aren't maximizing your full potential because you can't seem to ignore this intense urgency from within, pleading with you to do more with your life, to do something that you love. Maybe you feel stuck. Time is passing, your routines are waiting, and you just can't do anything about it. Or maybe you don't feel worthy…*how could I be important? What makes me special?* Then you're back where you started, before ever giving your feelings a fighting chance. It's as if you're opening your eyes to see the sun shining through your window…the day looks promising, but instead of getting up, you're swayed by the urge to close the blinds and stay in the sheltered darkness and comfort of your familiar bed. You toss and turn before falling back to sleep because there's something inside of you, fighting for the light.

You're not alone. Most of us are running in place. We may allow ourselves to dream of another life, but it seems that reality will always jolt our imagination, reminding us that "it doesn't work like that." Over time we become trapped in a low vibration—a feeling of unworthiness, sadness, and hopelessness. We're glued to the things we're familiar with because fear won't allow us to deviate from our tracks. When faced with problems, we tend to tighten the reins on our ambition instead of embracing change and jumping on an opportunity for growth. Why? Because we obsess over calamities and responsibilities, *ON OUR FEARS*. The thought of altering even one little thing in our repetitive lives is terrifying, even if it's for the greater good. We wonder, *What will happen if…? What would have happened if…? What's going to happen if…?* As we're reminded of the limits of time, we fear, *How will I die? When will I die? What will happen after I die?* We dwell on everything that's happened and fear everything that might. The times that we laugh, love, and feel joy seem so insignificant in the shadow of tough times. Is that just the story of life? Is that how it works? *Or*, are we so lost in reality that we become lost within ourselves? Does our wonder of *what could be* get shut down just as it did when we were children, when we were told certain things don't and can't exist? Is this possibly what's wrong with us?

The answer is YES. It's *obvious* we don't do the things that we are meant to do because we're tied down to things not meant for us. We are distracted from truth and take comfort in lies to avoid taking risks. Risks are scary, but they keep us alive. They help us break limits and help us persevere through failures. Risks allow us to **choose** our direction. But we more than often, choose to just stay put, constantly falling back on the thought, *the risk will outweigh the reward.* This is a fear mindset. The opposite way of thinking that attracts all the love; all the good things meant for us in this life.

Let me break it to you…this "reality" that we live in, isn't real. It was created by man-made fears that transformed into limitations over time. We fear life so much that we limit our abilities to the point where self-doubt debilitates us and controls everything from how we act, to what happens to us. What am I talking about? We create our own reality; we choose to live the way we do. We choose to be unhappy, fearful; we choose our circumstances; we choose to welcome degeneration in every aspect of our human lives …we just don't know we're choosing it. Why are we like this? Because we don't know who we are; we can't see it. We were never told the truth. We were never taught that we have the power to not let circumstances control us; that we are much bigger than what we see and feel about ourselves, and that there *is* a purpose for our existence.

DEAR HUMAN...

When we finally discover the truth, our dreams become our reality...*by our own will*. It's called **an awakening**—a conscious recognition of the soul that begins with changing your life, changing your course, and allowing yourself to be guided with love through every decision you make. First you must open your mind to become aware of not only your true self, but of this universe, so that you can experience peace and joy, inevitably.

Acknowledging that all the good and all the bad in your life is there for a reason, and not meaningless, is what will shake you and set you free. You'll become a powerful, knowledgeable, happy being, capable of living your dreams. If you don't see that or understand it yet, you will after you read this book ...and I'm not being cocky. You're going to take something, *something*, from all this information and prove to yourself that the world works differently than you had once imagined. I've learned things I never thought were possible, and it made me realize how *ridiculous* the way we live our lives is. We don't see it because we're too busy "dealing." WE ARE SCREWED UP. We need to wake up; we need to transform in major ways. If you want to know how to do that, I can certainly tell you, but you must be open to it. You must be ready for *something else*. Are you? If so, keep reading...

CONTENTS

Part I DEATH OF THE EGO

Chapter 1 THE WEIGHT OF THE WORLD 19
    Breaking points are turning points
    What's a Superhuman?
    It's a mistake, not a death sentence
    The "F" word

Chapter 2 PURSUIT OF HAPPINESS 29
    Burning desires
    Accepted or rejected
    WARNING Parents
    It doesn't sting anymore
    How to not ruin your child
    It's not them, it's you!
    Grow a pair!
    Revenge is a dish best …not served
    No one is perfect
    A knife in your back

Chapter 3 FACE EVERYTHING AND RISE 79
    When fear comes to life
    She loves me, she loves me not
    Airing out dirty laundry
    Is it your fault?
    Give it a giggle and get over it!

Chapter 4 GHOSTS OF MEMORIES 95
   Is your past haunting you?
   Time is fleeting
   Remembering love, not pain
   Spirit guides

Chapter 5 UNDOING THE DAMAGE 105
   Raising and lowering kids
   Reversible damage
   Poisoning the children
   Walking in their shoes
   I'm innocent!
   Blame shifting

Chapter 6 DON'T DRINK THE POISON! 119
   Forgiveness isn't about them
   The Four Agreements
   Are you self-aware?
   Round and round we go
   Breaking the speed limit
   Raising Superhumans
   Sleeping with the enemy!

Chapter 7 LET GO, OR BE DRAGGED 137
   Why can't you let it go?
   The Sedona Method
   That voice in your head
   Breaking through prison walls
   How to get rich
   The Law of Attraction
   Why me?
   How to do magic
   A realist doesn't live in reality
   Half-full or half-empty?
   Breaking habit!
   Secret to freedom

Chapter 8 RELAX! YOU'RE FINE 165
   Should I give them the finger?
   The real meaning of FEAR
   You got skills!
   How to be a goal digger

Chapter 9 KILLING THE EGO 177
   Id, Ego & Superego
   The Ego Is One Hell of a Drug
   How to kill the ego
   I came, I saw, I surrendered
   How to be attractive
   Stop loading your fear gun

Part II BIRTH OF THE SOUL

Chapter 10 WHO AM I? 189
   Shhh, nature is speaking
   Souls and skin suits
   Real recognize real
   Tragic inspiration
   Many Lives, Many Masters
   You ARE forgiven
   Lesson learned?
   Fairytales are not far from the truth
   Astral Traveling
   End time or start time?
   Dead doesn't mean gone

Chapter 11 THE RAW TRUTH 207
   The World's Alarm Clock
   Playing the "opposite game"
   Oh baby I like it raw
   Antidote
   Brain Game
   Say no to GMO
   Good old Mary Jane
   Set it off

Chapter 12 REAL EYES REALIZE REAL LIES 249
Rainy Brain, Sunny Brain
The eyes never lie
Eyes are the windows to…your health
Baby blue

Chapter 13 BEAUTY AND THE BEASTS 263
Humans are the savages
How intelligent are animals?
RED ALERT!
Still Breastfeeding?

Chapter 14 WHO'S GOT YOUR BACK? 277
Brain gains
F what they say!
No longer a victim
Sleepwalkers

PART III LIFE

Chapter 15 NATURAL BORN HEALERS 293
The Healing Power of Water
Words kill
The most magical element
Trauma drama
You're a powerhouse!
Meditation over medication
Mr. Miyagi wasn't playing
Think and Grow Rich
You can change the world
Superhuman tips

Chapter 16 THE END…BUT JUST THE BEGINNING 323
The revolution won't be televised
Embody the change!

PART I
DEATH OF THE EGO

CHAPTER 1

THE WEIGHT OF THE WORLD

"You will never be happier than you expect. To change your happiness, change your expectation."

—Bette Davis

Have you ever been so emotionally overwhelmed that your stomach physically hurt? And just when you thought you were done with the shit, your gut rumbled? Every time I tried to be happy, I was held back. Belly aches, headaches, heart aches… it was always something. Sound familiar? Welcome *friend*.

While I had never been diagnosed as depressed, I used to be very down about life; things were constantly going wrong. I didn't get it because I thought I was a good person and bad things don't happen to good people, right? WRONG. Bad things happen to everyone! Yes, some cards are worse than others, but how each person plays the hand they are dealt is what determines how things will *continue* to go in their lives. I learned that I was creating my own universe of misery and while I'm in a good place now, it *was* a rocky road to get here. Take what I've been through and recognize how I came out of it so that you can apply the lessons from my mistakes, to your life. *Your road can be much smoother.*

• •

To me, happiness is being totally carefree in mind and body. It's the feeling you have when you laugh from the bottom of your stomach. Your mood is elevated and all you want to do is smile. I always thought it was something that begins to slip away as a child grows, never to fully return. Going through bad relationships, watching my parents argue, dealing with personal issues, coping with the deaths of loved ones, and living with a violent sibling, I figured it was all downhill from there. Not only was I unhappy, but I was angry. I let my past experiences alter my state of mind which ended up altering my body.

Looking back I see myself perpetually, yet subconsciously eat my way to a temporary state of happiness because I didn't like my life. I was stressed out, in pain, unhappy, unhealthy, overweight, and feeling very badly about myself. I would describe it as hopelessness—hopeless with people, with myself, with life in general. My brain had spun a web of negativity and I was trapped in my own misery.

How did I snap out of it? What was it that changed everything? What allowed me to let go of regret and see the true beauty in this world, the true beauty in myself? What's changing my eye color? What's changing my body? Most importantly, how did I discover happiness? AWARENESS THROUGH SELF-OBSERVATION. You can't correct a problem until you're consciously aware of your own mistakes! As light always cancels darkness, the light of my new awareness will always cancel the darkness of my past. Simply put, I live in the moment.

• •

I feel like everyone is in search of happiness, yet the world is filled with sad people. Everyone's always arguing, complaining, feeling

THE WEIGHT OF THE WORLD

sorry for themselves, or talking about their misery…and it sucks. If you feel like you fit in here, THERE'S A BIGGER PICTURE THAN YOUR CURRENT UNHAPPINESS! I've seen it and I want to show you.

Regret is a word we're all familiar with; I especially can relate. I used to wish *so badly* that I could take back certain moments, you know, rewind time. It would drive me crazy, yet I'd repeat the very things I was beating myself up over! What was wrong with me? It was the constant return to unhealthy relationships and the way I treated my body. Trust me, I knew I was making poor choices, but I was stuck. I was so unhappy with myself that I ran back to the things that were causing my misery, searching for a source of comfort. And even though I'd feel guilty or angry with myself, I couldn't stop! I knew where I wanted to be in life, I just felt I couldn't get there.

> I KNEW WHERE I WANTED TO BE IN LIFE, I JUST FELT I COULDN'T GET THERE.

Rushing into so many poor decisions led me to regret *everything* about myself, to become haunted by what could have been, by *who* I could have been. The same question unceasingly ran through my head: *What if?* What if I didn't get involved in bad relationships? Would men still be walking all over me? Would I be less fucked up? What if I didn't experience so much betrayal? Would I be naïve, or would I have no trust issues? What if I had stayed home the night my brother went crazy? Would the blood have been mine or could I have stopped it? What if I didn't have hardships in life? Would I be weak or happier? What if!? What if!? WHAT IF!?

Is there something *you* regret? Whether it was something life changing or something as small as *I wish I would've said that differently*? Well let me tell you… it's all bullshit! When we regret past mistakes, we're trying to re-do the past. The past is over; it's untouchable, so why do we continuously reach for it?

SUPERHUMAN

What I've come to understand is that spending life trying to figure out life, is a waste of life. It doesn't matter how badly you want to know how it would have turned out *if...* you'll never know! Everything that you do and everything that happens to you leads to something else. Metaphorically speaking, we enter our doors of choice but once they close behind us, they're locked forever. So, it's important to not only choose the right doors, but to stop trying to open the ones from the past! Upon looking back, there really were no wrong doors if you eventually got yourself to the right destination. I didn't always understand that; I blamed my circumstances for my shortcomings, not my choices.

• •

THE TURNING POINT:

The epiphany that everything in my life was in *my* control, came to me when I hit rock bottom. After years of feeling mentally abandoned by my loved ones, disgusted with cheating boyfriends, *disgusted with myself,* let down by every one of my friends, and just plain sick of getting nowhere…SUFFERING had finally caused me to reach my breaking point! I saw my world at a standstill and realized nothing was going to change; it wasn't going to get any better, unless *I* made it better. The truth is that sometimes the darkest times in our lives help us see the light; they awaken us to a different way of living.

> BY GAINING AN UNDERSTANDING OF MYSELF, I WAS ABLE TO TRANSFORM INTO WHAT I LIKE TO CALL, A SUPERHUMAN!

How did I make this change? Through "**Self-Observation!**" This was my awakening: the beginning of my personal transformation, the unveiling of truth. By gaining an understanding of myself, I was able to physically, mentally, and spiritually transform into what I like to call, a **Superhuman**! What is my definition of a **Superhuman**? Does it mean that I think I'm superior to others? No, it means that I'm superior to the old me, better than I ever imagined I could be, better than I ever imagined I could feel! It's an empowered, constructive, emotional, and physical state of excellence, enabling me to do whatever I want to do with unshakable confidence. Do you want to know how I achieved this, or how I maintain it? It's really simple if you could learn to do one thing for a change… focus on the inner you! How do you do that?

1—Listen to how you feel inside
2—Observe how you behave

You will begin to understand why you do what you do. When you figure that out, you can change anything you're not happy with.

• •

I began this process by observing everything I was doing, good and bad, and then examining the root of the behavior to gain an understanding for it. Why was this important? Because you can't correct mistakes until you know why you made them! By taking responsibility for the direction of my life, I was then able to change its course. Without that responsibility and awareness, I was powerless; I was a victim to people, events, and circumstances.

The first major issue I tackled was REGRET. I knew I needed to get over the past! I was torturously "holding onto memories" of experiences that I couldn't change and simultaneously trying to figure out if I didn't *do that* or *go through that*, then maybe *this* would have happened. You've probably done the same, right? It's a ridiculous longing for different outcomes instead of seeing mistakes for what they truly are …valuable **lessons**! When I realized how backwards my thinking was, I snapped out of it and understood that the experiences I regretted actually did me some good! For instance, I grew wiser from dealing with devious people. Suffering is the best teacher for transformation and change. The "sting" presents us with possibilities and opportunities that lie just beneath our pain. Once we dissolve pain or regret by **releasing** it, possibilities and opportunities will surface.

SUPERHUMAN

As human beings, we're capable of incredible things if we don't let emotions get in the way. When we eliminate negative feelings, we're in a good mood, we're feeling positive, we're confident…we make better **choices**! I know it's hard to *always* do *everything* right, but every conscious effort we make to be happy in the moment and make a good choice will be recognized and rewarded. Good choices bring about new opportunities and experiences that we weren't destined for when we were allowing negative emotions to control us.

Are you following me? Let's say you hit someone who upset you and now you regret it. First, understand and accept that you and only you let yourself get to that point. Then when you find out where the emotion originally comes from, you can release it. This is what will allow you to FEEL and act differently next time around and make a different choice, a BETTER choice, which will change everything.

Starting to understand? Whether it is something as quiet as a thought or something as loud as an action, it will create something else, like ripples in time; every single choice changes our future. Moral of the story: We can't keep repeating negative behaviors and letting emotions run our lives if, in the end, they screw everything up!

Do you see how *you* affect your life? If you don't yet, then ask yourself this… have you ever missed out on something because you failed to seize the moment? Why did you fail? Was it because of anxiety, insecurity, feeling unworthy, sadness, or anger? I can almost guarantee you missed out because of a negative feeling. When I identified this issue in myself, I stopped harboring those bad feelings and finally felt peace. *You can do this too!*

• •

We can never fully embrace a state of peace if we're constantly in a state of regret. To regret is to live in the past. We're only alive in the present! So, what has this hold on us? What's causing us to make poor decisions and then lament over them later? I'll give you a hint; it's a four-letter word, the "F" word …FEAR; it consumes our lives.

THE WEIGHT OF THE WORLD

We fear everything about ourselves, and our experiences affect us so strongly that we're scared of our past, we're scared of our present, and we're scared of how our past affects our present! WHY ARE WE LIKE THIS???

Think about the many narcissistic, angry, and unjust people in this world. The cruelest ones are usually the most fearful because they were so damaged by life. They had to create a rock-hard exterior to protect and guard themselves. It makes sense but it shouldn't be that way! Our traumas need to be released, relinquished! In any form, they are diseases of the mind, the force that controls everything the body does and feels! THOUGHTS ARE **POWERFUL**. Are your traumas affecting you? Are you *snoozing* through life or are you "**awake**," living every day to its fullest potential? Are you *really* happy? *I wasn't.* Anger was stored in my body every time I felt regret or let others affect me, and while it made me tough, it BLOCKED any love I could have for myself, any chance to really be happy …until I learned to let it go. Now I maintain happiness by staying in the moment, enjoying the moment, and not looking back. When we look behind us, we can't see the possibilities ahead.

> WE CAN NEVER FULLY EMBRACE A STATE OF PEACE IF WE'RE CONSTANTLY IN A STATE OF REGRET.

• •

To achieve a state of peace, there's something else we *must* do to intensely experience it. After my awakening, I overcame something I had struggled with for many years, something that made my blood boil and my emotions run rapid. I was able to **let go** of my anger and **forgive** my brother for everything he did that negatively impacted my life. Those things had seemed unforgivable until I learned how stupid anger is, and how easy forgiveness truly is, from reading the book, *The Healing Power of Water*, by Masaru Emoto. It explains it so simply and I'll get more into that later but, I want you to know that my true realization of being at my happiest was whenever I was in a state of pure love, not feeling hostility from within. Why? Because when you release anger, love takes over. It's extraordinarily euphoric to be free of negativity, to be purely loving. It's peaceful! And forgiveness is not only about others, it's also about letting go of any bad feelings you have towards yourself! Not being able to forgive someone, *especially* if that someone is you, means not being able to fully move forward with your life, not being able to allow yourself to **just be**. Don't you want to achieve tranquility in this chaotic world? Peace and joy can be experienced right now by simply letting go, by forgiving. Can you let go? Will you? When?

Choosing, consciously or unconsciously, to hate or to be angry will negate love, peace of mind, and of course, happiness. YOU CAN'T BE HAPPY WHEN YOU'RE ANGRY; it's one or the other! So, for a lot of us, "letting go" of our pain is the ultimate forgiveness. We're freeing the emotion, and freeing ourselves by forgiving someone else but, we may just not know how to do that yet.

• •

The more you know about life and how it works, the easier it will be for you to *truly* forgive. Just saying *I forgive you* doesn't always release the frustrating emotion you're holding onto. Why? Even though it's a positive action, it's not the action of "letting go"- the *ultimate* forgiveness, the release of negative energy from YOUR body. I talk a lot about living in the present moment and allowing things to "just be," because it's bliss! The sense of "everything's ok and everything will be ok" takes over and any bad feelings skedaddle! When you fight against the will of the world because you can't understand it, you resist the beautifully lit flow of life and instead stay captivated by the dark. Darkness is there to show us how to find the light; it's a lesson; a metaphysical experience that leads to self-growth …if we can allow ourselves to see that. So, give value to both the good *and* the bad in your life. Everything happens as it's meant to and all you need to do

THE WEIGHT OF THE WORLD

is be the best you, you can be. You do that by making good choices and knowing that no matter what bad choices someone else makes, it's all part of the plan and will iron itself out.

• •

"Darkness cannot drive out darkness; only light can do that. Hate cannot drive out hate; only love can do that."
—Rev. Dr. Martin Luther King, Jr.

CHAPTER 2

PURSUIT OF HAPPINESS

As you read my story, you may feel you can't relate to my experiences on a personal level because perhaps you haven't been through similar things. However, my story may help you understand what we all experience when it comes to hardships, what makes hardships *hard*: fear. Anything unpleasant is meant to empower us. If instead it brings us down, we've accepted a negative feeling that stemmed from fear. When we allow those kinds of feelings to take hold of us, they only create more hardships and more fears. I allowed negative feelings from my experiences to grow into more intense emotions as time passed. These feelings affected my quality of life, my happiness…for one reason only…I accepted them!

When you accept negative feelings, you accept fear. Anger, sadness, and frustration are all fear-driven emotions, and when you hold onto them, you leave no room for love or happiness or any other good feelings because YOU'RE NOT LOVING YOURSELF. *You* can't have love for *you*, if you don't protect yourself from hurtful feelings. The power to reject them comes from within, from "the knowing" of your own self-worth. If you're not using that power, you're either scared or you're just not aware of it. Be aware and be brave, and understand that anything you experience in life, no matter how bad, can be received as good if you see the reality in it. How? When you read my story, think about yourself. Think about the choices you've made. Have you allowed something someone said or did to continuously affect you for too much time after the act? Have you repeatedly made bad choices? If so, then pay attention to the lessons I learned from my mistakes, the ways I learned to pull myself out of suffering, and you'll be able to understand too. I did it by coming to simple understandings about life. When you can finally make sense of it all, you can stop feeding into the things that hold you back. I've successfully changed many aspects of my life including, but not limited to, diet, attitude, and awareness… and now I want to help you. It's all so easy once you know how to do it! I want people to not just be reaching, barely touching their dreams, but to wrap their arms around them with the biggest bear hug! Do you want happiness? You can have it. IT *IS* OBTAINABLE.

· ·

One day, I took all my adversity of being mistreated and mistreating myself and used it as fuel to ignite a **burning desire** within. I desired change and simply made it happen. How? I transformed my mind, body, and spirit by digging deep within, and allowing myself to see things I never saw before. There's much more to this universe than the average mind can imagine without the knowledge of it.

    I want you to understand this…WE'RE ALL SPECIAL; we all have a purpose for being here. It's the things we go through that usually keep us from discovering it or acting on it, when they should be the very things that make us march courageously toward it! We experience both pain and happiness for a reason. The pain is not there to torture us, it's there to guide us, to help us become aware of our life's purpose. If you let it defeat you, you're missing the whole point!

    From lesson to lesson, we have the chance to change. Those who wake up and learn their lessons change the course of their lives for the better. Those who don't are trapped; they see no way out. Open your mind and your heart and you will understand why you had to go through things. Don't lose faith in life or in yourself because there is a reason for everything, and there's no doubt in *my* mind that I'm on this earth for a reason. It's my responsibility and my dream to share this with you, to tell my story, to tell the truth.

> DON'T LOSE FAITH IN LIFE OR IN YOURSELF BECAUSE THERE IS A REASON FOR EVERYTHING.

Right now, I'm happy! I feel great, and I feel like I look great. Fuck great, I'm *fantastic*; better than I've ever been! However, things weren't always this way…

MY STORY

I grew up in a small town on Long Island, New York. I can't remember much about being young, but I remember elementary years were happy times for me, with many friends and very few cares. I accepted everyone; I liked everyone. As I got older, things changed. Personas developed and disappointment in people became a growing problem. I felt those moments of happiness slip away as reality shifted.

• •

There were a few different groups that I bounced around, but my main clique was "the popular" girls. They were the root of my growing disappointment.

It started when my best friend became jealous that I befriended a girl who had just moved to town. She acted spiteful and it was shocking to me because it was new, it was hurtful, and it marked the beginning of my loss of trust in people.

You probably know how it feels when someone you trust turns into your enemy. Most people do and it's painful, but there's always a lesson to be learned. I didn't see the silver lining back then, but I do now. You can too, by remembering that pain is meant to give you strength and awareness of self-purpose.

When middle school started, things only got worse for me. The girls would constantly talk shit about each other, and I felt I couldn't rely on anyone; I resented it. It made me develop a trust complex because I thought, *If I can't trust my friends, who can I trust?* The truth is that I was partly to blame. Where was my head at when I continued to hold onto those friendships? Distancing myself, thinking maybe things would get better in my absence over and over again, was like repeatedly running into a brick wall! Don't get me wrong, it's great to forgive but when there's no change after forgiveness, what's the point of sticking around? This cycle continued throughout my school years, going back and forth between friends. Why did I do it? It was because I missed people for their good qualities! It's easy to forget the bad when you miss someone. That's a big reason people return to unhappy relationships. The truth is the person in the wrong doesn't deserve the other's companionship if they continue their behavior, and the other person doesn't deserve to keep being let down. It's a **choice**…a conscious effort to not allow someone to influence what we know is right. Being aware, thinking realistically, is how we make good choices.

> PAIN IS MEANT TO GIVE YOU STRENGTH AND AWARENESS OF SELF-PURPOSE.

• •

Growing up, one thing that kept me sane was always having a group of guy friends. I could see the blatant difference in how they acted. *BOYS* just want to have fun. There's no jealousy about who hangs out with whom and you better believe that if there's shit talked, it's done to your face. I always felt comfortable around them despite being looked at as "the bad girl."

PURSUIT OF HAPPINESS

It's important to know who you are and what makes you happy. If I had to end up with a reputation to be myself, then what exactly was I losing? Friends who really didn't care about me? When you're a kid, trying to fit in is a big deal. If sacrificing your soul by changing who you are or what you believe in is required to hang out with certain people, you're only doing yourself an injustice! Parents should talk about that with their children; they should teach them to be genuine and honest so they can weed out people who will do them no good.

• •

When kids start getting into trouble, it's usually because of a crowd they want to impress. It's up to them to choose friends and to choose how they make those friends. Have you ever seen a bunch of kids interact? There are leaders, followers, dictators, troublemakers, peacemakers, and rankings among groups. Don't you want your child to have a positive role? Don't you want them to choose wisely? Talk to them! Let them know what good and bad character looks like so they can spot it in others! Give them *real*, honest direction and they'll be able to make good, confident, personal decisions! If you build your child's self-awareness and integrity from an early age, you'll see how it helps them make good choices throughout their lives.

Let's face it! School is tough for kids and it seems to be getting harder for the newer generations. Bullying is a serious issue. It's disgusting that we're teaching our children to live with so much fear in their hearts…and I'm not only talking about the victims of bullies. The bullies are the kids with the most fear. At that time in their lives, most don't understand that reputation and "fitting in" doesn't matter!

After school is over and you're in the real world, you find far more people who will accept you for you. You meet people just like you who enjoy and believe in the things you do. School, high school especially, is a joke. Ten years down the road, you forget most of it because you grow and experience so many things. The problem for kids is that it's almost impossible to be aware of that while they're *in* the situation. That's why so many kids feel misunderstood. So many take their own lives because they can't see how great and different the future will be. School is temporary. Emotions are temporary.

If you are a parent, you can set your children up for success by helping them understand that things will change. Give them the tools to pull themselves up out of their lows. If you're ignoring, rejecting, punishing, disowning, or hurting your children because you can't understand or don't believe in what they're going through, you're not only harming them but you're also harming yourself. How? By allowing fear to edge love out of your heart. You're missing out and stumping your spiritual growth in this lifetime. You're missing your lessons! Just because *your* mom and dad taught you something was right, doesn't mean *they* were right.

Breaking through fear can only happen with love …and that begins with communication—positive, uplifting, constructive communication. Talk to your kids about anything and everything. Give them hope. Give them opportunity. Give them the ability to talk to you about anything, no matter how uncomfortable it makes you.

• •

If you feel ostracized, unaccepted, or unloved because of your appearance, race, sexuality, gender, or whatever, please know that the only reason this is happening to you is because of other people's fear. It is their faults and their fear-based agreements that make them act the way they do …it's not about you! Fear is passed down from generation to generation because people are scared to believe in or do things outside of what they were taught by their caregivers, so they accept agreements and project what they believe is true onto others. They're scared that if they go against something they were taught, it will threaten their wellbeing. It's a lack of love, not only for others, but for themselves. Why? Fear only holds you back. Fear keeps love out of your heart. It's deep rooted and detrimental to your wellbeing, and at the same time, someone else's. Isn't that sad? What a struggle kids live through because of ridiculous, unloving agreements passed onto them from their caregivers, who need to wake up and let those agreements go themselves.

We're all one; we're all connected. When we close off love because of a fear, we're blocking our connection to universal harmony. Every connection we close moves us further away from being happy. Are you a million miles away from happiness? If so, fear controls you. Love is lacking in your life. If you feel attacked by fearful people, you need to have love for them, as unjustifiable as that may seem. The choices that YOU make in this life matter. What anyone else does or thinks should not phase you if you're doing what you're supposed to do to create your own happiness. Being rejected by your family, peers, or whomever, only means they're lost in their own fears and it really has nothing to do with you. If you love yourself, have love for others, make the right choices, and do the things that make you happy, the universe will work in your favor. If it doesn't happen right away, it will one day. So, despite the hate you may feel in a world that seems so small around you, there are so many loving, accepting people out there. Be strong, because one day you'll be glad you got through everything and had the chance to meet them. But *always* remember, to love yourself.

> **STAY TRUE TO WHO YOU ARE, ALWAYS, BECAUSE THE PEOPLE WHO ARE GOOD FOR YOU WILL RESPECT THAT.**

If I had a child, I would tell them, "Stay true to who you are, always, because the people who are good for you will respect that. When you're genuine and being the best you can be, you'll attract more friends than anyone could wish for."

• •

Just a quick note: If you're that kid who feels different and alone, I was you! I was miserable because I didn't know why I was like that. Not only did I feel mentally complicated, but I felt like my friends' lives were a lot less complicated than mine. What I didn't know until later in my life is that there's actually a reason for it. People who "go through it," who have more profound hardships than others, were given them as gifts to make an impact not only in their lives, but in the lives of others. We all learn from and teach each other, but some people are here to learn how to pick themselves up from their troubles, in order to guide others. If you are the person who can't understand right now why you're "going through it," it is because you are more spiritually attuned than others and are on a special path. You may **feel** more; your senses may be heightened. Embrace them. Love your life. Love yourself. Trust me on this!

• •

Are you afraid to be yourself? Does it seem like the real person inside you doesn't fully experience life because you're faking it; covering yourself up with a mask? If so, then let me tell you something…you'll find when you step out of your comfort zone, out from behind your unneeded disguise, you'll see the world from another perspective, allowing new opportunities and experiences to find you. How? Every action or decision brings forth a different scenario into your life. When you allow things to flow naturally, not forced, opportunities will come. Don't be scared to be you!

• •

Besides me trying to fit in, there were more serious issues in my school. The main one was a mix of age groups. When younger and older kids are combined, bad influences tend to surface.

The middle school I attended was combined with the high school, serving grades 7-12. This is a BIG mistake. Parents beware! A middle school *should* be separate from a high school. That one- to two-year age difference is a big deal. When kids entering middle school, fresh out of elementary, see the things that go on in high school, they want to do the same. A major problem with *my* school was that senior boys wanted to date 7th and 8th grade girls, and the girls were intrigued by it. It was something that happened back then, but we didn't talk about it. When I look at the younger generation, not only is it getting worse, now they're flaunting it! This disturbs me because I remember my thought process at that age and I also know the consequences. I hate to see others make the same mistakes I did. I want YOU to avoid them.

• •

Middle school is when real life began for me. Teenage rebellion kicked in like a stomach full of tequila; I did whatever I wanted, whenever I wanted. There was no controlling me. I was so fed up with my friends and family that my angst made me either lash out or eat my emotions to the point of exhaustion. It made me completely lose sight, seeking out those "not-so-productive things" instead of focusing on more positive things, like my creative abilities.

A big part of my distress was my brother, Sal. He was experimenting with drugs and began to act out in unusual ways. When his behavior turned violent, I became distant with my mother because I was angry that she allowed him to continue. She defended him relentlessly which enabled his actions. I started to resent her. We had been close; Sal destroyed that. He began to destroy me. So I looked for an outlet in other places …bad places. One of them was a guy named Emilio.

• •

I developed friendships with senior boys that I knew through my brother. As the little sister, I wasn't relevant before. Now that I was post pubescent, the conversations seemed to linger.

Emilio's group was the main group that hung around me. They were all "bad boys" and that intrigued me. They brought something new and exciting into my life, allowing me to escape my friend and family troubles. However, I was just having fun and didn't see any of them as boyfriend material, *which is probably where I went wrong.* A group of guys usually won't hang out with a younger girl just to be friends with her. I didn't see it as a problem because I would hang around my other guy friends with no pressure to date. I just enjoyed being the girl of the group and they let me have that role, at least for a while.

• •

A stronger bond developed between Emilio, Jon, and me because the other guys were often with their girlfriends, so it was mainly just the three of us hanging out. In retrospect, it's obvious that was part of their plan; they wanted to see which one I liked. Truth be told, I liked neither of them! Both were only friends in my eyes. I should have told them that because…

We were hanging out together one school night when Emilio kissed me. A little later, Jon asked me to walk to his house with him to get something. It was freezing outside so he held me close, but the gesture was definitely an unexecuted move.

When we returned to Emilio's, he was sitting on his front steps in a white tee. Condensation flowed out of his nose; his eyes followed us intensely. It reminded me of one of those cartoon characters who gets so mad steam shoots out from its head! He was mad, *really* mad.

> CHOOSING TO LEAVE THAT WARNING ALONE INSTEAD OF LEAVING HIM ALONE, WAS A MISTAKE.

Feeling Emilio's raw, negative energy hit me harder than the cold. It scared me and I thought, *We only kissed, man, relax!* I should have taken that as a warning because it wasn't the last time I would experience fear as a result of his emotions. It also wasn't the last time I would notice a change in his eyes, something eerie. (Remember this later when I talk about the eyes.) Choosing to leave that warning alone instead of leaving *him* alone, was a mistake. Obviously, I knew he liked me since he kissed me and then got jealous of Jon so, that's where I should have nipped it in the bud.

• •

Emilio started asking me to spend time with him alone. The more I agreed, the more he tried to push a relationship. Of course, I knew it was stupid to hang out with him, but I figured if I kept making excuses not to date him, he would eventually let it go and we could remain friends. The story I stuck with was that my brother wouldn't like it, which wasn't completely the truth. 100% honesty would have been my best bet because he saw a way around my answer. He was interpreting it as, *I like you, but my brother wouldn't like "us."*

Don't mislead people; it's wrong. Honesty rewards us and dishonesty punishes us. Being truthful would have set things straight. In Emilio's mind, I liked him. In my mind, I knew he thought I liked him, but I really didn't, and I didn't tell him that. My mistake created trouble.

He was persistent and began getting frustrated. The day I gave up was when he threw his beeper against his bedroom wall. *Yes beeper, this was the year 2000.* I had reiterated to him that my brother wouldn't want us to date and BAM! Little red pieces of plastic flew everywhere. I relented to get him to calm down because there was no part of me that wanted to be his girlfriend.

You're probably wondering why I gave in. To be completely honest, I was scared and lonely. When you're young and you don't feel love from your family, you accept it from anyone. Another contributing factor was that I was interpreting his anger as, *He must really care about me since it bothered him so much that he couldn't be with me.* What I didn't know was that he had major issues, one of them being control.

Please, don't make this mistake! Be wise with who you allow into your life, especially when you're experiencing low points. When your energy is low or negative, it will encompass your universe, attracting people who feed off it. You'll begin to feel you need those people no matter how toxic they are! The trick is for you to be the one who loves yourself, always …because then the love of others (toxic or not) will become secondary; you won't *need* it.

• •

My parents were so wrapped up in Sal's tribulations that I felt left in the dark, like *I* didn't need love and attention as well? (In retrospect, I didn't). I stopped talking with them and pushed them away, resorting to other people for love. WARNING PARENTS: When your child pushes you away and you don't know how to deal with them, DON'T just leave them alone. This is the moment they want you the most. I wanted my parents there for me at that time even though I showed them the opposite. In their defense though, I was as hard as a rock. I could have reached out but was too prideful to be vulnerable; it was comfortable for me to be stubborn and angry. Don't be like that! Love yourself first, then accept your parents for who they are and understand that nothing they do to you is personal. Give them a chance. Even if they say the wrong thing or offend you in some way, don't just shut them out! You can't change people, but you can change how you deal with them! Look past your hurt and see them for who they really are because when you enable that awareness, you're open to forgiveness, to acceptance, and to love, which is followed by the ultimate…happiness.

• •

As my relationship with Emilio progressed, I actually grew feelings for him. He had a side I wanted to care for but also to receive love from. When he was good, he was good. I felt like I was his world, his everything. It felt like the love I had lost from my parents was replaced with his…"love."

We talked about having sex, but he never pressured me. When I was ready, he asked a few times if I was sure. It seemed like I was in the hands of someone who loved me, so why not? It was my choice, *even though you probably think he talked me into it.* However, he did talk me into something else, *drum roll…* unprotected sex! I think he might have given me the line, "If I pull out, there's nothing to worry about." BULLSHIT. You can still get pregnant people! Not to mention there are STDs ranging from some that can be cured, to some that can kill you. Protection is so important even though some people, *including some of your parents*, don't want you to know about it because they think it's going to lead to you *having* sex. Knowledge is power! The more you know about it the better you will be able to take care of yourself. If I had someone lay out all the facts, I never would have engaged in such risky behavior. I'm thankful I was lucky enough to not get sick or pregnant, but don't think you're invincible. Things are multiplying out there at an alarming rate. If you're a parent, TALK TO YOUR KIDS. Don't regret it later or have them resent you. I never got "the sex talk" and I should have. Every kid should! I was having sex at 14 and neither my parents nor my school informed me of shit. So there goes that theory of "influence of sex knowledge;" it was me being a teenager! WAKE UP PARENTS!

• •

Emilio's behavior began to change shortly after we had sex for the first time. He started to question my loyalty. It made me lose comfort in him. I was confused and unaware at what that "lack of trust" said about him. He always claimed he trusted me so much and knew I wouldn't lie to him, but now when something came up, I was a liar. I can see very clearly now, that his paranoia was a major sign that something wasn't right.

Soon it seemed as if he didn't believe me about anything. *That was Emilio, insecure with a random range of unhealthy thoughts.* I never knew how sick he was until his jealousy was full blown. It was gradual at first but as it intensified, I wanted out.

He would constantly accuse me of things that didn't exist, attack me verbally, then physically. It got bad when he started to grab and shove me so hard that I'd fall to the ground. His rage-filled grip often left bruises on my arms ...*and* heart (emotional blockages *are* real).

He would also punch objects or walls as I fearfully pictured my face at the receiving end. Why did I allow this? That's when love became diluted with fear. I kept our relationship to myself, so I didn't have anyone to talk to who could advise me on what to do; no one was saying, "Get away from him!"

Before a relationship reaches that level, you need to walk away. Never mind walk, run! When you see little signs in someone that make you uneasy, like an unjustified temper or a strange look in their eyes—how someone looks when they're up to something or thinking bad thoughts—they are only warnings for what is to come. I saw little things growing into problems, but I ignored them. For instance, I noticed how the way he spoke to me changed. In the beginning, he was as sweet as pie. As he became more comfortable, he grew more controlling. His whole tone changed, becoming more of an authority, talking down to me. He'd say I wasn't allowed to do something or hang out with someone, scolding me like a child! Look out for these controlling behaviors because they're signs of dominance. You are not a pet, you're a *person*. No one should tell you what to do.

I look back and ask myself, *Why did he feel like he could do that?* He saw something in me that allowed it, possibly an insecurity or yearning to be loved, or maybe both. It was as if he knew he had me, so he could start treating me however he pleased. That is never ok. No matter how lost in life you feel, you should not sacrifice your self-respect to feel love. Remember, you're NEVER responsible for the behavior of others, but you are ALWAYS responsible for *your* actions. You are in control of you.

• •

Dating Emilio was a detriment to my whole wellbeing, but I stayed with him through every tearful apology. People who have never been in an abusive relationship don't understand why the victim doesn't just *get out*. It's hard to understand this unless you've "been there." I'm not condoning staying; I'm just explaining it. Emilio conditioned me in a really screwed up way. He built me up with love and trust, then put a hold on me that was wrapped with fear. I feared he would harm, or even kill me or a loved one, so I sacrificed myself by living through it.

Allowing Emilio to fill the void where self-esteem and love was lacked, was where I went terribly wrong. Maybe if I had felt more love from my parents, I would have been able to talk to them, and the whole thing might have been avoided. Whether that would have resulted in a better or worse life, I'll never know. What I do know is that it ultimately made me stronger, strong enough that I can let *you* know, that it *is* avoidable. There are many cases where something like this or even worse happens and we don't talk about it enough. We need to talk to our daughters AND our sons, so they know how to avoid abusive relationships. We need to educate them early on how to stay in healthy, loving situations only. That starts in one place…the mirror; taking a look at ourselves and the examples we are setting. We can all learn to recognize signs of controlling behavior, disrespect, change of personality and demeanor in ourselves and others. We can all learn how to stop acting on emotion and talk things out! That ego which tells us that expressing our emotions in a healthy way is embarrassing, is destructive! Talking about feelings is healing. It's a release and it's not happening enough. Open communication will show a child their parent is aware and there for them. COMMUNICATE.

> WE NEED TO TALK TO OUR DAUGHTERS AND OUR SONS, SO THEY KNOW HOW TO AVOID ABUSIVE RELATIONSHIPS.

I just wanted someone I could talk to. I remember crying alone every night, wishing I could tell someone, but I feared Emilio would find out if I did. Every time he was in his crazy mindset, he tried to mind-fuck me by threatening to harm my family. I believed him and I was terrified. Every day became a mission to not wake the sleeping giant.

• •

One night my friend Chloe had a party and Emilio didn't approve of me going. I went anyway. A few drinks in, someone busted in to tell me *he* was outside. My heart sank. I could swear I was in slow motion, walking to the front door like walking down death row, approaching my fate.

Without a word, he pulled me so hard across the street that my feet dragged on the blacktop like a doll. Then came the accusations that I had hooked up with someone. The scolding and incoherent yelling was followed by him throwing me down on a neighbor's lawn where he did one of the most disgusting, disrespectful things he could have done…he spat in my face.

Before I could open my eyes, I felt myself being scooped off the ground and thrown into a car. Panic struck as I worked myself up into an asthma attack, begging him to take me to the hospital. Instead he drove around aimlessly, continuing to yell. Truthfully, I felt like I was about to take my last breath in that car, and no lie, I think that's what he wanted.

The torture wasn't over. Emilio brought me to his house and laid me down. My breathing became less labored, but my body and mind were in total shock; I couldn't even move. He cried, apologized, then tried to have sex with me. I let him. I didn't want it to happen, but I felt hopeless. I had no energy to fight him off and I didn't try. The scariest thing was that right after, in an angry voice he whispered, "You know I can fuck you whenever I want to fuck you." Then like a flip of a light switch he cried again, kissed me all over my face, and said he couldn't believe he spat on me. He went on and on all night talking about how I didn't deserve it, how he loved me so much.

As I write this, it's surreal to re-live, because these are things I haven't thought about in years, yet they're so vivid and as horrifying as those moments were at the time *and continued to be for a long time after,* I've learned to let them go; there's no sting anymore! It's like I'm re-calling the past of a different person because I have no emotional attachment to these memories. It's unbelievable. What I want now is for *you* to get to that point and to PREVENT things like this from happening in your life. I want you to have the courage to get away from someone who's hurting you and to not allow them to repeat it. And also, have the knowledge to stay clear of people who will! If you've been through things that have damaged you, release them and free yourself. The memory may remain, but the pain is not permanent! GET RID OF IT!! No one can repair what's been done but YOU. You have the power within, to dissolve the emotion. Use it!

• •

NO MORE STING: Your mind, your body, and your heart all belong to you, but they are not you. You are a soul. A soul is able to free a human of its burdens when the human becomes aware that the soul exists. When you become aware of the soul or "wake up," you will see that you are an incredible, infinite, energetic manifestation and your body is like an electrical suit that controls all the things you do, think, and feel. Due to a "connection issue," most suits are running haywire. When you fix the connection to your soul, you become *it*—an unconditional loving light of energy—not a miserable body that dwells on its pain! You're so much more than your physical body and what your body experiences.

Stop pitying yourself! Start experiencing life on a different level than just the physical! Ultimately, you're unbreakable because you are infinite energy. You're just borrowing a body. YOU ARE A SOUL. Don't let the things you feel affect you so much. Don't let the most disgusting thing someone did to you affect who you really are. Listen, if most people on earth "wake up," *and this is no new news to anyone who is awake,* life would be unimaginably beautiful. Being awake brings clarity. Clarity brings peace. Peace brings beauty. You are most beautiful when you are at peace. Translation for the average human mind: It's impossible to be a douchebag when you are awakened to, and in tune with, your soul; it's impossible to be miserable. You become a person who forgives because they understand people are fucked up from other people. You forgive because it heals you and gives you peace. You become a vessel of light, an example to show others how to live. You become radiant on the inside and radiant on the outside. You become you.

> YOU FORGIVE BECAUSE IT HEALS YOU AND GIVES YOU PEACE.

You are not you when your thoughts are overpowering your life. Trauma is a disease of the mind. It's set off by something physical or emotional that has been accepted instead of released. When you don't release what has happened to you, the disease will fester. This causes both the mind and body to malfunction, making you torturously experience pain over and over until it eventually kills you. Think of it on a simple level: when you're upset your stomach hurts, right? Now, can you see how emotional blockages in your body that resulted from trauma can cause pain, sickness, and even disease? Can you understand that these blockages, and ultimately illness, can be cleared with intentional spiritual healing and releasing? Can you understand how ridiculous and abusive it is for us to let things affect us? If your answers are yes, then you're ready to "wake up"…and I'll bet you're starting to understand now that shit just doesn't matter! Trauma is fear, and fear is an illusion! Pull the stinger out, shake it off, and continue on with your life! Pain is not a part of you! It does not belong to, or belong in, your body! **You** decide to keep it and agonize over it or set it free and heal. Choose what **you** do, from here forward…

• •

Every time Emilio and I fought, I'd leave him. He would cry and beg for forgiveness and I'd always stay strong …*temporarily*. While he was clearly at fault, I was allowing him to play with my mind. I should have listened to my gut that kept telling me, *Tell someone! Get away!* Instead, I allowed my fears to dominate what I knew was right. Your intuition is a gem. Value it. Trust it. It's there for a reason.

Sometimes people make choices that lead to some great happening or opportunity and they say, "I don't know why I did that or how I knew to do that, but I'm glad I did." The how, the why is because their intuition told them. The best way I can put it so that you can distinguish if it's just your mind talking or truly your intuition, is that it's like a resonation throughout your being. You don't literally feel your body vibrating, but you'll have an all-over sense of "just knowing" …you feel it, *strongly*. Get it? If you **feel** something take over all reason, all logic, all fear, all wild-running thoughts and you can't ignore or deny it, don't.

I ignored it; I paid the price. I've also learned my lesson and hope you learn that lesson here, from me. Neither physical nor emotional abuse should be tolerated, ever. Both are connected, because they affect one another. In my case, the mental abuse was probably worse than the physical, but it eventually changed how I treated my body. It polluted my mind, allowing for unhealthy lifestyle choices. If you're in that kind of situation, logic and reasoning can run amuck, so rely on your intuition. It can pull you out of a life of misery.

If you see any signs of impending abuse, get out. If you've already endured it in your past, let it go. Don't let that person control you any longer (learn to forgive).

• •

After about a year of trying to hold onto the relationship, things finally came to a head. There were a group of younger girls who were always up my ass. It turned out that he had sex with one of these, *not even teenage,* girls. I confronted them both about the situation, but he denied it and so did she…not that I needed confirmation, the feeling in my gut was enough.

SUPERHUMAN

The truth came out anyway because charges were pressed against him and he was arrested. It was the most stomach-turning, hurtful thing I'd ever been through at that time. One of the vilest things one can do is touch a child. Being involved with someone like that made me feel disgusted not only with him but with myself.

• •

After he was bailed out, Emilio stuck with the story of his innocence. Several failed attempts to convince me made him realize I was *done*, and his harassment turned into stalking. Stalking is a big problem because sometimes the victim ends up dead. When I was young, I watched a Lifetime movie based on a true story, *No One Would Tell*. In the movie, the boyfriend was charming at first, until he grew possessive and killed his girlfriend when she tried to get away. Emilio turned into that boy in the movie; he even eerily said a few of the same lines! That's why many times I thought he might kill me, and in some cases, that's unfortunately what happens. I was so overwhelmed with fear at the time that I was terrified to tell anyone…but I should have.

It's scary when you see someone you thought you knew turn into a crazed person. Being a young girl, I didn't know how to handle the situation, so I carried it around with me. We need to discuss this topic more with young adults. They should know the signs to look for early. As soon as Emilio's personality started to change, I should have left him. First, when his temper worsened, and then when he started telling me I couldn't hang out with certain friends. His temper and jealousy were the first warning signs before he became abusive. When it got to *that* point, I know I should have broken up with him, but I was too afraid. I was terrified to tell anyone, but people started to see it and talk.

The truth will always come to light. Don't be afraid to expose someone who's hurting you, because people *will* find out. If you hide it, you're just going to put yourself through it, however long it may be, until someone notices *or* something worse happens. Why punish yourself? Help yourself instead! Tell someone! *I* went wrong there, but now *you* can avoid my mistake.

• •

My brother heard everything that had happened, fought Emilio, and told my parents about my relationship. They didn't know much because I was always sneaking around, so they insisted I tell them.

I was in a hard spot. I didn't want my estranged parents to know my personal life, especially since they asked if I had been sexually active! If they had been more open with me about sex, I either would have not been having it or I would have been able to talk to them about it. I felt they had no right to know.

• •

Sometimes parents want to discipline their kids or get involved after things have already gotten out of hand. The mistake is not being present from the beginning, to show them the way. What happens is the child is suddenly out of control and the parents have no idea how they got like that. The household turns chaotic as the child and adults are communicating on two completely different wavelengths. I've seen it happen, especially with *my* family. If things are at that point, the adults need to take a step back and realize maybe they went wrong somewhere. Then they can try a different approach. What's the first move? **Communication**.

While my parents are good, caring people, they are not conversationalists. We don't sit down and rationalize how to work things out; we argue. I learned to be argumentative from not being able to talk openly. And don't get me wrong, debating your point can be a valuable skill as long as both parties come to a resolution or understanding at the end. That wasn't our type of arguing. It was explosive; I felt I had to hide things and keep everything in, resulting in displaced emotions which were expressed in the wrong ways when a situation arose. I felt they had betrayed me in many ways; when they enabled my brother's behavior, when they lied to me, and when they were not my friends when I needed them. It made me distant, and when they tried to reach out, I pulled farther away.

Trust is vital for a child. To help raise a **confident** person, parents should give their child comfort and assurance. A child needs to feel they can count on their parents. If trust exists, the child will be able to learn from them productively. If it doesn't, who can the child turn to?

When everyone around me broke my trust, I felt profoundly alone. Being betrayed over and over again during tough times when I needed respect and honesty instead of deflective lies, is what created emotional blockages. I angrily tried to figure out life on my own and it was a struggle. Believe me when I say that lies damage lives. TRUST and COMMUNICATION combined are essential to any successful relationship because they form the foundation for everything, especially in a family dynamic.

• •

The important thing is *how* you communicate. People tend to understand each other when they're speaking at the same tone, at the same speed, and with the same body language or non-verbal communication. In the book, *You're The Best!*, Frank Nicoletti, with whom I'm honored to be acquainted, explains the concept of rapport and how important it is in communicating. He states, "The most effective way for communicating with anyone is by **mirroring** and **matching** his or her physiology. By matching someone's posture, facial expressions, gestures, voice tonalities, body movement and even breathing patterns, you connect on a deep psychological level." Let's say you're mad at someone and want to work it out with them. When you approach them, they're calmly sitting down, speaking softly. Because of your anxious energy, you

> WHEN ENERGETIC AND PHYSICAL COMMUNICATION IS SHARED, SO IS THE FEELING OF IMPORTANCE!

remain standing, speaking loudly and abruptly. This makes you the dominant speaker, and more than likely, makes the other party feel as if they are less important or not being heard. If you had sat down and mimicked their behavior, both of your feelings would not only have been conveyed to each other, but energetically understood.

When energetic and physical communication is shared, so is the feeling of importance! Whenever I would fight with people I'd always try to get louder and angrier than they were. That was my ego attempting to dominate, but it didn't make them understand my feelings any better. All it did was cause miscommunication and the problem was never resolved. Now when I mirror someone else as I talk with them, they seem to appreciate it and the conversation flows in both directions; both sides are being heard. This usually results in an understanding, sometimes a solution. Try it; it's interesting to see what happens.

• •

Back then, my family and I definitely weren't on the same communication wavelength, but I eventually threw in the towel. I confessed everything about my relationship with Emilio, thinking it would heal something in my fucked-up life. However, they forced me to press charges, because for one I was being stalked, and two charges were being pressed against my brother. I appreciated him defending me, but now I was in a mess. I was livid. I didn't want to handle it that way. This resulted in much deeper trust issues.

It took a long time for me to forgive them for what I went through, especially my dad; he was the one who demanded I do it. I kept thinking to myself, *What the fuck have my parents gotten me into?* I wanted no part of it but felt I had no choice.

The whole situation stole my spirit, or what was left of it. I remember holding back my tears and fists on the way home. I felt robbed of my own free will; I felt forced into a choice I didn't want to make. I was disheartened, angry, and numb all at the same time, but I didn't show it; I always had to be the strong one. My mind had been well trained over the years to hold in emotions …well, hold them in until they bubbled to the top (this is where releasing would have been helpful).

Boy, did those emotions bubble…as soon as we got home, I unleashed my fury on my parents, leaving my relationship with them at an all-time low. That was a point in my life where I felt I had absolutely no one. I can still picture exactly how I looked that day, because it was almost like an out of body experience. I remember the clothes I was wearing, my hairstyle. I remember walking out of my house and down the street, feeling numb. It was like I was completely removed from the rest of the world …like everyone had betrayed me. I didn't know what to do with myself. Have you ever felt that low?

• •

I can understand how some people feel so troubled that they believe the only way to peace is by taking their own lives. Their emotional struggle, created from lack of love and trust in humanity, becomes so overwhelming that it blinds them from seeing anything worth living for. If you ever feel like that, understand that the pain is temporary and that you'll always have someone to pick you up. Who? YOU. How? By loving yourself! If you're desperately seeking love from an outside source and can't obtain it, it's because you're lacking it from within. When you pity yourself, you are choosing a negative path to darkness; the universe only rewards **positive choices**. Uplifting and loving yourself, no matter what you're going through or have gone through, is how the universe rewards you with love; it only sends it back to you when you're open and willing to accept it FROM YOURSELF. There are no freebies in life! You must do the work! Hang in there, make the choice to love yourself regardless of circumstance, and you *will* heal.

Pain is not necessarily bad. It feels bad in the moment, of course, but what *keeps* us feeling bad is the simple fact that we hold onto it.

PURSUIT OF HAPPINESS

Why do we hold onto it? Because we miss the point of it. When we can't see what it's really there for, we can't get rid of it. It's just a test and we either pass by using pain to help change something for the better, or we fail by letting pain bring us down and accepting it as our own. Allowing someone else to damage your life is like waking up every day, looking in the mirror and saying, "I hate you," while the other person goes on living their life. It doesn't make sense! Accepting someone else's negative words or actions means you're accepting fear and lacking understanding of who you really are and what matters in this world. *You matter and the only way you can see that is if you have love for yourself, if you truly* **know** *how unbelievably incredible you are as an infinite, energetic being of the universe, regardless of any flaws or faults. So who cares what someone else thinks or said or did! Care what you think or say or do!*

> YOU MATTER AND THE ONLY WAY YOU CAN SEE THAT IS IF YOU HAVE LOVE FOR YOURSELF.

• •

I found myself constantly pondering, *Why was I put through that?* I couldn't make sense of it and I held onto that experience for a long time. It haunted me, making me accumulate a huge amount of anger. It wasn't until years later that I realized… it wasn't 100% their fault! *I* made the choice to keep my relationship a secret… *I* made the choice to stay with someone who tried to control me… *I* didn't realize I was more in charge than I thought and didn't have to do anything I didn't want to do. It was *my* choices that caused these spin-off events. And at that time, my parents joined with the enemy in my eyes but now, I can see that it wasn't even personal! Why? Because anything anyone else says or does is about *them* and not the other person. It was *their* view of the world; it was *their* idea of how things should be done. I made up my mind that it was because they didn't care about me since they didn't try to understand what I was going through or take my feelings into consideration. What it really was, was their attempt to control the situation; the "idea" they believed. I just needed to accept them and their views, and to take control of my own life, to take some of the responsibility, to love myself, and then to conclusively… release it ALL!

• •

One important challenge in parenting is learning to be more like a friend than an authority to your children. I always hear adults ignorantly say the opposite. When all else fails them, what a child needs the most is their family, their foundation. They need someone to trust, to talk to, a shoulder to cry on. When there's too much authority, they lose that sense of security in the people they want it from the most. That's how I felt, and how others do too. It's like when a father is too strict with his daughter because he fears she'll become sexually active. What usually happens is precisely what he fears! That's focusing on the negative which puts that energy out there, making it a reality. Do you want to know how to do it the right way? Be open, be honest, and give your kids the freedom they need so that they end up trusting you enough to tell you things. It will help them make the best decisions.

While my parents didn't love me the way I wanted, I didn't get love from myself at all! As I grew angrier, I pushed them further away and they took more steps back. This is important, parents: When your child is slipping away, don't stop reaching for them! Work to get back in their life somehow, regardless of what happened. No matter how many failed attempts it may take, show them love every day. Talk to them and do things with them. For the kids: No matter how mad or let down you are, don't give up if you feel your parents don't love you. They may not know how to connect. Everyone is human and makes mistakes. People know what they were taught. If you talk with them and allow them in your life, maybe they'll learn things from *you* and become better parents. That's not a possibility when you completely shut them out, which was exactly the choice *I* made. There was no way they could relate, and as a result, it ended up hurting me because I grew more and more alone.

I get it: you have problems with your family and desperately want to feel loved by them. It's completely understandable, but don't ever forget to love yourself. Love is an amazingly powerful force that initiates miracles, especially when channeled inward.

BACK TO THE STORY

Back then, the only thing I got out of the situation with Emilio, besides anger, was a restraining order—a piece of paper that held no weight against his craziness. He continued to stalk me, but the cops did nothing. How can a restraining order work if someone is allowed to violate it? It's such a screwed-up system. People who get these "magical" pieces of paper sometimes end up dead. That's why YOU should stop the madness in its tracks. Don't let it escalate like I did!

Emilio and his friends would drive by every day like it was a game. They'd stalk me and my cousin Tommy, and then go play basketball at the school to intimidate us because the school was near both our houses. Some of Emilio's friends were affiliated with a gang, so he knew I would be scared. Anywhere I was, there they were. I became imprisoned by the fear in my own mind.

• •

After weeks of being stalked in school, outside of school, having scary run-ins with Emilio, being guarded by classmates and teachers, and walking around with weapons (yes, I'm serious), I thought to myself, *This is fucking insanity.* I knew my fear wouldn't go anywhere if I let things remain as they were, so out of frustration I finally mustered up the courage to take control back. My mindset was, *He can try to kill me but I'm not going out without a fight.*

SUPERHUMAN

First, I called this girl Emilio had been using as a pawn to intimidate me. I found she didn't want to have anything to do with the situation, and we ended the conversation in peace. All it took was one phone call to relieve some anxiety. I felt empowered, ready to take the whole thing on.

Next, I grabbed a big grey box cutter (kids, DO NOT try this at home), stuck it in the waistband of my sweatpants, and walked to the basketball courts. With my head held high, I approached the gang member who scared me the most and asked why he was harassing me and my family. He put his hands up as if to surrender, and with a smirk asked why I had a knife sticking out of my pants. I ignored the question and demanded he stop stalking me and my cousin. The guy had the nerve to deny it and to flirtatiously request my number! I almost broke into laughter because it was a moment of relief, but I kept my game face on, and he finally agreed to stop bothering us. That day, the weight was lifted from my shoulders. I knew all these scare tactics were bullshit; Emilio had nothing.

My fear of these people was nothing but a creation in my mind caused by one person who really shouldn't have had any power over me, yet I allowed him to have it! I showed him a weakness and he used it to his advantage until I finally gained something that we all need in this life, **courage**. It's what finally sparked something in me to fight back, to take charge.

As timid as we may be, we all have courage inside us. It's **choosing** to call on our inner strength that allows us to use it. Will you use it?

• •

Many times, we avoid situations or people because it's momentarily easier not to face our problems. What we're really doing is being fearful, leaving us stuck. We're scared to pursue what we want because the steps to get there seem threatening. Does that even make sense? Shouldn't you strive for the things that make you happy even if it may be a little scary along the way? Are you purposely staying put to feel safe? My advice: grow a pair! Give yourself a push and take a chance. You can't score a goal if you're paralyzed by the goalie! Confront your fears with courage and watch as they vanish.

In fearful situations, stay grounded. If you're scared, you're demonstrating weakness. You'll be respected when you stand up for yourself because when you cower, others feed off it.

Of course, there are some exceptions to being courageous, like confrontations that you know will turn violent; in those cases, it's best to walk away. In other situations, you need to be confident and not budge so that people know they can't overpower you. Stand tall, keep your head high, make eye contact, speak truthfully and calmly, but be very bold. It will take you a long way in life.

• •

While it took courage to stay strong around Emilio and confront the people who scared me, it's what needed to be done. When they saw weakness and fear in me, they took advantage. Stand up for yourself and don't let anyone abuse you in any way. Please don't let fear run you! If you dwell on what scares you, it will take over your mind and eventually your life. If you believe you're strong and can overcome your current troubles, you can, and you will!

Do you feel you're being controlled, stalked, or abused, and fear you can't handle the situation? Seek help. Many times the person doing it knows you won't tell, so they take full advantage. Be courageous. Do what's best for YOU, find someone you can trust, and just spill the beans! You'll feel the weight come off your shoulders because you're not only changing fear into self-love, you're also asking for help which there is absolutely nothing wrong with, That person can assist you with a solution or way to deal with your problem. I know how it feels to be alone with such a scary thing. No one should feel like that…and no one has to!

• •

SUPERHUMAN

So, are you ready for the ending to the story? I found out Emilio was arrested again. I thought, *This is my opportunity...my closure.* I anxiously anticipated visiting him in jail and scolding him for all the pain he'd caused, envisioning him sitting across from me as I figuratively painted a bird's eye view of his life. However, that's not what happened. He jumped bail and fled to Peru! It was bittersweet because I knew he was gone for good, but I also knew I wouldn't have a chance to confront him. I would never get to heal that part of my life...or so I thought.

For a long time, I relived the day I gave into him when he threw his beeper against the wall. I regretted it *so* badly. Over and over, I questioned: What if I had just stayed strong and said no? What if I had chosen Jon? What would my life be like? Would I not have been as hurt? I held onto all of that as I jumped into my second relationship. What I didn't know I needed to do was find a way to come to terms with it first (releasing, forgiveness, acceptance, love, and gratitude) so that I wouldn't be so vulnerable in the future.

· ·

Mark came around when the trouble with Emilio was ending. The new relationship allowed me to find love in someone else at a time when I thought I was broken. He helped me through a lot by making me laugh and feel loved at such a low point in my life ...at first.

Mark was a good-hearted but lost person who carried a lot of pain because of his father's death. It wasn't the type of pain you see. He was the outgoing, popular, funny kid. That masked what he felt inside which ended up being very bad for *me* because…

He was another cheater! Another liar! People would tell me the things he did, but when confronted, Mark stuck by his "truth." I always knew what my **gut instinct** was telling me, but he was a manipulator. He probably saw some vulnerability in me and figured he could use that to his advantage. And he obviously did because I stupidly always moved past it.

PURSUIT OF HAPPINESS

Say you're clueless and don't know when someone is manipulating you. Take a minute to think about a few things: Are the person's stories consistent? Do you often catch them in lies? Do you have more than one person telling you things that he or she is denying? Do you feel in your gut that when they tell you a story, there's something not quite right about it? This is what Mark would do when confronted: act like he was offended and angered by the accusations. Many times, when someone gets overly defensive, they have something to hide. If you're accusing them of something they didn't do, then they should feel confident enough to not get excited. His reactions were dead giveaways.

His Plan B: He'd pull some story out of his ass. As he filled in the details, the more we talked about it, the more things wouldn't make sense. His defense mechanism was to cover it up by turning the story around on me. He was such a terrible liar because he lied so much that he couldn't keep up with his own bullshit! That's how I learned to catch him on his lies. All I had to do was ask a bunch of questions and he would eventually screw up his own story. However, even though I could tell he wasn't being truthful, sometimes he would confuse me to the point that I questioned my own intuition. You know how they say to always go with your first instinct when taking a test if you're not sure of the answer because your first is usually right? In the back of my mind, I knew the right answer, but I switched it anyway. His stories caused me to doubt my own logic, *probably because I didn't want to believe the truth.* I wanted to stay in that comfort zone instead of doing what would have been best for me, saying, "Goodbye, Mark!"

As soon as you feel someone isn't being honest, chances are they're not. Don't trust your mind, don't trust your heart, trust your gut; it never lies. If you don't have emotional security with your partner, what foundation do you have to build your relationship on? **Trust** and **communication** are golden. When you lack one, the other, or both, the bond weakens.

How do you want your life to be? Create your future by making the best possible choices. How do you do that? Use your natural, intuitive power to feel what's right and wrong. It will tell you how to choose!

• •

After a while, it became difficult to ignore the rumors. My conscience constantly told me Mark was a liar. His ex-girlfriend claimed things that I didn't want to believe yet felt were true. She and I fought for many years. Unfortunately, it's quite common in love triangles for the two being cheated on to go after each other. In those moments of hurt and anger, I wanted to take it all out on her, but from a clearer perspective, Mark was really to blame. In the *clearest* perspective, *I* was to blame. I shouldn't have taken him back.

If someone is going to selfishly hurt two people and then sit back to watch while they fight, they're not worth it! When you're in a relationship, your significant other should not be giving their affection or attention to anyone else. It's a betrayal, plain and simple, and that hurts. So if it happens to you, don't blame the other person and don't give your partner the power to ever do it again.

"You can't start the next chapter of your life if you keep re-reading the last one."

—Unknown

When I finally caught Mark in a big lie, instead of fighting with the other girl or walking away, I directed my anger directly at him. He became verbally abusive. It didn't matter if *he* cheated; *I* was a slut, a whore, this and that. I never cheated on him; it was an illogical defense. I'd never cheat on *anyone*. It's wrong, hurtful, disgusting, and disrespectful, and reveals an insecurity or character flaw. There were, however, a few instances when we were broken up that I took the opportunity for revenge. It was an immature way for me to justify the pain he had caused, to neutralize the sting from his past infidelities. But two wrongs don't make a right!

I should have left Mark the second I saw signs that he was no good for me, some that were almost identical to the signs Emilio displayed. It's ok to make mistakes in life, but to consciously repeat them is not acceptable. I knew it too. I started to think, *Well, this is all too familiar,* but instead of heading for the hills I ran back into his arms! Why? It's probably because I kept thinking back to how he helped me through my first relationship, and I didn't want to lose him. I didn't want to leave that comfort zone (which is something most of us struggle to step out of.) The most healing thing I could have done would have been to thank him for that, or just be at peace with the fact that he did that for me and continue my journey, awaiting someone better. Instead, I grew spiteful and sought out revenge so I could get past my anger and keep him around.

> **IT'S OK TO MAKE MISTAKES IN LIFE, BUT TO CONSCIOUSLY REPEAT THEM IS NOT ACCEPTABLE.**

• •

Mark and I continued to see each other regardless of whether we were broken up or not. One time while we were hanging out, *just as friends*, his weed dealer covertly made a little sign with his hands for me to call him. Being mischievous, I got his number from Mark's phone. My thought? *Why not, after all he's done to me?* It intrigued me that this guy was so willing to stab Mark in the back.

I guess you can call it karma because during our little rendezvous, his girlfriend walked in! It was awkward and I felt bad for her, but on the other hand, I was satisfied with what I did to Mark.

Revenge felt good …at the time. In the long run, it caused more problems because the dealer's girlfriend was after me, and Mark became even more jealous.

SUPERHUMAN

"Anger ventilated often hurries towards forgiveness; anger concealed often hardens into revenge."
—Edward G. Bulwer-Lytton

Revenge is *not* a good thing. It stems from pride, because you're feeding your ego with a negative action. I used it to "fix" things. But what was I really fixing? Nothing! I was suppressing a feeling by covering it up with another. **Forgiveness** and **awareness** were the tools I needed. Forgiveness frees your soul, making you a better person, and awareness allows you to see the bigger picture. I didn't allow myself to take a break and realize that. I was too caught up being hurt and angry.

> REVENGE STEMS FROM PRIDE, BECAUSE YOU'RE FEEDING YOUR EGO WITH A NEGATIVE ACTION.

I'm sure there's been a time, if not many times, when you just couldn't get past something and you *had* to get even. What was the driving force that caused you to act? Was it really what the person did or was it something inside you? Please understand that what other people do in this life is ALL ABOUT THEMSELVES. They demonstrate their perspectives and misconceptions by reflecting what's deep within them onto others. When you understand that, you can accept it and you won't want to be spiteful or vengeful. "Getting even" is like adding two zeros; there is no gain.

• •

Note: If revenge feels necessary for you, let it be the kind where you leave a bad situation and better yourself because of it. Let them see how well you're doing without them. Let yourself see that.

• •

Each time Mark and I got back together, confrontations would happen more frequently than the time before. I was insecure about trusting him and he was extremely jealous. The break-up to make-up to break-up to make-up cycle, made us crazy! We became so deeply embedded in our unhealthy relationship that it eventually got physical. He would grab and pull me so roughly that I had finger marks down my arms. This brought back memories of my previous relationship and those emotions resurfaced. I remember thinking to myself, *Kate, are you really going to do this to yourself again?* It turned out my poor gut stood no chance against my unstable heart! The feeling that I was back in the relationship that I had no closure from comforted me. Since I never stood up to Emilio, Mark became the scapegoat. And *that* my friend, is a perfect example of the not learning your lesson, not listening to your gut, not stepping out of your comfort zone to better yourself kind of thing, that keeps us stuck and continuously unhappy with ourselves!

As a result of my poor choices, I had pent-up feelings which made me act out…*more violently than Mark did.* When I caught him in a lie, I would immediately hit him.

One year, on Valentine's Day, he said he would be at a friend's house. However, it turned out he was at his ex-girlfriend's house. I punched him and beat him with the roses he had the audacity to give me that very moment. It made me feel so liberated, but for the wrong reason.

Why was it not right? Even though Mark was wrong for lying, I was wrong for putting my hands on him! It was even more wrong for us to get back together! After it happened, we both sat and cried for a minute, but I left laughing with my girlfriend, who had watched everything from the car, because I felt liberated. Not only did I think he deserved what he got, but I also felt I was finally done with him. *Of course, I wasn't.* I eventually took him back. I always did. More stupidity! More of not listening to my gut…not listening to the OBVIOUS. I should have said, "Screw this," and walked away the better person, for good! Or, I could have broken up with him when my emotions were not sky high and left it at that. The situation needed to be diffused first, and then set free.

SUPERHUMAN

It wasn't until much later, after years of reflecting on that night, that I finally stopped being so hurt by it, because I realized how crazy and irrational I had been. I was embarrassed by my actions because they were immature, and while I don't agree with the way I handled it, I understood why I reacted that way. I wanted to deal with the problem right away, but violence is never the answer. Remaining in a situation that was unhealthy for me had warped my mindset, and instead of giving us both time to think, I acted. Instead of walking away from him, I stayed.

Another useless tactic was not answering a guy's calls when they messed up. It gave me a sense of control when I made them reflect on what they did and let them "sweat it out." Mark especially sweated it out and I always enjoyed it. I was once again ignoring my inner voice's advice. I was playing a game to make him miss me when I knew I would take him back. This brought on no real change; there was nothing stopping him from doing it again since he saw that I'd return eventually, ultimately giving *him* control over *me*. So in the end, all these tactics failed me.

Do you see how none of it was beneficial? The relationship was beyond repair and I was trying to use my crazy logic to fix it. You should always take time to think about the situation before you approach it. Really think about what you're doing wrong that keeps allowing it to happen in your life. Remember, you create your reality! As wrong as someone else might be, you control what *you* do in the situation; as for everyone else… stop trying to control them! I should have had the satisfaction, not from hitting Mark, but from leaving him!

• •

Realizing you have total control over yourself is one of life's most liberating moments. Have you ever peacefully walked away from someone who did you wrong? If so, then you probably know that feeling of empowerment. You no longer have any need for control over something you can't control, and you feel fucking amazing!

PURSUIT OF HAPPINESS

FREE! You feel like you finally did something good for yourself and it makes the other person look at you differently, different in a good way. They see your maturity and it smacks them in the face with their own *immaturity*. When you handle a situation with intense emotion and irrationality, it causes nothing but conflict because you're both competing to be right. Being right or on top or whatever, comes naturally when you just do the right thing. I've felt the empowerment from walking away many times, but along with it, I've also felt the regret that comes from giving in and allowing for repeated infidelities.

> BEING RIGHT OR ON TOP OR WHATEVER, COMES NATURALLY WHEN YOU JUST DO THE RIGHT THING.

Those little back and forth games became a thing between Mark and me. Instead of leaving each other alone, we continued fighting over our irresolvable issues, just to hold onto each other. Sounds absurd, right? It was, but it happens a lot. It's hard for people who love each other to accept they're not meant to be together, so instead of breaking up, they "deal" with each other's faults. They continue to compete for the higher role in the relationship, to compete for control. Do I hit close to home? If so, then you must understand that letting something go is sometimes necessary in order to experience something better. When you finally make that positive move, life will reward you.

• •

If you're in an unhappy or unhealthy relationship, look deep within and ask yourself, *What's the best decision for ME? What's the best decision for MY life?* If your thoughts race, don't try to decipher any of them; they're only there to confuse you. Go even deeper, beyond the voices in your head, until you can hear only one, clear voice …your own. What am I talking about? Your intuition! It will always show you the way, but it's up to you to head in that direction.

SUPERHUMAN

We often ignore our intuition when we think we're in love. Hence the saying, "Love is blind." It makes us look past everything that's wrong and hold onto a false hope that our partner will bring peace into our lives. Why is it a false hope? The only place we can find true love and peace is WITHIN OURSELVES. If we're blind to the truth, we can't fix our situation and no one else can either. Staying in a relationship and hoping that our partner will make everything ok, is unrealistic.

We begin a healthy relationship by knowing and loving ourselves first. Why? If we don't know who we are or how to be who we are, how can someone love us if we're not showing up as we truly are? It sets us up for failure because the relationship isn't genuine. Even if someone could see and love who we really are when we don't recognize it ourselves, we'll resist their love, if not consciously, then subconsciously. We won't be able to believe they love us if we don't see what's loveable about ourselves. Get it? And we won't be able to see their bullshit either! As a result, the relationship will never function as beautifully as imagined. Nobody's going to bring the comfort, the love, the peace into your life like YOU can. It's the same for the other person. If they don't love themselves, they can't love you properly or accept your love. My point here…learn to love yourself first and then let your intuition choose who's right for you.

> **NOBODY'S GOING TO BRING THE COMFORT, THE LOVE, THE PEACE INTO YOUR LIFE LIKE YOU CAN.**

• •

An eye-opening incident happened one night after leaving a club with Mark and his friends. After an exchange of words, he violently pulled me out of his car. We got into a physical altercation in the street and he left me in the middle of a bad neighborhood at 4:30 in the morning. Ironically, when I tried to call people to come get me, my phone died! That's when two boys approached me. I thought, *Ok, it's time to take off my heels and fight or this will end badly.* To my surprise, they were nothing but concerned; they called a cab and shared their blunt, along with many wise words.

The boys asked why I would allow someone like that in my life. They said there are so many guys out there who would never treat a girl that way, and I deserved better. Maybe it was the desperate situation or maybe it was just hearing something like that come from strangers, but something struck me. Sometimes when you hear what you were thinking come out of someone else's mouth, it helps awaken you to the truth. I was lucky for them to have found me.

Something terrible could have happened to me that night, all because I chose to stay involved with Mark. I realized this as the cab pulled up to my house; I had an epiphany. I looked up at the bright blue sky that marked that new day and thought, *He will never have the power to do this to me again because I won't ever give it to him.*

• •

The times that Mark and I got physical with each other accelerated the demise of our relationship. I was happy about *that* aspect of it. I didn't deserve that and neither did he. As good as it felt to hit him for his mistreatment of me, it wasn't the right thing to do. We were both in the wrong for staying together. Our relationship was a world of hurt, anger, and violence, none of which should coexist. Unless it's in self-defense, it's just not ok to hit someone. The cycle of abuse often continues, so I'm grateful I was able to recognize why I was acting that way and put a stop to it.

If you have a lot of personal issues, you will more than likely be presented with a person who brings out the things you need to fix in your own life. PAY ATTENTION! THIS IS IMPORTANT! It's not a punishment. It's the universe's sense of humor; it's trying to teach you a lesson! Despite what *they're* doing wrong, it's your job to see something about yourself in what they do, to recognize opportunities for a **change within you** so you can grow! The impact of the relationship's trials and tribulations can be of great help for you to see this, regardless of what transpired. The good, the bad, and the ugly are all learning tools you pick up along the way to build your life. Use them wisely.

• •

Even though Mark caused a lot of heartache, he showed me that I made the same mistake twice. I became aware that I needed to make better choices. The first choice was to just enjoy being single!

The best advice I can give to teens is to enjoy your youth. Don't get caught up in a relationship because you'll meet *so* many people. I know how it feels to be lonely, and when you find someone to confide in, it feels good, but don't let that rule your life. Figure out how to dig deeper and pull out what really matters. Most importantly, love yourself and have fun! Enjoy being a kid!!

• •

To enjoy what was left of *our* adolescence, my friends and I decided to go to Cancun to get away from our cheating boyfriends and just have a good time. It was sort of a release and a way to say *fuck you* to them. It was a "fuck you" (unintentionally) to my parents too because they were beyond worried. They didn't want me to go and we argued for a while, but there was no way I was missing out.

• •

We arrived in Mexico on March 21, 2005. On the second or third night, while we were dancing at a club, a bouncer approached me. He said I was invited to VIP. One of my favorite groups was there so I thought, *why not?*

In VIP, I was fed shot after shot and met a lot of people. The vibe was strong, and I was having a good time. That's when a guy sat down and chatted me up for a while. He said he wanted to show me something backstage.

PURSUIT OF HAPPINESS

I was beyond my limit at that point, so I let him lead me through a claustrophobic, cave-like hallway. When I looked behind me, I noticed a bouncer had followed us. He had a stern expression on his face; it unsettled me.

My fight or flight instinct kicked in, and I blurted out that I needed to tell my friends where I was, or they'd worry. With a fake smile, I said I would be right back, but he was hesitant to let me go, grabbing my arm. As my adrenaline pumped, I pulled away and ran, but the bouncer who was behind us tried to keep me from getting past him! He blocked the narrow hallway with his body, so I pushed him with everything I had and ran out of there.

It was stupid to follow that guy, but at least I got out safe. I didn't see the danger until I felt an uneasy presence around me.

We have **intuition** for a reason so it's important to listen to it. I can always sense when something is ominous. When you go out or go to another country, stick with your friends. And just a little passed down advice; what my mom always told me… never put your drink down! So many bad things happen because of the mix of alcohol, freedom, and people looking for a victim. Don't be foolish.

• •

A few more incidents happened on that trip, and some really bad things could have happened to us. One time, Chloe and I decided to get off the bus that was taking us to the club because we got in a fight with our friends. Two drunk girls walking in the dark, in the middle of nowhere…*great decision!* Another night, I was almost arrested for punching a guy who had spit on my friend. I'm very protective of my friends, but I also think I flashed back to when Emilio spit on me. Either way, it was a stupid move. To top it all off, we missed our connecting flight and got stuck in Miami International Airport for over 24 hours!

Even though we were 19, we were like lost puppies when all that happened. It showed me that I wasn't completely ready to be on my own. When we're young, we feel we have everything under control. No one can tell us anything because we think we know it all. My parents used to tell me this and I always blew it off. Sometimes it's best to listen! I don't regret Cancun, because overall we had an amazing time. However, sometimes we must look beyond what we want to see the bigger picture rather than what looks good in the moment, and always make smart choices when our life depends on it! I made some stupid mistakes that could have severely affected me. Worse things could have happened on that trip, and in many other cases, they have. We could be having a blast one minute and the next our precious life is ripped away from everyone who loves us. We must learn to look at all the angles and perspectives and then make good choices. Make ALL your choices good.

> WE MUST LEARN TO LOOK AT ALL THE ANGLES AND PERSPECTIVES AND THEN MAKE GOOD CHOICES.

Do you see how simple mistakes can easily lead you down a road of destruction? When you don't see your value, it's easy to be careless with your life. It's easy to let your emotions dictate your choices. Want to know what's also easy but not a popular choice? Recognizing your worth and treating yourself with the utmost respect. You are such a precious, incredible being who can live a very long life if you take care of yourself. Plain and simple…love yourself, always. Don't be careless.

• •

After Cancun, I returned to reality and life was back to basics. Most of the girls reconnected with their boyfriends after getting over the false hope that the trip scared some sense into them. I'll be honest, even I was on and off with Mark again. While the relationship was no longer violent, it still wasn't meant to be.

You've probably experienced how good things are in the beginning of a relationship, before they turn to shit. Why does this happen? It's because of the *love notion*—an infatuation with this perfect person who can do you no wrong. But then suddenly, a "new person" shows up.

Avoid my mistakes! Don't let the "honeymoon" stage of your relationship fool you, regardless of whether it's the first honeymoon for you or the 15th! The subconscious programs of others give them the ability to make you or break you. It's up to you how it turns out. You need to observe them, understand their motives, accept them, learn from them, and then weigh the worth of the relationship. Otherwise, it's self-sabotage! If you ignore the fear of an imperfect person, you'll never be able to have a successful relationship when the honeymoon stage is over. NO ONE IS PERFECT. Release the fear by exposing it for what it really is. Love is blind only if you have your eyes closed! So pay attention to the reality of your relationship, the reality of who your partner is and not who you want them to be.

• •

Eventually I had the strength to move on. I figured, *I better leave on a high note before this goes back to the way it was before.* After that revelation, I felt such freedom from not only being single but from releasing the negativity that Mark and I had dragged out for so long. When you walk away from a relationship it's always hard at first, but it *does* get easier.

I went through a lot of sadness and missed my exes, but eventually the feelings just went away. I remember my girlfriends and I would cry hysterically to each other every time we broke up with our boyfriends; it was silly. We'd say, "I don't know how I'm going to get over this." Guess what? We all did! You can too!

• •

While I was single, I had a few boyfriends here and there, but nothing serious. I refused to let my heart go "there" again, until I met Joe.

By that time, I was tired of the club scene, but my friends forced me to go with them. I remember standing there, drink attached to my mouth, attitude ready to fire. The bartender pointed out a group of guys, telling us they were football players and before she finished her thought, one of them had his arm over my shoulder. I wasn't interested or in the mood, so I threw it off. He was relentless because I had to forcefully remove his arm *three times*. That's when his friend intervened with an apology and asked us to join them in VIP for shots.

I met this guy and I was drunk, but I can remember feeling an undeniable connection or chemistry (whatever you want to call it). It didn't last long because he had to run out when that same friend of his was getting the boot. I said to myself, *Oh well, I guess I'll never see him again.*

Not even a week later, my friends coerced me into another club night. I looked to my left and was surprised to see a familiar face. It was Joe!

I busted his balls about him sitting next to me, saying that he must have been stalking me. It was weird how I thought I'd never see him again and there he was, on the next barstool! When things like that happen, let them play out, because that's the path you're supposed to travel. That's the person (the soul) you're supposed to meet at that time, at that place, in your life, and in the cosmos. That's how *I* look at it because I don't believe in coincidences!

• •

Joe and I connected and enjoyed each other's company. My trust for him grew stronger and faster than anyone I'd ever been with and that scared me because I'm usually an untrusting person. He trusted me too and I felt I finally had a good guy.

We talked about marriage and where things were headed. Believe me, I'm not naïve so I always thought, *Maybe it's all bullshit,* but it felt right. It was a breath of fresh air to have a guy like him—someone I trusted, someone completely different from my previous boyfriends. I can honestly say I fell in love with him after only two weeks of dating. I was in love once, years before, so I recognized the feeling.

PURSUIT OF HAPPINESS

My friends were skeptical, even though they didn't verbalize it. They thought I was infatuated with his status. To me, personality and chemistry are what matter; fame or money cannot win me over. I've never been a person interested in that. Having dated both rich and poor men, all I ever wanted was connection, passion, honesty, love, and loyalty. I sensed that from Joe. I just felt in every bone of my body that he was right for me. Otherwise, I would have headed for the hills because he was an athlete; athletes are known to cheat!

• •

I didn't tell many of my friends about Joe, but the few I did, I thought I could trust. However, there was something in Hannah's eyes whenever I talked about him: an envious look. Her fake enthusiasm was obvious too. When you notice that in someone, it's a good idea not to trust them.

Looking for deception? Whenever I talk with someone, I observe everything about them—their eyes, their expression, their body language, their energy, their speech, and their tone. The eyes give away a lot about what a person's thinking. Pay attention the next time you talk with someone. Clear indicators of deception are jittery behavior, no eye contact, looking other ways when answering a question, and uncalled-for defensiveness.

I should have seen Hannah's red flags, but I figured it was nothing. Who cares if she's a little jealous? I never saw anything bad in Joe's eyes. I felt his sincerity from the way he talked to me, his openness, his attitude, the way he treated me, how he looked into my eyes, how he held me close and touched me, and how he wanted to spend all his free time with me. I had never been with a guy who was so genuine. It's what I always longed for but never had.

One day when I was driving home from his house, I remember thinking the reason I went through those past relationships was to show me what I was currently seeing. That there *are* good guys in this world, and I wouldn't have appreciated him as much if I hadn't experienced some bad ones. That's when I made a promise to myself to let go of everything I feared in a relationship and let this guy in. But…

Things got rocky. I didn't keep my promise and began holding him at a slight distance. I think I did this because the feelings I had for him were so real that I was scared. In my free time, to drive myself crazy, I reverted to negative thinking and worried he would cheat on me and become one of those familiar faces from the past.

The relationship began to sour when he went home for a visit. He wanted to get me on a plane but that was a major step for me. I was too nervous to meet his *entire* family. He even expressed a few times that he was annoyed I wouldn't let him meet *my* parents. Every time he brought it up, I brushed it off. Why? Because I was anxious (fearful) about it. He was angry with me and I don't blame him. It's frustrating when you're trying to move forward with someone who's stuck in the past. Don't be that person. Let your past go!

> IF WE DON'T ALLOW OURSELVES TO EXPERIENCE LOVE, WE MISS OUT.

Joe deserved a chance. My past experiences had created a mental roadblock that I knew how to get around but felt safer being stuck behind. Whether or not he would have turned out to be an Emilio or a Mark, the **courage** to let go and let life happen would have set me free. I got past the other relationships, so if my relationship with Joe went south, I could've dealt with that too! My anxiety was holding me back. Because of it, I'll never know where the relationship could have led me. To quote Anaïs Nin, *"And the day came when the risk to remain tight in a bud was more painful than the risk it took to blossom."*

Joe had swept me out of my comfort zone. As in love with him as I felt I was, I fought with it instead of embracing it. We must take chances in life. If they don't work out the way we want, we must learn from them and move on. If we don't allow ourselves to experience love, we miss out. I made that mistake because the way I acted changed the relationship in a negative way.

• •

The bad energy began cycling between us. He became distant and untrusting, and I was worried he would cheat. At first it was just an underlying fear that made me not get too close to him, but eventually it drove me crazy, making me think all kinds of things. It ruined our relationship. If you live in fear, the reality of what you're constantly fearing, will be created.

One night, Hannah and her friend ended up at Joe's hotel. He thought I had sent her there to spy on him. He went along with it, entertaining her, thinking it would piss me off, but the truth was that I had no idea she was there! When I confronted her, her excuse was that she had to drive her friend to see Joe's friend. She claimed she stayed in the lobby the whole time, but her ulterior motives were exposed. He told me that she went into his room, laid on his bed all night, and when she left, she had the front desk call his room so she could ask for his number.

Instead of an apology, all she had for me was attitude and denial. A few weeks later, she sent me an apologetic text, but ironically it got cut off right before she explained why she did what she did. I'm glad it got cut off, because I didn't care. I was more at peace by just walking away from her, for good. The biggest problem, HER biggest mistake… was letting the truth come from *him*. She wanted herself some NFL football player, and her friendship with me didn't trump that! I had known something was up because of the way she looked every time I spoke about Joe. What I didn't expect was for her to betray me, then lie about it. It's shocking when people show you a completely different face than the one you see every day. It happened many times in the past with friends, but somehow, I let myself get fooled again. I didn't want to believe she would be like that. I'm always trying to look for the good, despite seeing the bad. What I've learned though is that no matter how old I get or how real people seem, some people will hurt me in a second. It sucks, yes, but it teaches me to recognize them more and more, to realize who's out for me and who's out to get me. You can turn your betrayals into knowledge as well.

• •

In addition to what happened with Hannah, Joe had to move to New Jersey the next day. Even though we had talked things out, it was just weird at that point. Trying to get out of my funk, I vented to my girl Josephine. She was completely there for me, which I appreciated. Erica, one of my closest friends, took Hannah's side. She couldn't understand how I could still talk to Joe yet write Hannah off…even though she admitted what Hannah did was wrong. We grew apart, which sucked, because I really thought she was a lifelong friend. But, everything happens for a reason.

There are friends who will knock you down, and there are friends who will pick you up. Be grateful for both kinds because they all have a purpose in your journey.

• •

I think friendships are actually harder to walk away from than relationships. Your friends are supposed to be there when someone screws you over. They're the ones you're able to tell things to that you wouldn't tell another soul. So when they betray you, it's one of the worst feelings; it's almost like they've died because they're no longer in your life. It's worrisome too, because they can become an enemy with your secrets, and your weaknesses, roaming around with all this ammo on you! However, you can move on and **learn** just like you do with boyfriends or girlfriends. Learn who you can trust.

Take this valuable lesson to heart: What other people think of you does not matter and should not matter! What you think of yourself is all that should matter to you. People have talked about me throughout my life and I've honestly never given a shit what they said. Some things were true, a lot wasn't, but that's not the point. The point is to be ok if something comes out that you'd rather keep private. Because who really cares? We all do stupid things, have dark secrets, and embarrassments, yet life goes on! No one's judgement can stop the world from turning. We all live, we all die; anything that transpires in between is temporary and gone with the wind the second the moment passes. So in the humblest way, fuck what anyone thinks of you. That attitude carried me through life with ease, at least in *that* area of "the struggle of existence." And a struggle it may be, but life is truly beautiful when you can take something powerful from all the madness, when you can focus on the exquisiteness of your nature and look right past the dumb shit that happens to you.

> EVERY EXPERIENCE IS MEANT TO HELP YOU GROW. ARE YOU BLOSSOMING FROM YOURS?

We're like seeds planted in the cold, dark earth, pushing our way through the soil, withstanding the elements, reaching for the sun, to eventually, hopefully, unfold each petal of our beauty. Remember, every experience is meant to help you grow. Are you blossoming from yours?

• •

At the time, I was holding a grudge that was making me once again, feel regret. I regretted not committing more to Joe and I regretted trusting Hannah. Looking back on that now, I see I was punishing myself. I needed to **forgive and stay in the moment**, to forgive them and to also forgive myself. I needed to just live my life! I couldn't change the past and neither can you! DON'T REGRET. Live, learn, and be present!

Joe and I never recovered. Whenever I visited him, he brought up what happened and sincerely apologized for it. He said he was sorry for ruining my friendship, but I let him know that he actually did me a favor. I got to see who Hannah truly was. The apologies, however, didn't make things better. We kept in contact for two years, but it had been over from the start. Long distance relationships don't work, especially when trust has been severed. What matters is that I loved and lost and I'm perfectly fine with that because it was an experience which taught me lessons. For one, it made me realize I needed to let go of my past and start fresh with the next guy, to not punish him for what others had done to me. It also showed me that sometimes it's just not meant to be, no matter how strong my feelings are for someone. Consider that the next time you're holding onto someone. If you get the feeling you should let go, let them go! It's easier than you think. And guess what? The universe doesn't allow people to be separated for too long if they're truly meant to be together. Sometimes the timing just isn't right. Sometimes *they're* just not right. Whatever it is, release your need to control and set it free.

No matter what happened between you and an ex, learn to release bad feelings. No matter what happened between you and ANYONE, learn to release bad feelings. If they did you wrong, all that means is that they inflicted their own pain onto you because it was too much for them to handle. You deserve better than to allow it to keep hurting you. And never wish them pain. Wish them healing, because that's what they need, and that's what the next person they encounter needs. Even the worst things can be forgiven (not to do them a favor but to do yourself one). Forgiveness is not a weakness; it's a strength. If you feel *you* have done someone wrong, make amends for your soul *and* theirs. Whether that would be saying sorry to them, to yourself, or to both of you, just make it right somehow so you can carry on with your life without holding onto the past. Forgiveness is NOT A WEAKNESS. It's one of the strongest things you can do.

> "Holding on to anger is like drinking poison and expecting the other person to die."
>
> —Unknown

CHAPTER 3

FACE EVERYTHING AND RISE

Does forgiveness seem too difficult for you? Try forgiving someone who basically ruined your life.

The war between my brother Sal and I began when I was born. I guess you can say it was a sibling rivalry, but ours was deeply psychologically rooted. I've seen other brother-sister relationships; some are bad but they often can coexist. This wasn't the case for us; I can't recall a time we *ever* got along. He always put me down, always tried to belittle or hurt me. It was the root of my insecurity.

• •

When I was about 11 or 12 and Sal was about 13 or 14, drugs became a big part of his life. They set things off in his brain and his temper grew uncontrollable. He had these fits and he would scream at my parents, throw things around the house, break furniture, or sometimes hit my dad. His verbal outbursts were so illogical and so incoherent that it was impossible to reason with him. This went on every single day for years; it was terrifying.

SUPERHUMAN

Sal would call my mother and me every name in the book. When I was the main target, he would cruelly attack my weight. I developed stronger body issues than I already had, which I carried for a long time. He would also scream in my mother's face and curse her out until she was in tears, like it gave him satisfaction to break her down. I grew resentful towards *her* because she never put a stop to any of the madness. She forgave him every time, for everything, and moved on until the next day; it frustrated me to the core. I felt captive in my own mind.

• •

I will never forget one day when Sal was enraged, because of the way his words resonated with me. He had flipped out, screamed at my mom, and then decided he was going to take a shower. Something about the way he spoke that day gave me an ill vibe. As soon as I heard the water turn on, I grabbed a knife.

My body pumped adrenaline as I paced up and down the stairs and around my room, not being able to reason myself into calming down. When I sat next to my shaken-up mother I said, "Mom, I'm going to use this if I have to," showing her the knife.

She chuckled a little and said, "Don't be silly." I'm not sure if she tried to act strong for me or just didn't know the extent of the situation, but it bothered me that she laughed at a time when I was so scared for her. I couldn't make sense of it and the frustration became overwhelming.

One time when Sal was fighting with my dad, I happened to be in the middle of it, literally. He was throwing things around the house as I sat at the table casually eating my McDonalds™. I was used to the fighting at that point. While taking a bite of the cheeseburger, I felt something strike my head so hard that it wasn't even painful, just intense. I realized what happened when I turned my stiff neck and saw one of the wooden dinner table chairs on the floor. He had hit me in the head with a fucking chair! My dad immediately chased him out of the house.

FACE EVERYTHING AND RISE

Sal came back and apologized. Not even looking in his direction, I dismissed the "I'm so sorry" and told him to go away. If I acknowledged it, I would have enabled him like my parents always had. He couldn't get away with it with me and he hated that.

He frightened my parents, but he never scared me personally and he knew it. I always envisioned myself taking a punch—or something worse—for them. Their lives were more important to me than mine. What I *did* fear was him doing something when I wasn't there to protect them. It was like the roles had reversed and I became the parent, worried like a neurotic mother.

• •

A few times, things were so severe that the cops were called. I remember my dad had pinned him to the ground to stop Sal from beating him. Sal was so uncontrollable that he began head-butting my dad. I ran over to hold Sal's head down, crying with him, begging him to stop. It was traumatic.

One time I came home to flashing lights. If you've ever used the expression "my heart was in my throat" then you can relate to how I felt that night. I was convinced that the worst had happened. Anxious and terrified, I made my way through the police where I saw my brother being rolled down the walkway, strapped to a stretcher.

As he struggled within the restraints, he noticed me and frantically said, "Kate! Kate!" I was frozen for a moment, shocked by the sight. When I snapped out of it, I ran inside as fast as I could to see both my parents. I took a breath then swallowed…my heart fell back into my chest.

• •

Every time the cops came, Sal went to a hospital, only to make atrocious phone calls to my parents, begging for his freedom with tears and apologies, selfishly torturing my mother's emotions. The final decision was always to get him out. I pleaded for them to make him stay. I didn't know whether it was the right place for him to be, but I knew he needed real help and I couldn't understand why no one else agreed. In the end, *my* emotions were tortured.

> MY CONSCIOUS LIFE WAS ONE CONTINUOUS NIGHTMARE. ONCE IN A WHILE, I COULD WAKE UP AND BREATHE.

Each time he was in the hospital, the relief that came from his absence was like nothing I can describe …but I'll try. Imagine you are having a lucid nightmare and your heart is pounding. Now imagine the comfort after you wake up safely in your bed. As you exhale, you realize it was nothing but a dream. My conscious life was one continuous nightmare. Once in a while, I could wake up and breathe.

Every time they got him out, he would be good for a week because he was scared to go back. Then a whole new cycle would evolve. The same exact scenario happened *every time* but somehow my mom had this nonsensical hope that things were going to change.

I would say, "Mom, he's going to go right back to it in a week or two."

She would respond, "No, he's doing so much better."

Unfortunately, I was always right.

· ·

December 24, 2006 was the night my fears came to life. My family and I were at my aunt's house for her usual Christmas Eve party. We had food and drinks and family. Perfect equation, right? Not exactly.

When we got home, Sal went to his room and I went to mine. He was drunk and on drugs or medication, so he started to chant. This was something he did to be "heard." I knew his chants were directed at me and they made me uncomfortable, so I called some friends. I just wanted to smoke some weed and get the fuck out of the house! I could feel in my bones that he had it out for me that night.

FACE EVERYTHING AND RISE

To avoid confrontation, I quickly left and walked up the block where my friend picked me up. When we got to our friend's house, I left my phone in the car to charge. After about two hours, I went to get it. My stomach turned when I saw my cousin Tommy had called a bunch of times; something wasn't right.

We promptly left. When we got close to my house, the street was blocked with cop cars. I called Tommy back and he told me to come over immediately, so I ran to his house down the block. Usually, I would have run right into my house, but something held me back. I couldn't do it; I knew this one was bad. There have been very few, if any, times in my life where I felt I couldn't stand alone; this was one of them.

When I got to Tommy's, the look on his face made me want to faint. He didn't know what to say so I begged him to tell me. Finally coming out with it he said, "Your brother stabbed your dad."

My whole body went numb as I fell to my knees. I began to panic, asking questions like "Is my dad alive?" and "What happened?" He didn't know. On top of being in distress, I was also ridiculously high. I can't even describe how I felt that night.

• •

I was beyond grateful that my dad survived, but I couldn't help being bombarded with emotions. It was an "I told you so" moment: *Now you can finally see what I begged you to see for so long.* Along with anger: *Why the fuck did they let this happen?* And then self-torture: *Why was I not there to stop it?*

Christmas morning was unlike any other. While most people were opening presents, I soaked up blood. Looking around at the horror, I was almost in a trance. It wasn't the blood that bothered me, but what it symbolized: a reflection of my fears and all the years of built-up frustration trying to tell my parents something like this was going to happen. I was angrier than ever—angry at Sal, at my parents, and mostly at myself. The biggest emotion I felt about the whole incident was guilt. I regretted not being there.

• •

I contemplated a move to Florida many times in my life. The thing that always held me back was knowing that I would regret it if something happened and I wasn't there to stop it. Well, it happened, and I was MIA right in NY. The thing that really screwed with my head was that Sal wanted to kill *me* but took it out on my dad. The fight was about me. I found that out the day my dad came home from the hospital. He was in a bad place, not being able to sit still or calm down. Emotions poured out of him as he released his thoughts, anger, and pain. While reliving the situation aloud, he slipped and said that Sal had talked about wanting to slit my throat that night. I'm sure Sal said a lot more, but I know my parents won't ever tell me all of it.

I had left the house that night because I knew he was after me. He had acted the same way before when he punched a hole in my door trying to attack me. I didn't realize he would redirect his anger. So since then I've held onto the guilt, telling myself if I had been there, maybe I could have stopped it. On the contrary, I get a strong feeling that if I had been there, I would have died that night. There's that "what if" again! I needed to stop trying to do the event over in my head and instead just let it go. There was nothing I could do about it; it was over.

If you're feeling guilty about something you cannot fix, release it. Guilt is like regret because you're holding onto the negative energy from a past experience and no matter how badly you wish you could change it, you can't. There was a reason it played out the way it did. Let it go; set it free.

• •

FACE EVERYTHING AND RISE

After Sal's release from jail, my father tried to mend their relationship. I didn't know how or why. I didn't get it. I imagined though that to forgive someone that quickly for something to that degree, must mean you truly love them. Of course, my dad held onto some anger (how could he not), but that was his son. He bravely allowed love to conquer his fear, which is incredibly inspiring.

My fear was not so much conquered at the time because I didn't understand forgiveness like I do now. When someone wronged me, I cut them out of my life, but held onto the anger. My dad just wanted everyone to heal. To mend the relationship, they started having Sal come over (at the time he was staying in a halfway house). For me, the nightmare returned.

• •

As I tried to live my life, I encountered fresh obstacles. I found out Sal had told people the reason he did what he did was because my dad was abusive—an utter lie. My father never raised a hand to us in any way. He barely raised his voice! He's a hardworking man who took care of his family; both my parents did. They both love us. My dad didn't spend as much time with us as we would have liked, but that's something Sal needed to forgive him for to heal. He really did love my dad he just wanted his attention and approval so badly, and not being able to get it was disastrous to his psyche. We have a choice to accept the people and things we can't change, to let go of feelings and just be happy with ourselves and others, so we can enjoy our short time on this earth. In my brother's case, the grudge he didn't release strengthened his anger.

You try to kill your father and then when he still accepts you and tries to heal your relationship, you slander his character to make yourself look better? That thought kept running through my head. I couldn't make sense of it and it enraged me, especially after I heard the horrendous things Sal was saying about *me*. My emotions grew *beyond* sky high as my mental state dropped lower than ever. At times, I felt I needed to be put out of my misery! What I really needed to know back then, was what I know now—that anything anyone else says or does is about themselves. It's not personal. That knowledge helped me come to terms with it.

• •

When Sal visited, I would leave. Honestly, I have no idea what I would have done if I had been around him. I've never wanted to intentionally hurt someone like I wanted to hurt him. My parents didn't understand that and didn't realize how worried I was for them. It was bad enough before when I feared him harming them, now since it happened, I was constantly reliving it (living in the past). So when he came over, I found people to hang out with, drove aimlessly, or sat in my car, curled up with my head in my hands in some random location. My world was upside down. I was hurt from being alone, from being frustrated, and from feeling betrayed. It's horrible to feel you have no one who understands. My mental and physical wellbeing grew worse. I was worn down and not taking care of myself. Can you guess what I needed at that point? Self-love.

• •

Just when I thought things couldn't get worse, one night my parents came home said Sal would be sleeping at our house. You have no idea how I felt; I was out of my body and out of my mind, feeling so many emotions at once. I'm surprised I didn't have a breakdown.

Long before Sal did what he did, I had been promised over and over about the things my parents would not allow him to do, things that would jeopardize my feelings or our safety, and they broke their promises every single time. So while this behavior was nothing new to me, it always shocked me. When a parent does this, they're creating an underlying traumatic event which gives that person a complex, or something worse. They felt it was important to give Sal what he wanted, to keep him at bay. However, not keeping their promise to me that he would never stay over after the incident was like a bullet ripping through my soul. It started with, "Sal will only come once a week," to, "It's not fair that you don't allow him here more." Then, "Sal will never sleep over, don't worry," to, "He's sleeping here and that's that." Over and over they reassured me that *this* or *that* wouldn't happen, and it backfired every time. Him sleeping over was like every nightmare I've ever had becoming a reality right then and there. I broke at that very moment. The fear of him repeating what he did hit me so hard that this time around I didn't want to be there. I couldn't allow myself to be present. I couldn't allow myself to stay, after all the years being let down by the people whom I was only trying to protect, while secretly wishing they would protect me.

I spent many weekends in hotels and many holidays alone. I thought my running away would show them what the situation was doing to me and cause them to change their ways. I also just wanted to drown in my sorrows. Why? It was the only thing comforting me in some screwed up way. In my own mind, I was alone in the world and misery was my only company.

Why did my parents let that happen? Did they not love me? Back then I would have said they didn't. Now I can see that it was just how they felt things needed to be done, whether it was right or wrong. Remember the charges they made me press? That was another attempt to control a situation—their idea of how things should be and not them neglecting my feelings, like I felt it was. They thought because I was strong, I could handle it. Turns out, they were right. It's too bad I didn't know that then, but you can apply that knowledge now, anytime you *just* can't grasp why someone did what they did. Sometimes, most of the time, there's something you're not able to understand in the situation—sometimes not at first, sometimes not for a while, and sometimes not ever. It's up to

> IN MY OWN MIND, I WAS ALONE IN THE WORLD AND MISERY WAS MY ONLY COMPANY.

your ego, your life experience, or your level of open-mindedness that will or won't allow you to see other perspectives and live your life with peace in your heart. So drop your ego, trust in the universe, be forgiving, loving, accepting, understanding… and you'll "get it."

I made numerous attempts to reach my parents. They never *clearly* saw how Sal was destroying our family, how he was destroying me. I tried to calmly reason with them many times, but sometimes I couldn't help but lose my temper. Because of that, I think they thought I was just an over-emotional teenage girl, but I'm not an emotional person. My friends would joke that I was emotionless because I rarely got upset like most girls do. As for my parents, however, I was begging for them to see how much the situation was impacting my life. I carried such a weight on my shoulders and all I wanted them to do was lift it. I needed to lift the pain for myself, to love myself even when I felt no one else did.

• •

I wrote the following at a very low moment:

10/31/07

It's like everyone in my life will always betray me. My mom promised she would never bring Sal over here in the morning again without telling me because the last few times, I freaked out. For a while, it was all good and I built a sense of trust with her that she wouldn't do it again. However, this morning I woke up from having a nightmare to the sound of his voice coming from downstairs. In the nightmare, the killer kept coming from Sal's old room into mine and shooting this guy in the head. I could see the guy get shot, but when he was running from the killer, the guy was me. I was trying to run through the crawlspace in my room to get away from him. It was a very gory dream. Coincidence? I don't think so. She doesn't understand what this does to me, no matter how emotional she sees me get. Or maybe she doesn't care. I don't know. All I know is it's the same pattern with men in my life, friends, and worst of all, my own family. Everyone just keeps hurting me over and over. That little bit of forgiveness and trust in my heart tells me it's all over when things are good, until I feel that knife pierce through my back again.

    I was so enveloped in negativity that I couldn't see the positive – this was an opportunity for growth and change. You might say, *The positive? In a situation like that?* Yes. No matter what's going on in your life, if you expand your awareness and refuse to limit yourself to a one-sided reality, you'll find positive in anything and everything. I needed to use my pain to grow stronger, smarter, and to let the past go, to focus on the present, to focus on MY life.

• •

This was a very trying time for me. If *anything* troubling is going on in *your* life, seek help. Therapy is a great way to bring up emotions so you can release them. My family would have greatly benefited from counseling, but since they're secretive people, I think they were afraid of it. *I've* even said for a long time that I would never "air out my dirty laundry," but one day I decided to see someone.

    The pain had become unbearable. I went to the psychologist's home and sat in her dimly-lit basement, which was strange but at the same time comforting. I let go of EVERYTHING. I told her it *all* from start to finish, using many tissues to wipe the tears that effortlessly flowed. As I dominated the conversation, she said very little, but the few things she did say profoundly touched me. At one point she stopped me and said, "I just want you to know that you are a very strong person and I'm sorry that you went through all of that; it must have been very hard on you."

    Hearing those words while my emotions were already high as a kite was like a release, excuse me, an *outpouring* of years of emotional attachments leaving my body, finally putting me at great ease.

SUPERHUMAN

I've had many people tell me I'm strong, but I've never had anyone convey it like that. Sometimes an outside perspective, a person who doesn't know you, can help you see things that you can't.

When I left, I took a deep breath of fresh air, feeling not only peace of mind but like my body was as light as a feather. It was euphoric. I drove home with the biggest smile on my face, feeling free for the first time in a long time.

Seek help when you can't help yourself. There's nothing wrong with it and absolutely everything right with it.

• •

Something I didn't see before has also helped me cope. It took long torturous years of feeling sad and angry to finally pull something out of me. While I was mad at my parents for what they were allowing to happen and mad at my brother for what he did, I wasn't seeing where *I* went wrong. At my deepest point of searching for answers in the confusion, I realized…I let it all get to me and I didn't have to! That was the start of my **awakening**. Suffering not only woke me up but it pushed me out of bed! I began to understand that since there was nothing I could have done because I had no control over their actions, I should have just carried on with my life instead of letting it affect me to the degree it did. I let fear take over instead of letting love in. Love would have guided me. Instead I was resentful, hateful, fearful, angry, frustrated, worried, depressed; I was all of the things that were useless, yet damaging to me. As a result, I let my grades slip, I dated the wrong people, I ate terribly, and I was unhappy (I had created my reality). If I would have STOPPED THINKING about it all so much and just lived in the moment, it wouldn't have affected me the way it did. While it's nearly impossible to ignore things that are happening in your home,

> I LET FEAR TAKE OVER INSTEAD OF LETTING LOVE IN. LOVE WOULD HAVE GUIDED ME.

FACE EVERYTHING AND RISE

if there's nothing you can do, you'll need to find a way to be at peace in your own mind. Like my transformation into a **Superhuman**…if I had made this change back then, I could have transcended my emotional turmoil into personal empowerment much more quickly. And while I can't change that about my past, I can use that knowledge in the present. You can live vicariously through me to see how this can help *you*, right now.

My mistake was worrying about my parents and not focusing on myself. Voicing my concerns and opinions didn't change how they handled the situation, so I should have realized then, to let go. Let go of what? Fear, anger, frustration, and not accepting what I couldn't change. Worrying took a portion of my life away. I dwelled on the situation instead of doing what I'm doing now and concentrating on *myself* for once. I'm letting go and letting life happen. You too can live in the moment and allow love to guide you, because the truth is, what's beyond your control is not worth a second of worry!

If you feel trapped in the chaos of your own home, seek refuge in something that can take you away from your troubles, whether that's music, meditation, a sport, a hobby, or anything constructive. Use that energy, especially your high-powered emotions, to do something creative, something you love, something that will benefit you. NEVER allow anyone to direct your life. You control you! And don't forget, even if you feel no one loves you, love yourself! AND love others unconditionally; people are screwed up in different ways, for different reasons, and it's really not their fault …even your parents.

• •

Now I can look back and realize how far I've come, but it's sad that I let it affect me so profoundly. I was my own worst enemy, possibly even causing bad things to happen by focusing on the negativity. Who knows? What I do know is that love conquers all bad in this world. It's the strength to use it in the times when we would most likely express the opposite that makes us most powerful. My choice to love myself and love life by accepting all that is, is what turned suffering into living. Finally accepting and forgiving MY BROTHER, showing him unconditional **love** ...is what turned suffering into living. I could have easily continued being angry and feeling sorry for myself, dwelling on what happened for the rest of my life, but I woke up. Don't you want to live? Choose to be awake in this very moment no matter what has come before it. Choose to take control of your life.

• •

As long as you're mad at someone or looking at them thinking, *She's such a bitch*, or *He's a dick for what he did*, you're not open to love because you're not embodying it. It's closing off your heart which in turn, closes theirs. When you show someone love and respect despite their actions, you will get a different response than expected. Love changes the way they see you and will cause them to reflect on themselves. It's like a shock because people who attack expect to be attacked in return. When they're embraced with love instead, they don't know what to do. They'll have a moment of confusion, sometimes enlightenment.

Responding in love was important when I worked on my relationship with my mom. I had held onto resentment because of everything that happened over the years with my brother. Every little thing she did annoyed me. It made things complicated between us because I always saw her as a beautiful soul, yet I couldn't get past her actions. It's funny though, because at the end of our petty arguments or the passive-aggressive webs we spun around the house, and despite how mad she made me, I always felt guilty. I noticed when I began to let my anger go, that beautiful soul of hers would appear brighter than ever. Why? Because the energy would shift and before I knew it, things were working in my favor! She would start to correct the things I was upset about without the presence of my emotions. It's like when a wife nags her husband. Despite all the things that he does to make her mad, if she backs off, he'll wonder why and try to fix things, all because of that shift in energy!

If you keep telling someone to do something or try to change them, their ego is only going to resist. Yes, EGO. It's not really them; it's their fear-filled brain telling them to act this way, to be defensive. So stop being angry with them. Love them! When you blow a cloud of love in the face of the ego, it has no choice but to step aside. Love conquers the ego because the ego is made of fear; FEAR AND LOVE CANNOT COEXIST, AS ONE CANCELS THE OTHER. Love is far more powerful. So ask yourself, would you rather fight until you're blue in the face to prove you're right, or would you rather just be happy? If in the end, your love or acceptance doesn't change their actions, then take a closer look and see what it really changed. Do you see it? It changed *you*.

• •

While I can't fix how I felt in the past, I can see something tremendous now. In all the times I felt alone and hurt, I kept fighting. My fight obviously led me to victory because I now stand taller than ever. I hold my head high and at the same time, I keep love in my life at all times. Yes, there are fleeting moments of darkness, but they always pass as soon as I call back the light; as soon as I remember the truth.

> MY FIGHT OBVIOUSLY LED ME TO VICTORY BECAUSE I NOW STAND TALLER THAN EVER.

Learn to find the positive in every hardship and recall it whenever you find yourself in the dark. Don't sit around waiting for someone to help you. Help yourself! Acknowledge what happened, accept it, let it go, and look forward to something that will do you good. Then figure out what you'll need to do to get there. Maybe something that happened will empower you to get there quicker because you're now wiser. And remember, it may be your own faults that have led you to where you are at this current moment, but you must acknowledge that to grow from it. When you realize where you've been and what you can do with the lessons you've learned from your past, you can go the distance in life. Most importantly, always invite love in your heart no matter what. It will be your greatest ally.

Do you want to love unconditionally? Can you forgive others so you can heal yourself? Would you like to know that no matter what happens, you will be ok, that you'll be happy? You must reach a point in your life where your mood or choice isn't based on the selfish, insignificant action of another person or circumstance. You also must learn to laugh at your own mistakes. Shake your head, give it a giggle and get over it! Getting over shit quickly is a great strength and you *do* have it in you. I've used all my hardships as fuel for strength. I've also turned around and laughed at it all because I know how necessary it is to find humor in life. Life is about being free, not taking things so seriously. You can do exactly what I've done to overcome your troubles. Be a warrior, wear your battle wounds proudly, acknowledge your victories… then, let it all go and live lovingly in the present moment! Just forgive!

CHAPTER 4

GHOSTS OF MEMORIES

I don't remember much of my childhood. Is this normal? I don't know and I honestly don't care! Why? I live in the present moment! However, one fond memory I'll always hold is of Pop, my grandfather, teaching me how to catch a pigeon.

I can see it clear as day. We were in his backyard standing under the Horse Chestnut tree. He wore high waters with suspenders and a trucker hat propped up on his snow-white hair. Slowly, we bent low to the ground with feed cupped in our hands and he told me to throw some. The sound it made on the slate pathway enticed a few pigeons that were perched in the tree. They were grey and white and tan and white with full feathered necks. As we remained still, they cautiously came over and pecked the feed from our hands. I mimicked his energy, being very graceful and patient and then… I snatched one up! The feeling of holding it in my hands was so rewarding.

· ·

Pop was a cool guy; he touched the lives of everyone in my family, especially mine. We all looked up to him because he positively influenced us, like how he taught me to catch a pigeon. It wasn't just that I caught a bird; he taught me to have patience so I could accomplish my goal. It's important to have strong role models like that in children's lives, people who show them guidance.

The little things you say or show your kids will influence them greatly. That memory stands out in my mind for all these years because I was so proud of myself. When you build a child's self-esteem it helps them later in life. One of the worst things you can do is to talk down to them or make them feel as if they aren't amounting to what you wanted. Whether you realize it or not, they're always trying to impress you, so shooting them down for failure is a blow to their confidence. I know *I* didn't hear "I'm proud of you" a lot. My parents never purposely made me feel bad about myself, but they also didn't recognize my achievements. I had the ability to do things, but I didn't have the drive, so I ended up slacking off a lot. Motivate your kids. Use **positive reinforcement** so they know good things come from good actions.

> YOUR CHILD WANTS TO BELIEVE YOU'RE AMAZED BY ALL THE GOOD THINGS THEY DO.

Your child wants to believe you're amazed by all the good things they do. They want to feel loved and hear encouragement. Positive reinforcement will help them grow confident and loving. How? They will be taking a positive experience along with them as they grow, which helps them cope in life. Whether an event was good or bad, they'll remember consciously or subconsciously the way it made them *feel*, by remembering the way *you* made them feel, and that will eventually turn into a behavior or an emotion. If it was a negative feeling, they may develop a fear. Here's an example: A little girl and her mother are at a grocery store. The child doesn't want to be there, so she starts whining and acting out which annoys her mother. The mom yells at her child in front of other people and the little girl becomes embarrassed. The mother just helped create a memory and feeling. It obviously wasn't a good one for the little girl because she was embarrassed. The bigger problem is that the experience could cause issues later like shyness, insecurity, or communication issues. She could also have difficulty getting what she wants in life because she will be afraid to ask for it. When she asked something from her mother, she was embarrassed instead of being shown the proper way to act. In the moment, the parent can't usually see the possible effects. They're acting on impulse from frustration or anger instead of reasoning with their child. Children may not have the comprehension that adults do, but they understand quite a lot when you talk with them rationally!

An insignificant moment to a parent could be very significant for the child. The negativity from that re-lived memory and feeling can resurface many times throughout their life, bringing out negative responses. These responses can disable the child. Don't you want to create confidence in your child? I missed out on job opportunities because of my shyness and nervousness, and I have no clue which experiences made me that way! It's not only the memories that we can recall that affect us. These are our subconscious experiences, below our level of awareness. People frequently act the way they do and are held back by things they can't remember.

Do you have any behavioral faults? If so, do you know exactly why you got in the habit of acting that way? If you don't, maybe a suppressed childhood experience is to blame. It may also be an everyday trauma that affected you. An everyday trauma is something that was experienced regularly. In the book, *Many Lives, Many Masters*, author Brian L. Weiss, M.D., states,

> "What I did not yet fully appreciate was that the steady day-in and day-out pounding of undermining influences, such as a parent's scathing criticisms, could cause even more psychological trauma than a single traumatic event. These damaging influences, because they blend into the everyday

background of our lives, are even more difficult to remember and exorcise. A constantly criticized child can lose as much confidence and self-esteem as one who remembers being humiliated on one particular, horrifying day. A child whose family is impoverished and has very little food available on a day-to-day basis might eventually suffer from the same psychological problems as a child who experienced one major episode of accidental near-starvation. I would soon realize that the day-in and day-out pounding of negative forces had to be recognized and resolved with as much attention as that paid to the single, overwhelmingly traumatic event."

He made this realization after hearing his patient, Catherine, recall a past life when she was a boy named Johan while she was under hypnosis. Yea I know, many people don't believe in past lives or reincarnation, but there's a lot of proof out there. Some things that affect us may have been carried into this life from another life we've lived and can be set off by similar events. Past life traumas, those daily traumas that influence us but we don't consciously recognize as abuse or neglect, and other suppressed childhood experiences that carry negative feelings—are hidden in our subconscious. We are not consciously aware of them. And while that may make it a harder to figure out where a negative response originated, we can be aware of it, and release every emotion that comes up along with it. I'll get more into that later.

Just being aware of our fears, emotions, and setbacks helps us recognize that we need to let go of them, no matter their origin. Whether you remember mom, or dad, or whomever being the root of your faults, or even if you can't remember at all, just let your negative emotions go *and*... don't let your children experience them in the first place!

• •

GHOSTS OF MEMORIES

We need to uplift each other. We need to make sure that we're all ok, because we're all going through things. When we let our feelings get in the way, they not only affect us, they affect those around us. While saying negative things to children is harmful to their growth, saying nothing at all is too. The ways we affect our kids, our family members, our friends, or whoever, comes from the way we choose to react, or not react to shared moments. The thing most of us have trouble with in all types of relationships is healthy communication.

· ·

When Pop died, it devastated my family. I was subconsciously crippled from the way everyone dealt with it ...we didn't talk about it! Death was a strange concept at that time because my cousins, my brother, and I were all young. We had never experienced a death before (besides animals.) On top of that, we were all heartbroken when we saw Lou cry because he clearly understood the loss, maybe even more than we did. Lou is my cousin with Down syndrome, but he is not to be underestimated. He's very smart and makes us laugh until our stomachs hurt with his incredible sense of humor. People love him, animals love him; everyone can sense his pure heart. It's amazing to be around his energy, he's always up for a conversation to see how you're doing and how he can help. Regardless of what life has given him, he sees the good in himself and in others, and he only wants everyone to be happy and healthy. We can all learn from people like that.

· ·

My grandma passed away years later, right after my graduation from high school. I never got to have the relationship I wanted with her. She was a strong, hard headed woman like me, so we clashed, but I always thought I'd better fix the relationship before she died, otherwise I would regret it. Oh my God, did I regret it.

A loved one is irreplaceable. Disagreements are nothing compared to the value of someone you love…a living, breathing being whom you have finite days with on this earth. We are here for a short time and none of us know exactly how short that time will be, so we need to make the most of it and let go of the little stuff. We need to be kind to each other. We must understand that our feelings, which turn into choices, which enable behaviors will affect the ones who love us, even if we can't see it.

> LIVE IN THE MOMENT…LIVE LOVINGLY IN THE MOMENT. SURRENDER ALL FEARS.

I expected my grandma to be around for a while. I thought I had time to make things right with her, but I let my ego overshadow my love for too long. Don't make the same mistake. If you need to make amends with a family member, do it NOW. The past is done, so let it go. Allow love to guide you. Don't wait until it's too late and you're burdened with regret. And yes, regret can be released, but we'll always remember what we weren't proud of; what we knew we were doing wrong at the time, yet did it anyway. So live in the moment…live LOVINGLY in the moment. Surrender all fears.

If you have lost someone and torture yourself over what you believe you should have done or said, or not done or said, *please* release your regret. Talk to them; I believe they're always there when you need them. I believe they can hear us. More than a few psychic mediums have told me that when someone passes, they go through a "review" and see why people were the way they were and did the things they did. There's no anger or anything like that on their part. Instead, they only feel love and understanding because they don't feel negativity like we do; they're fully loving energies. Remember, it's your agreements that have formed you into the person you are. Your HUMAN personality and behavior is a composite of patterns and characteristics developed through experience and conditioning, which you can release and relearn to become a better person. Regret is another tool in your book of life. Release it; it's not something to hold onto, but something to learn from. If you allow yourself to transmute it, it will teach you to not make the same mistakes with other people. It will teach you to never feel that type of pain again.

• •

My grandparent's deaths have left such a mark on our lives. My brother, my cousins and I were traumatized not only because we loved them so much, but because the deaths affected our mothers, which affected us. They were so distraught that they failed to adequately comfort us. There was a distance …a painful emptiness. Because of it, I learned to shut off my emotions. I saw my mother shutting down during an emotional time so I learned to shut down my emotions too; it's what I picked up subconsciously. Our mothers are amazing, caring women who would do anything for us, so I know it's no one's fault; people grieve in their own ways but, that's the reality of it. My cousin Tommy and I have discussed it a few times and our feelings are mutual. Our "blunt-loop therapy sessions" were comforting because I realized more about why I am the way I am. I also realized, I wasn't alone in this. YOU are not alone in "this." Communicate. It's *so* very important.

I'm blessed to have someone like Tommy. He's not only family, he's also a friend. He's felt let down in his life too, so we can relate and communicate openly, as adults. I'm also grateful to have my cousin Ashley, Tommy's sister. She's always been like an older sister to me, and over the years, she's become one of my best friends.

• •

There's no right or wrong way to grieve, but my advice is to not push away from your other loved ones, especially your children. They need you for guidance during this hard time, and you probably need them too! The purpose of family is to have a structure built on love and support so that together you can share memories and moments. They will help you process your emotions, as you do the same for them. Just because you may feel you have more pain than someone else, that doesn't mean you have to deal with it *by* yourself. Let's take charge of experiences by sharing them. No matter how bad things were, we will remember the love and support there at that time, not the bad memory.

I've seen some of my friends lose their parents when they were young. Their lives became chaotic afterward because they didn't have the comfort they needed, which is so sad. It's traumatic to lose someone at any age, but it's especially hard for a kid. When we're young, we're still trying to understand our lives and ourselves, so the death of a loved one can be a major trauma. While things like religion teach us about it and try to comfort us, we will still have a lot of unanswered questions. What's most important is to have others who will guide us through it. We're all here to help each other; no one should be alone. The voids we don't heal will be filled with emotions that will turn into suppressed negativity. No one needs that. There's always someone to talk to, whether we choose a professional, a friend, or someone who "coincidentally" happens to be there at the right time. If we don't have a Tommy or an Ashley, we *can* find comfort, even from complete strangers. There are many caring people in this world, as hard as it may be to see them sometimes.

Whether you believe it or not, we all have spirit guides, angels, god(s), or energies watching over us. When you become open enough to believe in them, you'll recognize their presence through signs, opportunities, "coincidences," and miracles that occur after you've asked for their guidance. ASK FOR THEIR GUIDANCE. ASK FOR THEIR SUPPORT. You will realize you are never truly alone in this world.

As we take on human form in each life, we may feel physically alone for short periods of time (which seem long from our perspective), but we are infinitely, never alone spiritually. When you understand and tap into that concept, by **waking up**, you will NEVER FEEL ALONE AGAIN. Take this from someone who used to feel so very alone. I'll never feel that way again, because even if no one on this earth has my back, I do, and so does the universe. Spirituality is something we cannot deny as conscious living beings.

• •

When you experience a death or another catastrophic experience, in the moment it's almost like life is over. While it's normal to feel bad, understanding that it's part of your journey, another hurdle to overcome, is being optimistic and that will only make you stronger. After the moment passes and you're still alive and the world is still turning, you realize that you got through it; you're still breathing! With each breath, release the bad feelings from your body. Remember how tough you had to be to get through those moments. Plant each memory with a seed of clarity and not confusion. If you can see how brave and strong you are as your life progresses, you can build on your optimism and overcome any hurdle life has placed in your way. How we handle death is how we perceive life. If you're an optimistic realist, you'll believe there's something bigger, a greater plan than you can wrap your head around, but you know it's there. Having faith in the universe will set you free.

> HOW WE HANDLE DEATH IS HOW WE PERCEIVE LIFE.

If you lose a loved one, stay strong because you *can* get through it. Love every day you're alive and cherish the blessings you have around you. If you don't have many, at least you have life. Be thankful for your memories and the privilege of loving someone, because not everyone experiences that. Don't focus on the negative. Let the pain from your trauma go and remember the good times. I believe everything happens for a reason and we'll all figure it out one day, whether we're on this earth, or beyond it. In the meantime, be happy.

• •

Besides a few childhood memories and the painful ones of past relationships, I don't have many more. Most of my memories are from home videos and pictures. I know I've smoked a lot of weed, but could it really have affected me to that degree? Maybe the trauma I experienced in my teenage years did something to my mind? Maybe there are things from my childhood that are affecting me? I have no clue. I used to fear that something traumatic had happened in my childhood that I had subconsciously suppressed. I've come to know myself very well over the years and I would like to think there's no missing puzzle piece. From what I know, the reasons why I am the way I am are because of my experiences and the way I was raised. *But,* if I ever do find something I would rather not know, I won't let it affect me! How will I do that? First, by energetically letting it go, and second, by reminding myself of who I am today. Today is all that matters!

You are not what happened to you. You are not the emotions you hold from your memories. You are not the keeper of negativity others have placed on you. You are *you*, as you stand right now, free as bird in love with the wind. The past is gone; it's not real, release it. What counts is the present moment. Live in it.

CHAPTER 5

UNDOING THE DAMAGE

Amber, a former friend of mine, developed BPD (Borderline Personality Disorder) because of her childhood trauma. I didn't know about it until I started dating her brother. She didn't like it and started showing her true colors. He told me that her parents would lock the two of them up in a room for hours when they were babies. The reason? They were busy doing cocaine. *Nice, right?* All this talk of love and there's a perfect example of the lack of it.

• •

Amber and I became friends in 2008. I was in orientation for a waitressing job and she sat across from me and my friend, Corrine. During the orientation, Corrine and I passed notes to each other about smoking a blunt after the training. Amber interjected to tell us she had weed so we agreed to smoke with her.

I really liked Corrine, but when I started a friendship with Amber, Corrine began to throw jabs and get mad at me. Corrine was a lesbian. Although we had a platonic relationship, she was jealous. That's how I knew she wasn't a real friend. It felt like my past happening all over again, but I was able to catch it before it went too far. (*See, bad friends do teach us good lessons.*) Instead of trying to salvage things with Corrine, I moved on.

• •

Amber and I were similar, from the type of music we listened to, to smoking weed daily, to home troubles. She would tell me everything, so we quickly became close. She also had a lot of issues. I began to see them the more we hung out.

BPD is tragic because its victims become self-destructive. Amber had done porn, had extremely low self-esteem, was bulimic, and did drugs. She also had conniving and manipulative characteristics. She would lie, steal, and have major fluctuations in mood. You might say, *Then why would you be friends with her?* It was just something that happened. We clicked and I couldn't deny the chemistry.

Chemistry might get me into trouble. It forces me to use my heart instead of my gut. *Hmmm,* kind of like my repetitive relationships. Amber had a hold on me, even though I felt she was trouble. In that sort of situation, we must weigh the good with the bad and determine what they'll bring to the relationship. Was I keeping Amber around to fulfill something in myself? Did I want to help her? Was she going to bring me down in any way? I think it was all of that. I felt a bond with her since we were similar, I did want to help her through her troubles, yet I also feared she could bring negativity into my life. However, I always give people a chance by not judging them and observing what they bring to the table. When I do that, I can see if I want to allow someone into my life. I've also used it as a tool to help me discover when it's time to let them go.

• •

The friends I've made as an adult share a common denominator. I'm pretty sure my energy attracts their energy, if you know what I mean. They sense I may be able to heal something in them, or help them through something, because they all reveal their life stories to me right off the bat. Many people have told me they can sense that I'm trustworthy, which I am, but from being "awake" I know there's more to it. My energetic field freely gives off compassion vibes, and at the same time, no bullshit vibes. People realize I don't tolerate nonsense because I never return it to them. It's like they feel I'll tell them something no one else will. They seek the truth in themselves by sharing with me, hoping I will give them constructive criticism… which I do. That's what makes a real friend; they're someone you can trust to keep your secrets, and who will call out your bullshit, not a "yes man."

The thing about *all* my friends (including childhood friends) is that they always asked my advice and I was more than happy to give it to them, but they rarely used it! It was always the same trauma and drama over and over, but as a friend, all I could do was keep listening, offer my opinions, and allow them to make their own choices. *You* may agree with the things I've written about, but unless you're willing to put it into action, this will be another book you throw on the shelf and forget about most of its content. Sometimes that's how it is though. I can give the most amazing advice, and sometimes not even use it myself!

We're not always ready for the truth and that's ok, but the more we learn to push through resistance and do what we know is right, what we *feel* is right, the greater we will become. While I may not be able to reach everyone, that won't stop me from planting seeds.

> THE MORE WE PUSH THROUGH RESISTANCE AND DO WHAT WE KNOW IS RIGHT, THE GREATER WE WILL BECOME.

My goal in writing this was to give people a guide to happiness. I want you to **feel** the truth and **see** how easy it is to fix your life…and then do it! Whenever you need to do something but are procrastinating or self-sabotaging, get up and do what you need to do without thinking too much! Push yourself! I want people to heal, to experience life. I'm just a regular person who went through some stuff and was able to pull myself out of my suffering with tremendous ease, all by doing simple things that cost me nothing. It's been said that the best things in life are free, right? Well, they are, and they're available to you when you're ready to accept them. Are you ready?

Time is of the essence to make positive strides in your life. If you don't, you're wasting valuable time being unhappy, being stuck in your ways. I spent many years like that. To snap out of it, I decided to try another way for once; I decided to listen to the good advice of others, the good advice that had resonated with what was inside me all along. If you listen to my mistakes and my corrections and then try it all out for yourself, you'll be happy you did!

• •

Amber revealed more as our relationship grew and I felt I needed to be there for her. I wanted to guide her in the right direction. I've always enjoyed giving my friends advice. Not only did it feel good to help them, but it also showed me something about myself. I had been through real things and grown wise from them, so much so that I could teach others.

Something I wasn't so wise about was doing drugs. Obviously, it was bad for me but I didn't realize I shouldn't be doing drugs with Amber. Smoking weed was innocent, but we got heavy into pills one summer.

• •

Our days consisted of smoking 3-4 blunts, taking up to 10 Vicodin each, sometimes Xanax, and driving around selling them. I recall being in a zombie-like state every day and night. It ended when I caught her cheating me out of money. I cut her out of my life for about two years.

After I got off pills, I realized what I was doing was horrible, horrible for myself and for others. Selling any kind of drug besides

UNDOING THE DAMAGE

weed (which is not a drug unless you're putting it in the medicinal category) is equivalent to ruining someone's life. The price a drug dealer pays, figuratively, is the price of their own soul. Plain and simple, it's bad karma! The draw of selling drugs is the fast money that comes out of it. It's the easy route and that's why more and more kids are getting involved. If education were stronger and there were more teachers who cared, fewer kids would become dealers. Kids need better direction on how to set and achieve their goals, not to read some useless nonsense written on the blackboard. I'll say it… most of the stuff we learn in school is useless! Find your true, creative potential and don't let anything stop you from marching toward it. See chapter eight if you need help with your goals.

• •

I'll never go back taking or selling drugs. When I imagined how much damage I was doing to my body, I became angry. I felt guilty that Amber had told me many times that she looked up to me. What kind of example was I setting? I was supposed to be showing her the way *out* of her troubles, not encouraging them! So instead of continuing to be angry because I couldn't change it, I used it as a learning experience like everything else. I promised myself I would never abuse pills again and never put them into someone else's hands.

Have you been there? Are you there now? If so, consider what you're doing. Drugs are killing at an unimaginable speed. They're only suppressing the emotions that need to be released.

• •

We take drugs to numb our pain and to silence our psyches, but what we're really doing is not dealing with our emotions. Not dealing is not accepting love. When you put drugs in your body, you cannot possibly love yourself. If you're assisting someone else in putting them in *their* body, again, you can't possibly love yourself. We're all one and what we do to others is projected back onto us. It's bad energy, bad karma. The money that you hold and spend has bad vibes attached to it. Whatever you buy with it will surround you with that energy. See chapter eight for the right reasons to obtain money.

•••••••••••••••••••••••••••••

When Amber and I hung out again, she hit me with one of the worst things she could. She did heroin. I was heartbroken for her. I also felt guilty. Could I have caused her to fall so low? She had BPD but I'm sure she was hurt when I ended our friendship. That's when I realized that same "what if" was haunting me again and decided the only thing I could do, was be there for her. So that's what I did.

•••••••••••••••••••••••••••••

One sunny summer day, dressed in brightly colored clothes that matched our moods, Amber and I took a ride to Jamaica, Queens, to get weed. When we got there, we picked up her friend B and some other guy. We hung out, smoked for a little, and stopped at a Dunkin Donuts™. Amber took a long time in the bathroom. I felt in my stomach what she was doing. I was angry.

When she got into my car, I demanded that she look at me. Her eyes were insane, on another level; I was so disturbed. B took her bag and pulled out two used needles from a hidden pocket. She swore they were old, but we decided to leave it alone since she was barely "there."

There she was, a nice-looking girl, hair done, all fucked up on heroin, with two syringes in her fifteen-hundred-dollar Chanel™ purse. I couldn't be there for Amber anymore. Sometimes it's best to step away from an addict, but I still feel sad about it. She became a different person, a shell of herself. Once someone's addicted like that, it's rare for them to pull themselves out of it, especially when they have deep psychological issues. I always wonder how she's doing and if she's even alive. I wish I could have helped, but without her acceptance and willingness, there was no helping her. Her family tried and I tried, but what was going on in her head was far more powerful than we were.

UNDOING THE DAMAGE

My friend's brother died at 22 from a heroin overdose; it was devastating. He was a good kid who had potential in life. While he tried so many times to get clean, it ended up killing him. Amber, if you're reading this, I wish nothing but the best for you and hope you're doing well.

• •

When it comes to addiction, it's not the drugs that are taking over, it's the person's personality, their demons, their fears. Those fears originated from past experiences and that's why therapy is necessary; it's a release. A life change using self-awareness, forgiveness, acceptance, and love is needed. AN AWAKENING IS NEEDED. If someone you know starts using drugs, the first thing to do is be there for them, but don't enable them. Let them know that you love them and how their behavior is affecting your life. Show them the light by explaining that the process of setting their pain free is very real and very possible. If they agree to get help, that's a positive step in the right direction. I've seen addicts, even my own brother, continue to use because they weren't getting the proper help. I always hear people say that the addict must want to get better for it to happen. While I believe that and believe they all *do* want to get better, I think it's up to their support system, *to a certain degree*, to bring that out of them and show them the way to a happier life. They need therapy, guidance, and love. It's very rare they'll decide or succeed on their own to get clean.

My parents were always there for my brother but a little *too* there. They enabled a lot of his behavior by giving him money and not enforcing stronger consequences. Don't let your love for someone overshadow your guidance; it will only be harmful to them.

• •

It seemed like Josh, Amber's brother, hated her, judging by the way he talked about her. What he really hated was everything she'd done to their family because he couldn't understand it. He reminded me of someone...myself. Yes, Amber had done a lot of fucked up things to them but to look at the bigger picture, she had a serious disorder. Realizing that helped me with my situation at home. Since Josh and I had similar things going on, it gave us both comfort to talk about it and helped me to not *hate* my brother. I despised him for a while, but the more I learned about other people, like Amber, the less I felt so angry. I realized that sometimes people just can't control themselves, and it's not their fault. It's their trapped, emotional pasts that are influencing their lives.

• •

Many times, damaged adults were abused, neglected, or mistreated as children. Sometimes they were just misinformed. Children are innocent, brought into this world as blank canvases ready to be painted. They learn almost everything they know from the people and things around them (agreements). When something happens that influences or impacts their lives, they carry that into adulthood. If it hurt them, the adult they become usually reflects that pain. Many people who experienced trauma as children end up developing disorders and addictions. Whose fault is it? It's no one's fault; we could say it's whomever made a negative imprint on their lives, but then we'd have to blame whoever did it to *them* and so on and so on. That's why the cycle of abuse is so devastating.

What can break that cycle? Love, acceptance, awareness, forgiveness, releasing, and... surrendering to the present! Re-wire the brain with a new understanding of self! These things are huge! They're not just little aspects of life; they're profoundly powerful abilities we don't use enough. We fight them instead of working with them!

UNDOING THE DAMAGE

When you encounter someone you would label a "bad" person or if that person does something to you… **just forgive**. Remember to be a **Superhuman** and act in a totally different way than expected to get a totally different expected experience. Don't let that person create a negative bond with you because of their imbalanced conscious scale. Balance your own by acting with love! Something really messed up must have happened for them to become that way, so think of them with compassion.

When I view people, I view them as souls, not bodies. Our souls don't control our bodies, our minds do! When pollutants are present, whether they are physical or mental, the mind influences the body to make certain choices. Those choices may be wrong but they're almost inevitable, due to the *abundance* of pollutants in the world. That's why we as individuals and as a society need to negate the negativity. How do we do that? With forgiveness and love! This will not only negate it but spread it in the form of positive energy from one person to the next. I understand, however, that some things people do seem unforgivable, such as the trauma caused by death or rape, but the purpose of forgiveness is not to benefit the perpetrator. It's to free the victim of the hold their pain has on them.

Release the feelings trapped inside you. Being violated in any way is a physical thing; it's a feeling. When a memory is recalled, the emotion surfaces and the body experiences the emotion. If you can get rid of those feelings instead of letting them eat at you forever, then do it. Feelings are only made up of energy that can be moved out of the body.

Now I'm not saying that all traumas can be resolved through releasing alone, because some people may need professional therapy, especially since some emotional releases can bring up other suppressed emotions or experiences. However, releasing is an efficient tool to help heal, and it costs nothing.

As low as you feel in life, you're only being held down by energy that can be shifted, *if you allow it to happen*. As I've said, memories aren't real. What we feel are the associated emotions or trapped energy that is tied to those memories. When we get rid of those feelings, we are free; we are at peace.

• •

Everything that happens affects us to a certain degree, but we all experience different levels and cope in different ways. Don't be judgmental toward others, because you never know how what they've been through has shaped them.

One way to diminish the number of damaged people is to create more awareness about child abuse. Kids should learn at an early age they should go for help if someone is mistreating them. We should also have stricter laws because many adults cross the fine line between discipline and child abuse. I believe no child should be hit. It physically hurts them, but more importantly, mentally scars them. Think about the bad energy coming from the hand of the parent. It goes directly into the child and they don't have a choice to accept it or not. It's a loveless way of teaching because it uses fear and what that does is shows them it's ok to be fearful, that "that's how life works." It also demonstrates that the parent hasn't created healthy communication with the child where they can get on their level of understanding to convey the message. When you can explain and reason with a child, they pick up that logic and use it throughout their lives. *That's* how life SHOULD work.

Also, pedophiles aren't being brought to justice. They're screwed up from something that happened in their lives, but we must stop them from screwing up more children. They're allowed back out there with merely a scarlet letter, ready to repeat their heinous crimes, many times to more severe degrees. The truth is that many of them are protected and right under our noses in this disturbing society we have created. It's horrendous and perhaps they need stricter penalties and have permanent, mandatory therapy along with random monitoring to prevent a reoccurrence. Something needs to be done. More children should be aware of this subject. They could learn more important life lessons in school, rather than the usual bullshit.

Another form of child abuse is feeding them unhealthy food. Just like emotional or physical abuse, it damages the child later in life (and sometimes sooner). People don't normally make the connection that what we eat affects our moods. **Nutrition** is important for keeping the physical body healthy, and for keeping the mind healthy as well! It's important for parents to know what the right food is. If you're a parent, don't ignore this. Set your child up for a long, healthy existence on this earth; don't play Russian roulette with their life.

> PEOPLE DON'T NORMALLY MAKE THE CONNECTION THAT WHAT WE EAT AFFECTS OUR MOODS.

• •

One day in psychology, we discussed the symptoms of BPD. Amber had every single symptom. I diagnosed her on the spot, putting checkmarks next to the symptoms she had; there was no doubt in my mind. A week later she said, "Kate, I have borderline."

I compassionately said, "I know." I told her I learned about it in Psych class and she made a face almost like she was insulted. My intention was not to insult her, but to communicate to her that I understood. I understood she was abused or mistreated during a time in her life when love was crucial, and the abused child grew into a damaged adult. I didn't judge her, I empathized with her.

Another person who I learned about in psychology, was my brother. I didn't empathize with him so much at first because I didn't understand that his issues were really to blame for his behavior. The things he did put little obstructions in my happiness because I spent so much time being angry with him. When I was able to understand, I was able to heal.

SUPERHUMAN

Mental illness is horrible for everyone. Misdiagnosis is even worse. Let's bring more awareness, less judgement, and a whole lot of healing.

• •

To sum it up without a coat of sugar…The world is like a prison. We're constantly controlled by fears, constantly in a dark place, constantly limited, and constantly punished. But here's the thing… we're all innocent. Our pure souls that mean no harm get tossed into circumstances, some that we have been put in and others that we have put ourselves in, knowingly or not. We are each held captive by our own mistakes, actions, inactions, feelings, and fears. We become prisoners because we choose unhappiness. Nothing good happens just because we are down in the dumps or because we experience some fucked up things. Things don't get better for us until we make them better. Pity doesn't exist in the laws of the universe. Creation and manifestation don't work to keep us happy. It's our responsibility to create happiness *from* them. In every moment we have choices, and the biggest, most rewarding choice *is*…the choice to be happy! In any moment. Under any circumstance. Yes, we can go through horrific things, we can do horrific things, but if we let those things destroy us, we are **choosing** darkness; it's not choosing us. We're not only choosing it, we are allowing it to grow. To choose light, to live in light, we must acknowledge where we've been, learn the lessons from it, and change for the better.

This is *evolving*. You want to keep learning; you want to use every life lesson and every bit of knowledge to elevate your consciousness to help you better understand life. The more you understand it, the more you will understand joy and how to experience it. Think about it. What is it doing for you if you stay in a dark place after something bad occurs? Do you have to prove something to someone? Do you

> THINGS DON'T GET BETTER FOR US UNTIL WE MAKE THEM BETTER.

UNDOING THE DAMAGE

feel it's wrong to be happy after some shitty thing happens? Do you need to prove something to yourself? That you don't deserve happiness? Is it wrong to push a bad feeling out of your system because people might look at you like you don't have a heart? Or maybe you'll look at yourself that way? Get the fuck out of here! It's no one's business when and why you are happy. Or if not happy, at least not drowning in sadness. Come on! Are you supposed to punish yourself every time you do something wrong or something bad happens to you, or are you supposed to make right from it? Learn from it!

It's ridiculous to suppress our joy and allow others to do it to us. You probably do it too! It's called judgement and it's a load of crap. You can't judge people because you never know what they've been through, or where their head is, so you're only making a false observation based on your own fear driven ego. GET OVER YOURSELF. Learn to be a loving human being! Start by loving the person you are, no matter where you've been or where you are. It is in *your own* power to create the world around you, to see through love-filled eyes and to experience life with a free heart. No one, nothing, not even the laws of the universe can change someone's life for the better, so why would anyone wait around hoping for happiness? Why are *you* waiting for happiness!? You already have it! You just choose it and it will choose you. The universe DOES work like that. It matches the vibrational energy of your thoughts, intentions, and emotions, so be mindful of what you are feeling because you are creating. You know exactly what I'm talking about because you've been experiencing this truth your entire life, whether you realized it before you read this or not. This world is not bad, it is us who are plagued with oppressive beliefs. So please, PLEASE, pretty please… in the words of Bob Marley, "Get up, stand up, stand up for your rights!" You are not really a prisoner. You have the ability, the right, to be free. GO!

    YOU: Universe, why are you making my life so miserable?
    UNIVERSE: Oh, this is not what you want?
    YOU: No!

UNIVERSE: Are you uncomfortable?

YOU: Yes, very.

UNIVERSE: Guess what I'm going to do for you?

YOU: Make me happy?

UNIVERSE: Nope! I'm going to keep making things hard on you until you stop feeling sorry for yourself.

YOU: Why would you do that?

UNIVERSE: So you learn how to overcome adversity. LEARN HOW TO JUST BE HAPPY.

YOU: Hmm, so my attitude and actions are the reason bad things keep happening to me?

UNIVERSE: Congratulations, the first step to recovery is admitting *you* are the problem! I'd like to reward you with this opportunity to better your life even further...

• •

Holding onto anything negative, big or small, only haunts us; it controls us and spares us no pain. If we want to be free, we must let go. We should stop being angry and saddened by the things that no longer exist. We must learn our lessons and live our lives the way we dream of living them.

If you were a victim of child abuse or neglect, don't let the mental abuse carry on any longer. Release the pain with The Sedona Method™. Understand that it was completely, utterly, not your fault. You were an innocent child, and you don't have to let your abuser affect your life any further. Forgive them... for yourself; love yourself; release, release, release; move on with your life and live in this very moment. You deserve to be happy.

> "The Universe isn't judgmental. It won't grant your wishes when you are asking for pity. The Universe IS freedom and it will grant you freedom when you choose to be free and make it your reality"
>
> —Jaclyn Wallach

CHAPTER 6

DON'T DRINK THE POISON!

One MAJOR step in my transformation into a "Superhuman" was when I learned to **forgive**. *Let's face it, that's a tough one for most.* But, we must get over what others have done to us to move forward in our lives. If we constantly relive past emotional experiences, we're holding ourselves back from being happy.

Would you like to give yourself something special? Forgiveness is such an incredible gift and the funny thing is, it's more of a gigantic surprise covered in wrapping paper and bows for the person who forgave, than it is a small act of kindness to the person who was forgiven.

• •

Who haven't you forgiven? Let's try a simple exercise: Think of a person who offended or hurt you, but you haven't yet forgiven. Got one? Good. Release them right now; release how they made you feel. Ask yourself:

The Sedona Method™
1—What is my now feeling?
2—Could I welcome/allow that feeling?

3—Could I let it go?
4—Would I let it go?
5—When?

Do you feel different, like something changed? How could this have happened without that person even being present, without a conversation or an apology? It's because YOU'RE the one holding the grudge, letting it affect *you*. They're not experiencing a debilitating emotion, *you* are…and you don't have to! As easy as it is for you to remember what they did, it's just as easy to remember that it holds no real weight in the present moment. Their past offense is nothing now, and you don't have to experience the emotion that came from it anymore. YOU have all the power. TAKE IT.

• •

Not forgiving someone is a constant reach for control. You're trying to punish them for the way they've made you feel. In the end, YOU'RE PUNISHING YOURSELF by holding onto that negative bond. You certainly can't get rid of the way they made you feel if you keep reliving it! And yeah, it may be impossible to *forget* what they did, but you can **release the emotion** tied to their wrongdoing. Doing this will release you from their painful hold. It's not your job to put people in a time-out chair. The universe takes care of that in its own way. Your job is to love yourself and not let others affect you.

> IT MAY BE IMPOSSIBLE TO FORGET, BUT YOU CAN RELEASE THE EMOTION TIED TO THEIR WRONGDOING.

When we forgive, we're demonstrating **love**; we're showing forgiveness to that person and to ourselves. That changes something in them, as well as something in us. I understand forgiving is hard; I've been there, but the greatest benefit of it belongs to YOU, not to the person you forgave! This is the most important distinction for truly understanding this esoteric principle. YOU get to rid yourself of the pain that is keeping you stuck! After forgiveness has occurred, even after a long time of being hurt, a weight is instantly lifted. You feel at ease because you've let go of the bad energy that was anchored to you, dragging behind you, serving no purpose at all!

• •

While I admit that I had some fault in all my relationships, I always stayed true to people. I was loyal and got played repeatedly, which led to my unhappiness. It was the same with friendships. Throughout the years I've had to leave behind most of my friends, even the ones I thought would be there forever. No matter how close you are to people or how loyal you may be, there will always be someone who will screw you over. You have the power to not allow them to affect you. How badly they screw you over is all on you.

People may do harmful things to you, but it's not about you. The book, *The Four Agreements*, by Don Miguel Ruiz, explains this well. We make agreements with ourselves about everything we learn or experience. Most of the time, these agreements are made, whether they're right or wrong, without us even knowing we're making them. For instance, as children we're taught what to believe and how to act. Can we say, *racism?* This is the only possible origin for ignorant concepts like that. We make sense of this world and ourselves through other people's influences. This eventually shapes us into the emotional, *or emotionless,* beings that we are because these influential thoughts become psychological programs that affect how we function every day; and while some help us cope, others cripple us from fully experiencing life. Your task is to **observe** which thoughts and beliefs are holding *you* back, so you can work on fixing them by making new, correct agreements.

According to Don Miguel Ruiz, the four agreements for a happy life are the following: 1) *Be impeccable with your word,* 2) *Don't take anything personally,* 3) *Don't make assumptions,* and 4) *Always do your best*. "Don't take anything personally," the second agreement in the book, is so important to understand because let's face it, people are fucked up from other people. The actions of others stem from their perspective, from the many agreements that have formed them into the person *they* are, so they have different views and morals than you do. While you can't understand their agreements because they're different from your own, you should understand that it's nothing to take personally. If we take things personally, we're sharing and accepting another person's beliefs, allowing them to infiltrate and influence *our* minds.

Remember when I explained that releasing emotions allows you to feel and act differently when faced with a recurring problem? This is where that tool can be used. When someone says or does something to you that would normally cause a familiar reaction or feeling inside you, you are now equipped with the ability to feel and act differently, because now you think differently! The agreement has a new meaning …or maybe no meaning! So, no matter how hurt or frustrated or angry you are because of something someone did, you hold all the power in *how* what they did will continue to affect you. Remember that peace is found in forgiveness, not in holding a grudge. You have the choice to just let go, to free yourself of a temporary emotion and keep it at that… temporary. People hold onto painful emotions all the time, not realizing they can actually get rid of them and feel good! Feelings caused by someone else's view of the world, a view that's so different from your own, are only there for a moment until you accept them as your own. Now the question becomes… how do you confidently overcome other people's agreements? With **self-awareness**! When you know who you are, whatever anyone else says or does to you doesn't matter; you don't have to accept it!

• •

HOW TO INCREASE SELF-AWARENESS: Start with **love**. When you're able to love and accept yourself by realizing that you're a soul

DON'T DRINK THE POISON!

just like everyone else, you can figure out who you are as a person and why you do the things you do, through internal and external observation. For instance, think about a time when someone wronged you. How did you act, or should I say react? Was it a positive experience? No? Then you probably acted on emotion and not self-love. If you flipped out, hit the person, got revenge, or acted in a negative way, it probably didn't cancel out your anger and instead it keeps offending you, correct? That's because you're lacking self-love and self-awareness—the tools that allow you to think and feel differently (positively), the tools that give you the ability to *shine* through the shade people throw your way. Increase your self-awareness by reminding yourself of who you are and why you're amazing instead of letting other's opinions and negative intentions get to you. Then you can make the best choices, choices that will change your life in incredible ways.

> INCREASE YOUR SELF-AWARENESS BY REMINDING YOURSELF OF WHO YOU ARE AND WHY YOU'RE AMAZING.

• •

I'm going to ask you something that I want you to ask yourself…it may or may not apply to you, but many people need to ask themselves this question: At what point are you going to love yourself and stop seeking other's attention and approval? When are you going to stop giving a shit what others think and do? When are you going to love you, for you? When are you going to be happy with yourself? When are you going to make those choices? WHEN? What time? What day? What year? What life? How about this one and how about now? Being happy and loving yourself has nothing to do with anyone else. Nothing. Remember that.

• •

What's that? Someone just took a shot at you? You know who you are and how great you are, so why do you care? *They* must be lacking self-awareness and self-love. *Now do you get it?*

Coming to love and know yourself will keep the people who take advantage of you over and over out of your life, or at a safe distance. If you know what I'm saying all too well, then you should ask yourself, *Why do I allow people to take advantage of me?* They may see a weakness, a lack of confidence that comes from lack of self-love and awareness, or maybe you allow yourself to be hurt.

The truth is that people who have grown accustomed to being hurt by others find it easier to continue being hurt; it's like they're asking for help to justify their suffering. It's twisted but true; pain is comfortable for some people because it's familiar. The thought of stepping out of a comfort zone feels threatening because it puts them face-to-face with fear. Change is scary! *But*, since fear is fake, when it's confronted with self-love, which is very real, it no longer has strength. You do!

Now there are instances of abuse that are of no fault of the victim. That's where it is especially important not to take things personally. As Don Miguel Ruiz states, "Don't take *anything* personally. Even if someone got a gun and shot you in the head, it was nothing personal. Even at that extreme." Abusers are merely demonstrating their "model of the world," their perspective. So, it's not about you, it's about them.

• •

Know your own weaknesses, faults, strengths, and qualities. They will carry you through life, depending on how you use them. Look at yourself as your parents' child. Whoever raised you and how they raised you significantly influenced who you became. There's truth to the phrase "You're turning into your mother," or "You're just like your father." My parents imprinted their agreements on me, and I accepted them. Some of their faults have become my own and it made me want to point a finger, but they're not to blame! They were conditioned by their parents, who were conditioned by *their* parents, and so on. Do you see the cycle?

The thing is, if we don't break the cycle by accepting and forgiving our biggest influences, we can't accept other men or women who come into our lives. Just like agreements turn us into our parents, they affect who we choose as our partners. I'm sure you've heard the theory that women pick men who mirror their fathers, and men pick women who mirror their mothers. People usually seek what they know, even if it's abusive.

Sometimes men with absent or abusive mothers growing up tend to treat women badly later in life. It's the same with women and their fathers. Sometimes it's the other way around, where the abuse or neglect they experienced makes them pick people who will repeat the same behavior. They allow it because it's what they know; it feels familiar.. Can you see how these psychological programs can affect people so dramatically in their lives and in their relationships? You should now understand why the programs need to change.

• •

Sigmund Freud believed that children develop their personality between the ages of three to five, while other professionals say ages one to three. Either way, those are crucial years, so who's making the biggest impression on them? The people they're around the most! Children mimic or model their caretakers as they grow because it shows them how to act. While other sources like their environment also influence them, parents are typically the biggest teachers.

Do you notice how many questions kids ask? Questions are how they learn about the world. The answers they receive create neuro-associations that contribute to the growth of their minds, setting them on a certain path in life. If you take a look at who and where you are now and find that you're not content, you may need to change some of the agreements that were put in *your* mind. When you let go of them, you turn away from fear and head down the path towards love, where a new life with new opportunities will appear. Why? Because you've changed a major part of who you are! When you think differently, more positively than you always have, these new thoughts will create new scenarios that will lead you to success. Failure is just lack of persistence, or being set in your ways. You can never fail if you keep reinventing yourself!

> NEW THOUGHTS WILL CREATE NEW SCENARIOS THAT WILL LEAD YOU TO SUCCESS.

If you dig deep down in your heart and feel that something isn't right, despite what you were told, you need to change that fear-based agreement. I'm learning to change the ones I feel are wrong. Don't be afraid to do the same! Embrace new possibilities and show future generations that it's ok to think outside the box that's labeled "What Mom and Dad taught me."

• •

Today, most children learn to fear and struggle through life, and what that teaches them about themselves is that the happy, loving child they are isn't good enough for this world. That that they have limitations! It's sad but true. Children are our true teachers, but because we're too controlled and too controlling, we can't accept that …or even see it! They show us how to live—how be joyful, fearless, forgiving, loving, and imaginative. As adults and parents, we stop them from using their full potential because we put limitations, boundaries, FEARS on them …on ourselves! Just imagine what kids could create and change in the world if we allowed them to believe they could do anything, that their imaginations were valid. Imagine if *we* believed that we could do anything…

• •

DON'T DRINK THE POISON!

Transcending boundaries is our biggest task in life, yet it's the most ignored and the most feared. Today is the day to step up and be brave so that innocent beings don't have to be brought into a dangerous world. We must look deeper into the universe and realize there are different ways to approach problems and different ways to avoid them. Different from what? Everything we've ever learned! We weren't taught to listen to our gut; we were taught to listen to our parents, our teachers, our environmental influences, OUR FEARS! When something isn't right, we feel it but don't listen. Why would we when there are so many other things put into our heads to make us think otherwise? Those jumbled thoughts only confuse us into making choices that create more problems in our lives *and* in the lives of others.

Let's cut the cords of limitations, not only for our future generations but for ourselves, no matter our age. Young or old, we're alive in this very moment and have a chance to change the course of our life. Will we? Will *you*?

• •

So many people don't know how to raise kids or even care to find out. The truth is they shouldn't be *having* kids! If they don't have their shit together and don't want to get it together by loving and caring for themselves, how are they going to love and care for a child? It's sickening to see people who are clueless continue to pop out babies. Screwed up kids turn into screwed up adults who take their issues out on the world. We don't need any more of that! We already have *way* too much!

Children need immense nurturing. Of course, many people are loving to their kids but when they don't demonstrate right from wrong through their own actions, the kids will most likely develop issues and have misconstructions about life. The parents who have it down are securely settled physically, emotionally, spiritually, and financially. They feed their kids healthy foods, distinguish right from wrong in positive ways, are a positive role model through ethics, morals, emotional, and physical health, have open conversations, have fun, give support, and endless love. They're creating **Superhumans.**

While it's impossible to raise a child perfectly, it's imperative to do things correctly, or as best as you can. You don't want your kids to have to work on their issues later in life, do you? I'm sure you want to set them up to grow strong and happy. My parents are good-hearted, loving people who tried their best, but they didn't really know what they were doing in a lot of aspects and things were beyond their control. It happens. I believe people should focus on themselves first. The most important thing to do before you even consider having a child, is to heal yourself. Find your purpose in life! Make some money! Then decide why, when, with whom, or IF, you want to have children.

I grew up with *many* misconceptions about life, but thankfully I was awakened to an opportunity to work through my issues as an adult. That's why I don't fault my parents for my upbringing, and I don't have regrets about it either. I want the world to understand that we have a chance right now to change ourselves for our kids, and *duh*, to change ourselves for *ourselves*. Work on being the best version of you before you bring a life into this world. Yes, we *all* get screwed up in some kind of way but as parents you kind of want to do the least amount of damage possible.

Whatever your situation may be, cut your shit, forgive, heal, and stop passing the negativity on! If you grew up lost or mad at the world, it's time for you to stop feeling sorry for yourself, to **forgive**, to stop this vicious cycle, to make good out of your bad.

> "There is no time like the present. The past is a memory, the future a projection; only the present, which is pure awareness, is real. We can continue with our lives, lost in our thoughts and memories, never changing, with every day a repetition of the past. Or, we can choose to stay awake and begin each day with a new start."
>
> —Frank Nicoletti, *You're the Best!*

DON'T DRINK THE POISON!

When you examine your agreements and can truly see them, you expose the truth: you don't really believe you should be abused or fearful. You will no longer need to use fear as a justification because you'll realize it was never true, and then you can heal. Negative influences from other people will dim your light. Letting go sets your soul on fire! Be you, your authentic self, and move past all the bullshit. FORGIVE. Forgive others to heal yourself, no matter what they've done. Without forgiveness, you are always punishing yourself first by holding onto your associations with them. When you're able to learn and move on from those people and experiences, you've grown, and most importantly, you become FREE! It's never too late to change. Release your past agreements and you will finally live like that happy child.

Remember, forgiveness is always a gift to yourself. It's not intended to benefit the abuser or the transgression they committed. It's merely your way of letting go and moving on from the past, living in the present moment. Let the universe, and more specifically "karma," offer the ultimate justice for any wrongdoing. It's called "God's boomerang" or "What goes around, comes around." Ultimately, there's always a price to pay for what you do. So be careful what you ask for and what you do unto others.

• •

I learned not to take anything personally but to also take some responsibility for the things people have done to me by realizing that I allowed them to affect me. Acknowledging that helped me get over it. Looking back, I saw I was a person who was there for everyone, so it took me a little while to figure out what I was doing wrong. I always forgave, which is good, but my mistake was that I didn't forgive AND carry on with my life. I forgave and then allowed people to repeat the same things over and over again, putting limitations on my life. It instilled anger in me! You have to realize that when someone isn't changing the behaviors you've forgiven them for, maybe it's time to let them go. Nothing is different but your acceptance of their wrongdoing. If they don't want to change, you can't force them! I should have accepted that. I should have released them sooner, along with my anger. What I wanted from them was the love that I should have been receiving from the one person who I needed it from the most ...myself.

When I finally started paying attention and started to *really* love myself, I set higher standards for others. I accept and forgive all, but respect, loyalty, and love need to be mutual in my relationships, otherwise it doesn't make sense to hold onto them. Why? People with drastically different views and morals will clash! When I encounter someone I cannot possibly vibe with, I look at it this way: their presence must have taught me something, or maybe they learned something from *me*, but that's the extent of the relationship. It is a lesson, not a long-term friend or a partner. That's why it's easy for me to say goodbye to people like Hannah. While I forgive her, I'm not built like her; I could never do to a friend what she did to me, so I knew it was time to walk away. You can choose to leave behind those who are no longer right for you too.

• •

Although it's always painful to experience betrayal, what comes from it is a gift.

All my relationships taught me grand lessons that I use in everyday life and I'm grateful for that. I haven't forgotten, but I have forgiven so I could heal. When I was holding onto anger, I was not only constantly regretting what happened, but also setting myself back emotionally and physically. Can you relate? It's such a relief when you finally let all that go! How did *I* do it? I stopped being down about everything and realized I have a whole life ahead of me to make up for it. Instead of wasting more time, I started that new life immediately by changing my attitude and freeing myself of negative energy. I'm now strong, powerful, and wise. I know not to make the same mistakes and how to weed out the mistakes that are about to happen. If I'm dating a guy who shows any signs of being controlling, such as telling me how to make personal decisions, or if he's not loyal, I'm gone. If I have a friend who's shady, I leave them alone.

Do me a favor…do YOURSELF a favor—take my experiences and don't let them happen to you! If you've already been through bad relationships, realize you can find lessons in those as well, even the current ones. If used as a mirror, your relationships will reflect things about yourself that you never would have observed on your own. I know I learned a lot about my character, and I like the Kate who came out of it *so* much better. Don't regret your past. Live, learn, move on, grow, then be happy with the new you! But don't stop there…keep improving in all aspects of life!

> DON'T REGRET YOUR PAST. LIVE, LEARN, MOVE ON, GROW, THEN BE HAPPY WITH THE NEW YOU!

• •

ATTENTION: You can't let (insert ex's name or friend's name here)'s actions dictate your life! You need to move on, do good things for yourself, and be happy! Easier said than done? Yes. Too hard? No. It's all about training your mind, releasing, accepting, and doing something positive, even if it's something as small as saying, "I'm not going to eat that piece of cake because I'm sad over him/her." Stop letting it take over your mind in that moment. You control your thoughts. Don't let your thoughts control you. Positive thoughts = positive actions. Positive actions = happiness.

• •

Marriage is another belief that has changed for me now that I've discovered I'm a free being. *I used to believe it was normal* …not anymore! I think that it's absolutely possible to be with someone for a long time, even forever, without marrying them. The piece of paper binding two lives is sometimes also what separates them because of that "locked down" feeling. Being exclusive with someone should be about pure love and intentions, not about an egotistical title. Truth? Marriage is often about fear. Many people grow anxious as they get older and rush to settle. That's such a mistake, *especially* when they bring kids into it.

While I loved my ex, Joe, and considered marrying him somewhere down the line, one little bump in the road changed everything. When an uninvited third party got involved, it ruined us since our trust and communication were off. My mind was set on the fact that the way we met and how quickly I fell for him were signs we were meant to be together, but in reality he was only meant to be in my life for a period of time to show me something about myself. Despite him telling me all about his life, I still didn't really know him. It takes time, experiences, and growth in a relationship before two people completely know each other.

Many people rush into marriage before they truly know anything about their partner *or about themselves,* and they end up resenting their spouse. They want to be loved so badly but don't love themselves. Self-love is beyond important. Lack of it, especially in a relationship, is a no-win situation, and I bet that's why a lot of marriages end in divorce. Love yourself and know who you are first, because if you don't, how can you believe someone else loves you for you? What would they love about you if you can't see it yourself? If you don't know and love yourself, you'll subconsciously sabotage relationships, never accepting true love.

> LOVE AND KNOW YOURSELF FIRST, BECAUSE IF YOU DON'T, HOW CAN YOU BELIEVE SOMEONE ELSE LOVES YOU FOR YOU?

Since I've come to know myself very well, I'm at peace with being alone or leaving a relationship. Until I can share my life with someone who has pure love for not only me but themselves, I'm happy

DON'T DRINK THE POISON!

by myself, even if that means forever! I find comfort in truth, not in the struggle of two lost souls trying to hold onto each other in a desperate, love-defying search for comfort, security, and approval. Of course, it's nice to have someone there, but I don't *need* it. Think about that the next time you're feeling lonely or afraid. There's something that needs healing in you, by you, before you attach yourself to someone else. It's important to be guided by the truth, not the pressure to have a relationship.

The moral of the story is that love isn't always what you think it is. While you may love someone or they may love you, it doesn't mean you have to be with them. Let me cut to the chase …no meetings are coincidental. People come into your life to show you something that needs to be healed inside you. *Everyone* you encounter has a purpose for being there, but it's up to you to figure out if they should stay, or if they're just passing through for a season. How can you tell? Tune into your intuition, observation, self-awareness, and self-growth. You'll **know** you share a mutual love when you both have matured in all aspects of it. Until then, let each person be a blessing of knowledge.

Also, understand that when someone loves you, they're not the only person out there who is capable of that. There are many others who can love you the way you want to be loved. Many people think they can't do better, or they'll never find someone who cares about them as much, so they tolerate things like abuse or neglect. It's all a choice! When you choose to limit yourself to those beliefs, you're stuck in them, becoming trapped in a distorted world of your own creation. Live, love, learn, forgive, and move on if that's what the voice deep down is saying, because… it's letting you know that you're meant to experience something greater.

• •

Genuine love is absolute selflessness. A person who is truly in love wants to do things for the other person …not for their own benefit, but to genuinely make them happy, like buying a gift just so they smile, not to get something out of it. And in order for a relationship to last, being selfless must be shared by both parties.

If someone constantly tells you they love you but shows you no love, they're just trying to hang onto you or want something from you …they're being selfish! If you're not sure and want to know if someone really loves you as they say they do, then your answer is right there. It shouldn't be conveyed through words but through actions! It's up to you to see that and make a choice.

Want to know an easy way to know how you feel about a relationship and if it's worth working on? Use the "Advantages and Disadvantages Releasing" from *The Sedona Method*. Make a list of the pros and cons, figure out where the "want" from each one is coming from (wanting control, approval, or security) and release each of them until the answer is revealed. When you clear your emotion-induced thoughts, the proper solution will come to you. The tricky but necessary part is listening to the answer, as hard as it may be.

> "Dismiss, also the thought that love never comes but once. Love may come and go, times without number, but there are no two love experiences which affect one in just the same way. There may be, and there usually is, one love experience which leaves a deeper imprint on the heart than all the others, but all love experiences are beneficial, except to the person who becomes resentful and cynical when love makes its departure."
> —Napoleon Hill, *Think and Grow Rich*

Bad relationships are just that—bad. The good is what you take from them. Stop rehashing the past! You'll only feed your negative feelings. If you use your experiences as stepping stones, you'll eventually get to the right place. People are put in your path as challenges to test and build your strength. In life, it's not what you were given that defines you, it's what you make of it. Forgiveness is how we heal and move on. We can't see the lesson if we're blinded with resentment. The next time someone hurts you, ask yourself, *What did I learn about that person that I can watch for in the next? What did I learn about myself?* The answers to those questions will enlighten you.

> "Every adversity, every failure and every heartache carries with it the Seed of an equivalent or greater Benefit."
> —Napoleon Hill

CHAPTER 7

LET GO OR BE DRAGGED

"Everything that is really great and inspiring is created by the individual who can labor in freedom."

—Albert Einstein

"Letting go" …let's get into it! We need a practice to rid ourselves of the most, excuse my language, fucked up shit that's happened to us because let's be real, just saying, "Ok, I'm over it," isn't going to do the trick. We must learn to say goodbye once and for all to our emotional attachments, and we need a solid way to do that.

For me, it started to happen when I *so* badly wanted to figure myself out. I gradually began to let go of each negative emotion that came up by realizing where it stemmed from (what memory/memories) and how it influenced my life. It was a kind of surrendering. What it showed me was that I was letting something that doesn't exist control the things that do exist now. That helped tremendously, but honestly, it was the hard way. After all, is it even possible to consciously recall every negative thing that affects us on a subconscious level? Probably not. That's why I want to tell you about what I've learned. Something that has not only sped this process up but made it so much easier. It's called The Sedona Method™. It's so simple; all you need to do is be honest with yourself and have a little bit of an imagination. I learned it by reading the book, *The Sedona Method*, by Hale Dwoskin.

The book's premise is that we are limited specifically by our thoughts, holding onto experiences from the past no longer exist. We create emotions in the present that really have nothing to do with who we are, since we're not our emotions or our memories; we are who we are right now! The things that have happened to us stimulate feelings which are tied to our memories, making them continuously feel real every time we recall them (whether consciously *or* subconsciously). So, when we sever those ties by releasing those emotions, we clear out the negativity that creates bad thoughts. This allows us to get closer to who we really are—peaceful and loving beings, our true nature.

Every feeling that we have is just that, a feeling! It doesn't define us! IT IS NOT "US!" When we're able to realize that and release or let go of the limiting emotions brought on by thoughts, those emotions *will* dissolve…and so will the negative thinking! This allows for a purer state of being, pure and free of all those disgusting feelings that rob us of our joy.

• •

The basics of releasing, according to The Sedona Method™, involve asking yourself the following five questions:

1—What is my "now" feeling?
2—Could I welcome/allow that feeling?
3—Could I let it go?
4—Would I let it go?
5—When?

LET GO OR BE DRAGGED

When you ask and answer these questions honestly and **imagine** the feeling going away, the energy you have tied to the emotion of whatever it is you're thinking about, will disappear. I'm not kidding! Picturing something in your mind *can* create reality. Through intent, the energy you're "seeing" and feeling leaves your body and frees up space. The more you release, the more your emotional energy is cleared and the closer you are to being a happier you. You're closer to being, well, you! The *real* you, not this destructive being controlled by thoughts and emotions.

How do you let go of the most painful feelings, the deep-rooted emotions that can cause you to be overweight, underweight, self-destructive, violent, etc.? To be completely truthful, it's not easy. Asking yourself to let go is simple but allowing old memories to come up and *really* feeling them won't be a walk in the park. Digging deep may uncover many buried feelings tied to those memories, but in actuality, it's ALL good. These buried terrors are coming to the surface, approaching their finale. **Feel** them; **release** them …as many times as it takes. When they're gone, they're gone forever, and you're **free**! How can that be? The bad energy shifts outward upon letting go! It literally moves out of your body.

Emotions are visitors. They're not here to stay unless we let our memories hold them hostage. Welcome them. Acknowledge their presence and purpose. Allow them to be as they are but stay true to who *you* are. Then, send them on their way. Tell yourself that these associations are done with; they're over. If there's nothing good coming out of reliving emotional memories, acknowledge that and mentally move on.

The key is to:
1—Let go of the past
2—Surrender yourself to the moment

UNDERSTAND THAT YOU ARE NOT YOUR EMOTIONS, YOU ARE NOT YOUR EXPERIENCES. While these things may have influenced your life to make it as it is now, they are not "the now." "The now" is the present moment, the only thing that's **real** and happening! It's a blank slate! Again, the problem is that many of our feelings are tied to our past experiences and we are dragging them into our present. We're "playing the past forward" and that's what keeps most people stuck. What's underneath it all, what everyone has in them but not everyone has reached, is the state of peace. When we release our feelings and eliminate our baggage, we get closer and closer to reaching it.

Remember, your past is over. You can't change it so why would you dwell on it? You're only punishing yourself for something you can't control. IT DOESN'T EXIST! Ask yourself, *What is this doing to me in the current moment and can I let it go?* According to *The Sedona Method*, just asking yourself to let a feeling go and answering with *either* a yes or a no, can cause you to spontaneously release that feeling. When I release an emotion, I can feel the negative energy leaving my body. Sometimes I go from feeling sad to an immediate smile …it's kind of weird but really cool.

This is my technique: With an inhale I picture the emotion being sucked into my lungs, and then with a strong exhale, I imagine it being blown out of my mouth, recycling back into the universe with positive intentions (I imagine it looks like thick smoke). It causes me to feel lighter and less burdened immediately. If the relief is not immediate, I repeat the process until I feel the freedom. And freedom, it *truly* is. You should try it!

Think about this… why do we sigh? We do it when we're not happy, right? It's to blow the negativity out! It makes us feel slightly better! It's a release! If this still doesn't make sense, take a long, slow, deep breath in, and a long, forceful one out. Now how do you feel?

• •

LET GO OR BE DRAGGED

To find a state of peace, you need to release your feelings and accept that the past will never change, but also accept that it's over with. Memories aren't real! They may have been real when they happened, but they are non-existent now. What you're feeling is that lingering sting of negative, emotional energy. So, when you become **aware** of these thoughts that are limiting you, you then have the power to set them free.

• •

Let's say you frequently think about a bad experience from your past. It's been holding you back, keeping you in pain, causing limitations, self-doubt, or lack of confidence.

Identify what it is specifically and TRUTHFULLY ask yourself the 5 basic releasing questions:

1—What is my *now* feeling? (It could be anger, fear, pain (physical or emotional) or whatever comes up… FEEL IT.)

2—Could I welcome/allow that feeling? (Allow it to be, don't resist it.)

3—Could I let it go? (Yes or No)

4—Would I let it go? (Yes or No)

5—When? (Now, 1 day, 1 year, etc. but don't worry. Releases happen fast if you're doing them openly/correctly.)

That's it! That's all you need to do. You may have to repeat this exercise several times or perhaps a dozen times, but you *will* feel the pain go away. When the sting is gone, you have arrived! You're free!! It's really that simple but not often an easy choice. Why? Because as I stated earlier, *letting go of our pain is the ultimate forgiveness* and forgiving someone who hurt us or even committed a crime is not something we want to let go of; sometimes it feels more comfortable to hold on to the hurt or anger. But letting go of the emotion is NOT a waiver of their act; they are still accountable for what they did.

They don't even have to know you forgave them! It just allows you to **choose** between your own peace or continued suffering, that's all! So, with this method you can choose to safely call on your emotions and release them from your body which then allows you to stay in the present moment but move on with your life. Or, you can remain stuck in someone else's action ...*it's up to you.*

Remember, letting go... forgiving... is always a choice; it's your decision. It's a release of *your* emotion, not a "pass" on a crime or injustice.

• •

The next step in my personal **transformation** was understanding what I was doing to my body. Once we fix the emotional, it's almost impossible to ignore the physical's cry for help.

My poor eating habits had existed since childhood but were especially encouraged by negative feelings growing up. I was in emotional pain so I would eat to gain pleasure *(a pretty twisted crutch)*. What the food did was push aside anything that was really bugging me by blocking my thoughts and engaging my senses. Unfortunately, it was just a temporary fix because my problems were still there after the food was gone! Tuning into that reality was what allowed me to finally fix it.

After working on letting go of the past, I was then able to forgive myself for where I was currently and only concentrate on making good choices in the present, for a better future. I wanted to see myself happy and healthy, with a whole new zest for life. I wanted to stop repeating my mistakes; I wanted to do things differently. These changes brought upon the decision to start eating healthy. After that, everything has just **flowed**. Life is now easier, and I see more positive things happening to me every day. Why? Because I took the **initiative** to better myself instead of letting life control me. When it comes to the universe, every good choice is recognized and rewarded.

LET GO OR BE DRAGGED

If you aren't happy and want to be happy, you must start somewhere, at some point, to make a change. If you don't, every day will be a repetition of "yesterday," which leaves you with the same exact feelings and the same exact outlook on life, and before you know it, you're looking back wondering where all the years went.

Do you want to better yourself? If yes, then let me explain something: each individual is responsible for their own future, for their own fate. Unfortunately, most people are in denial! They believe their circumstances made them the way they are or put them where they are. That's not it! It's every choice they made! Look at it this way: of all the people who grow up in poverty, there are always a select few who **create** wealth and make something of their lives. Why is that? It's what they allow to come out of their situation! The ones who remain in poverty have accepted their lives as is, instead of using the negative to make positive; they're falling victim to their circumstances instead of fighting against them.

Think about when a relationship turns ugly, there are two options: Option A, settle and be miserable, or Option B, break up and use the experience as a learning tool to find someone better. Can you pick the scenario which best foreshadows a life with a more positive future? Understand that both cases are the same person in the same bad relationship. The difference is what they decide to do (the door that they choose) will determine the outcome. Each decision will send them on a path that's completely unparalleled to the other. One bad choice will create the beginning of a downward spiral. One good choice will lead to many more. Remember how I said every thought or action creates a ripple?

If you feel *you* are headed the wrong way, take the wheel and steer yourself in a new direction! Most of us doze off and let circumstance drive. There's a reason we **feel** when things are right or wrong. **Intuition** is telling us how to choose. Whether we listen is up to us.

SUPERHUMAN

I ended up regretting a lot of my decisions because I would not only make mistakes, but I'd REPEAT them. I'd go back to abusive boyfriends, aware that it was wrong, but at the same time allow their words to mess with my mind …manipulation at its finest. I had trouble hearing my inner voice's advice always saying, *Just let him go!* When I finally learned to listen, as hard as it was, I felt free. Don't *you* want to be free?

• •

I want to let you in on something. The most incredible thing about self-awareness, self-love, and having control over your own life by making good choices, is the **freedom** that comes from it. It's like getting your hands on the right tool to break through a prison wall that you've wrongfully been locked behind for too long. This breakthrough comes to you for the simple reason that you've snapped out of playing the victim and are finally being YOU, doing what YOU want to do and not what any person, event, or circumstance tells you to do.

Understanding who you are, what you love to do, and putting that into action exposes your true self and allows you to fulfill your purpose, without limitations. You reach an extremely empowered state of being when your abilities, your talents, and your desires all unfold in front of you. And the more you persist, the more tools the universe hands you to keep breaking through walls. Having the courage and unstoppable drive to fulfill your self-purpose—the reason you're on this earth—is the most liberating thing you'll probably ever feel. Why is that? Because you're most powerful when you do what's right! Doing what you're meant to do is the best decision you can make, and the universe recognizes that. YOUR SOUL recognizes that.

I'm telling you this whether you believe it or not: YOU ARE SPECIAL. We ALL have purpose. We aren't meant for this conformation, this structure that society has scared us into believing is the way we have to live our lives. When we shut down our self-purpose, we conform to others' ideas and lose value in ourselves. *Your* desire, your pure love and inner creativity, is the key that unlocks your full potential. It's up to you to open the door.

● ●

Not allowing circumstance to control fate is how people with no arms or no legs play sports, run races, etc.; it's how people in treacherous conditions, lost out in the elements, survive and make it home. Think about victims of horrific violence who fought off their attackers! It's all about free will, a drive, a purpose to live the way you and only you plan to live your life…not the way life plans for you to live it. Our mind controls the direction of our lives. A positive mindset is what makes many people rich! Success often has nothing to do with luck, IQ, or circumstance, but instead with the power of mind.

It may sound strange but it's true: we physically create the world around us, mentally! Our subconscious mind has been scientifically studied to have a direct link to the physical world. When we feed it thoughts through experiences or self-communication, it believes these thoughts are true and moves them into physical matter. Since everything on this earth is made up of energy and matter (slowed energy), the feelings (energy) we create are put into the universe (matter), making things happen in the physical sense. How? Well when we have dreams or goals or ideas and strongly believe in their possibility and probability, that energy goes from our minds into our bodies, causing us to act in certain ways and make certain decisions. This leads us down a set of circumstances that will do anything and everything to make it happen. It's just imagination. When we create something in our mind and focus on it, our subconscious eventually believes it is true and creates it! The universe already wants us to have these things; they're already seeking us, we just have to open the right doors to meet them! Have you ever heard someone say that anything you ask of this universe will be given to you? It's true! It's called the Law of Attraction.[1] As we think, we attract.

Things that are meant for us are attracted to us as if we're the south pole of a magnet, with everything good we can imagine being the north pole of another magnet …but only when there's nothing repelling the attraction. Any negative thought or action we entertain causes a blockage or repel. What in the world am I talking about? WE CAN HAVE ANYTHING WE TRULY DESIRE BECAUSE IT DESIRES US …but the *real* us, not our ego.

Your vibrational energy matches what you create, so the higher the vibration you're emitting, the greater the attraction is to the things you want. When you do good things for your soul, you're gifted with an overflowing, fruitful flow of abundance from the universe; these things have been written in the stars long before you entered your body. Why? Because you *are* the universe. The universe is one with you. Ego is not you. Fear is not you. It's an illusion. Even your physical body is an illusion. So, when you understand that you are this divine power, you can create the world around you. When you make pure decisions based on love and not on ego or fear, there are things… *great* things… that you will find are ALREADY SEEKING YOU. It's like they come out of nowhere… they become available… within reach…up for grabs.

This is the path to true peace, a path that has been chosen for you but does not unfold unless *you* choose *it*. You may bring forth situations or "create" them by making choices, but they have already been searching for you all along. This is your divine destiny. When you discover and ascend down, through awakening, the path your soul has been longing to travel, you become aligned with your divine destiny. That ultimately means you can access an abundant life of peace, love, and joy …and many times, wealth. What could be better than that?

---

1 http://en.wikipedia.org/wiki/Law_of_attraction

LET GO OR BE DRAGGED

Have you ever been thinking about someone when suddenly they call you? What about an answer to a problem appearing right before your eyes in the form of a "sign" that seems far too coincidental? It *is* too coincidental! It's happening for a reason… you're creating it …with your mind! This is synchronicity with the universe, or flow, the opposite of resistance. When you desire something and allow your mind to expand in that direction by just being in the moment, doing the right thing, and believing things will work out, the world presents what you desire; it presents what is genuinely meant for you. That's why when you expect success and not only grow stronger, but stay **persistent** through failures, you eventually get what you want … you get what wants *you*. Get it?

· ·

If an obstacle seems impossible to overcome, you've made it impossible; you're being pessimistic; YOU ARE BLOCKING YOUR BLESSINGS. If you keep searching for a way around the obstruction, you're creating a path for success; you're being optimistic; YOU'RE ALLOWING LIFE TO FLOW. Pessimism = fear & failure. Optimism = love & lessons. People who earn riches in this world have set their mind on a goal. To them, failure is only a lesson. They SEE, FEEL, and BELIEVE in their dream and believe there's nothing that can stop it. That **intention**—positive thoughts mixed with emotion—creates the desired success.

"There is a growing consensus that emotional intelligence (EI) is just as important, if not more important, than IQ in predicting someone's level of success and life satisfaction."
—Hale Dwoskin

Seeing (literally, figuratively, or both), feeling, and believing in something we want, along with making positive life choices, is called manifesting a desire. We can also manifest undesirable things by putting that same energy or focus onto something we do not want… and most of us do that every day through our thoughts, emotions, and actions, without even knowing we're doing it. We manifest good things subconsciously too, but most of us tend to create exactly what we don't want. Why? We're unaware that we're making these negative things come to life! But how could we manifest positive circumstances when we were brought up to have doubts and fear judgement? When we weren't brought up to know how to use our energy constructively? When we weren't taught that everything we want out of life wants us and can be ours if we believe in it and go after it, no matter how ridiculous it seems to others? WE WEREN'T TAUGHT THE TRUTH—that the reality we know is full of LIES and limitations, which really are the only things that are ridiculous when it comes to our dreams. So much negativity has been shoved down our throats and it's time for us to spit it out.

Start to question everything. Say, *why not,* not why or how. Stand in your power. You know you intentionally and unintentionally make bad things happen at times—maybe a lot—and you see how things spiral. When you're down and out, you must know that nothing changes until you change. Things won't start looking up until you do. It shouldn't be difficult for you to now understand that despite any misconceptions the world gave you about yourself, you are powerful and have the ability to make all things in your control, go your way.

You are creating right now just by thinking, and it shouldn't be something that's hard to understand, but it is. People say this all the time…*I don't know why stuff keeps happening to me.* Stuff isn't happening to you, it's responding to you! Whatever way you think and behave, you'll get it back from the universe. But hold on for one minute, don't take my words out of context…not everything bad that happens to you is your fault. It's the things that you give your time, energy, thoughts, beliefs, and emotions to that unfold in your life.

• •

MANIFESTING THE GOOD: You know that feeling you get when you're excited about something? It's like an energy is coursing throughout your body, lifting the corners of your mouth, widening your eyes, and you can't seem to sit still…That's a reaction from an emotion, and when you can manipulate your body to feel like that according to your thoughts, whether it matches them or not, you can change the world around you.

Before I go any further into this, let me give you an example: let's say you want a new car but can't afford it. First, close your eyes and imagine that you have all the money you need to get a new car, and that you're going to pick one out soon. (Yes, I'm making you pretend…try not to be such an adult for a minute!). Next, bring up happy emotions; get excited, smile, jump up and down if you wish! *Really* **feel** that you are getting this car; *really, really* **believe** it. Picture it happening and how you look being excited to get it; picture having the money at your disposal, seeing the car that you want, feeling the steering wheel gripped in your hands, smelling the interior. Feel that child-like happiness in you. Now before your mind wanders back to "Adultland," take a long, deep, slow breath in (still imagining your car and being happy)…now release that want, that desire, with a strong exhale. Sit in peace and let the universe take your thought. Be free from ALL feelings for a moment. Your car most likely won't appear instantly in front of your eyes but repeat, repeat, repeat, and watch as the universe delivers you unexpected blessings of opportunities and/or monetary abundance that will, in fact, get you that car. You can…we ALL can…have anything we desire if we learn to override our psychologically-programmed, doubtful, li(e)mited, fearful brain.

The more positive thoughts you dream up in your mind, believe in, and feel with positive emotion, the more positive things you will create in your own life. The same goes with negative thoughts; like perverse mantras, calling them over and over again will make them happen. Why? How? Again, the energy you put out there moves into matter. Your thoughts are only energy, and a car (matter) is only energy...think about that. Sometimes things happen quickly, and sometimes they take a little a while, but with every repeated positive thought, emotion, belief, desire, release and action, opportunities and success will manifest in your life. So, think positively and do positively.

This involves retraining your subconscious to believe in your body, to believe that what your body is feeling is what is really going on in your life. Are you following me? Your subconscious trusts your body. When you see something sad, you cry and can be deeply affected because you feel and believe in what you just saw, and it affects your view of the world...sometimes it literally and personally affects your world. (That's why I don't watch the news; it's designed to keep our vibrational energy down!) So, if you force your mind to believe in your thoughts, you also must make your body respond as if that thought is true. In other words, believing is feeling because beliefs are passions. You *feel* passion. And with repeated positive thoughts and actions, your mind begins to change and pull you in that positive direction more often! *Sooo*, create your life! Imagine! Believe! It's so easy a child could do it!

• •

Imagination sparks creativity. Creativity showcases talent. Talent enables joy. Joy allows love. Love brings abundance. As the character Lorenzo from *A Bronx Tale*, says, "The saddest thing in life is wasted talent." This movie had a big impact on me when I was young because it had great life lessons. It made me want to keep fighting for the life I wanted—a creative, fun existence, where I didn't settle for society's boring standards. *That* lesson really rings true.

LET GO OR BE DRAGGED

If we're not using our gifts to create happiness, then that is indeed a sad thing. Each of us is here for a reason—to utilize something we're not only good at but enjoy doing. Why? It lights up life for us, and everyone we help, touch, affect, and inspire. This thing we call life isn't about working our asses off in hopes that we get what we want; it's about being in the right mindset to be confident, bold, and in love with what we're doing. It's about wanting what we have, wanting where we are, not beating ourselves up in the hope of getting somewhere else. Somewhere else comes naturally when we let it, when we're grateful and present in the moment. So, use your talents and your gifts. If you don't know what they are yet, you have some work to do on yourself first. Learn who you are—what makes you, you; learn what puts a smile on your face and warmth in your heart. Learn what true passion is. That will tell you everything.

The truth is, the path to a mediocre life is traveled by being a "realist." A realist is not open; they don't believe in an imagination or believe that they are creating reality through their thoughts. This is called cognitive dissonance—holding a thought or belief so strongly that you are closed off and unable to accept new information, even when there is evidence against your belief. That's why racism still exists today. It's why someone will die for a religious belief for which there is no proof. A mind like this works so hard to protect, rationalize, fight, and deny anything that goes against the belief that their ego is guarding. The funny thing is that these types of people are the ones living in an imaginary world! I get it though, it's all learned behavior.

If that's you, do yourself a huge favor…unlearn it now! The "reality" we were taught to see is a veil. It causes depression, oppression, conformity, control, manipulation, and a waste of the precious, valuable time we could be using to do good and feel good on this earth. Whenever I talk to "drowsy" or "sleeping" people about a positive mindset helping them move forward in their lives, I usually get this response, "Well I am positive, but I'm also realistic."

LIMITATION ALERT! They don't yet understand or have not tapped into the fact that they possess this magical power of being able to manifest anything they desire. That this universe with which we are one, is quite advantageous if we stop being so "adult," and pull out our magic tricks!

If you're not satisfied with living a mediocre life, if it's just not enough for you, if you have a burning desire to do more, to CREATE a pathway of no limitations built with bricks of creative imagination, cemented in with zero doubts, you must be open to new ideas always, but be stern with what you desire. Manifestation requires having absolutely NO DOUBTS, NONE, ZERO, not in yourself, not in your vision, and not in your "team" of like-minded, supportive people, a.k.a. your "Mindset" (as referred to in the book *Think and Grow Rich* by Napoleon Hill). Why team? Because no one "gets there" on their own. When you begin to manifest the things you desire, connections with the right people will also begin to manifest. With that, you'll inevitably lead yourself to success, to an extraordinary, exciting, FULFILLING life. Don't believe me? Try it! Use anything! Decide right now to wake up every morning and **think** about, **believe** in, **feel...TRUST** in something you want, and imagine nothing getting in your way. Let me know what happens...

• •

We make decisions based on how we feel. When we're at a negative emotional state we usually create chaos around us, like the saying, "misery loves company". In order for good things to happen you must make good decisions, plain and simple. If you keep allowing yourself to be negative, you'll attract more negativity. That's just how it works! If you allow your mind the privilege of positive thoughts, how can you not be happy? Life will reward you for being in a good mood! *It can't get much better than that.*

In the relationship example we discussed earlier, staying in a bad relationship as in Option A will most likely result in regret and a depressing life. Why? Because they are feeding a negative mindset. The person who leaves as in Option B likely will continue to make good decisions that will in turn, create happiness. They are transmuting (changing in form, nature, or substance) through a positive mindset. A is afraid of change and would rather wallow in their own misery, whereas B would rather grow from it and learn how to experience better things. The difference is in the way you think and react. If you keep your mind positive, your attitude optimistic, and you trust your intuition, the best possible choices will slap you across the face before you even get a chance to wallow!

● ●

When you constantly rehash the past and hold onto regret or misfortune, you become a prisoner of your memories. Let them go! If you don't want to regret things in the future that are happening in the present, weigh all your options and trust your gut! Don't make a rash decision that you'll end up kicking yourself for later on. Instead of being confrontational and saying things you don't mean when a disagreement occurs, talk it out civilly. If that doesn't work, walk away and find something to take your mind off it. Come back to what happened once you're calm. The proper solution will come to you when you clear your emotion-induced thoughts. How do you do that? Find a place for serenity and relax. It may help to take long, deep breaths or to write down everything on your mind. Try some releasing exercises to let go of the emotion. Maybe you can talk to an objective third party who will give you good advice. Use whichever method you prefer to help you sort out your emotional reflexes from your common sense.

The mind is truthful when it's at peace. When you take time to think without the influence of high emotions, you'll be able to see things in a better light. And every time you practice this, it will move your life further forward in the right direction.

Choosing a positive mindset facilitates the positive thoughts, emotions, and actions that bring positive outcomes. Do you want to reach your goals? Do you want to be happy? Picture and believe in only the good things that you want to see happen. This way, that's what your brain will see and create in your life. See good things always!

> "Psychological science has established a simple truth: how we view the world and how we interact with it change how the world responds to us. It's a compelling fact that's all too easily forgotten. Our way of being, our take on things, the attitude we bring to life, what I call our affective mindset, colors our world, affecting our health, our wealth, and our general well-being."
>
> —Elaine Fox

I have a question for you… do you need an umbrella? Is there a constant rain cloud following you, or is the sun shining every day? The book, *Rainy Brain, Sunny Brain*, by Elaine Fox, explains *why* some people remain so hopeful while others so hopeless. Through neuroscience, it explains why our view of the world is either optimistic or pessimistic, and how we can become optimistic. If you're not sure where you stand, look at your "glass:" is it half full or half empty? You would rather it be half full, wouldn't you?

• •

What is optimism? I would say it's a merge of mindful faith and confidence that causes happiness. It's not just seeing the world for the good but also accepting the bad and finding a way to overcome it. If you believe there's a way to deal with or get through anything, you *will* get through anything.

What's pessimism? To me, since I used to be a pessimist, it's an unrealistic, one-sided, hopeless belief system that only creates negativity. Have you ever experienced that feeling of *I can't do this?* Guess what? When you say you can't, YOU CAN'T...and then you're stuck.

An optimistic person's mind will automatically pull them toward the good and steer them away from the bad. How? The positive, optimistic brain causes the mind's eye to expand in different directions, to see things that weren't seen before. If something bad happens and you do nothing but dwell on your emotions, you can't see anything else. You're focusing on the negative or in other words, BEING PESSIMISTIC! If you open your mind and look for another way of experiencing what happened, thinking *this will only make me stronger*, it will indeed make you stronger. Emotions are ok for a moment, but we need to release them so we can move on with our lives.

• •

Happiness is brought on by not only being optimistic but by living in the moment (fully engaging in "the now"), being loving, forgiving, accepting, peaceful, grateful, aware, and…discovering self-purpose! When you know what you're here for (your purpose, your passion) and what you can do with it, life will give you everything you've ever dreamed! You'll be able to confidently go for what you want and believe that any adversity or failure is just an opportunity to grow! Nothing will stop you from getting what you want because if you can keep going after failure or misfortune, what else can stop you? When you're pessimistic, you don't believe there's a possibility for growth; you're seeing FAILURE written in bold, red letters. The thing is, you may just not know *how* to find the positive, but you can learn!

• •

We have what's called "Selective Attention;" it's what limits our senses. If we noticed everything in sight or heard every noise, our brain would become overloaded with information. So, if we want to focus on something that's normally unnoticed, we have to re-direct our attention. It's the same thing with our patterns of thought… we also *think* selectively. Just like we can focus in on an object we didn't notice before, we can focus our thinking on something we didn't think about before. How? By understanding ourselves like I mentioned, through **self-observation** and, changing our patterns of thought! If we fall into pessimistic thinking too often, we need to learn how to re-train our brains to see "the bright side." When we can finally see it, we can move our thoughts forward in that direction more often.

Practice strengthens our abilities. Re-training the pessimistic mind is how we develop an optimistic mind. When it comes to focusing on the good rather than the bad, we can make the "wires" in our brains *physically* change course by giving them different instructions to follow! I didn't even know I was re-wiring my brain. I repeatedly focused on the good and doubted or made less out of the bad, until it became automatic. That shift from fear to faith changed the quality of life for me. It can for anyone and that's why we need to practice anything we want to improve, including the way we see the world.

• •

What is the science of being optimistic or pessimistic and how do we "fix" what's wrong? When we experience certain pleasures or fears, chemicals in the brain create or strengthen pathways ("wires") when they're stimulated by our thoughts. These chemical communications make us feel certain ways which in turn makes us think and act on those feelings. As the chemical communications repeat again and again, they develop strong, fast, and advanced connections. The ones associated with unreasonable fears are the ones that need to be re-wired. They make us experience it unnecessarily and too often.

Elaine Fox uses a metaphorical example in her book: imagine a water pistol fight between the amygdala and the cortex. The cortex's team gets soaked by the amygdala's team because they're outnumbered. Or in terms of our brain, there are so many fearful alerts coming at the cortex from the amygdala, that the cortex doesn't have the chance to overpower or regulate the information. This is why, even though we may know there's no real reason to be scared of something, we can't overcome our body's response to it!

The amygdala is a part of the brain involved with processing emotions, fears, survival instincts, and pleasures. The cortex is responsible for our thinking, reasoning, understanding, or, in other words, our consciousness. When emotional information overpowers reasoning, the response is usually unpleasant. Think about this: There's a protective railing at the top level of the mall but you can't get too close to it, let alone look over it. The information (fear) in your brain has now trickled down into your body, paralyzing you. That overwhelming feeling is your "animal brain" or "ancient brain" at work. It's something that made humans act immediately in the face of danger a long, long time ago, still making you act a certain way now. It says *this is a threat* even though you know there's no real threat. Over time, it has grown unnecessarily powerful. Can we say *anxiety*? It's an overactive part of the brain that shouldn't be so active all the time! So even though we are aware that what we're fearing isn't dangerous, we can't help but respond as if it is.

How can we stop responding to fears? Practice and repetition. Practice shutting down your fearful, limiting thoughts every chance you get. Recognize them when they come, let them go, and repeat. It will take effort and time, but your happiness in this lifetime is worth it. If you want something bad enough, you have to just do it!

• •

Science is coming to understand that the brain's pathways or connections may not have just developed through life conditioning but through a combination of conditioning and genetics. Basically, the nature and nurture aspect may not just create connections but encourage the expression of genes that already have these routes mapped out for us; a predisposition to optimism or pessimism might be why some of us need that umbrella while others don't. Scientists are now looking at the genes which affect specific neurotransmitter systems and I think they're absolutely on the right track. What I learned in college and what I truly believe supports this; it's not environmental factors or heredity alone that causes emotional/physical problems. It's a combination or synchronization of the two; one strengthens the other. I also believe that changing our state of consciousness allows us to change the codes of our DNA; pre-disposition is preventable, reversible, and interchangeable according to our own manifesting. If we can fix the psychological and even physical issues that were programmed into us through consciousness, diet, and environmental changes, then let's do it! Let's rid the world of negativity by ridding our human makeup of it! Are you a pessimist? Do you often have limiting, negative thoughts? There's a way right now to begin the change, to re-train your brain!

• •

BREAKING THE HABITS: It's time for you to do this. It's time for you to be happy and live life freely. You don't have to be a prisoner in your own mind. I bring to you the concept of neuroplasticity—"re-wiring" your brain is a real option! Changes in connections or synaptic pathways in the brain due to changes in thinking, behavior, emotions, and environment can completely change one's outlook on life. It's confronting fears with faith over and over, as many times as it takes, until the brain finally realizes *everything's ok.*

When the brain is at peace, so is the person who owns it! We can change unnecessary and harmful connections that have developed in our brains and made us miserable our *whole* lives, by re-routing their pathways. Isn't that incredible?

• •

Are you ready to throw away your faulty umbrella? If so, I want you to understand that your mind, while being overly fearful, gives you

LET GO OR BE DRAGGED

a window to change how you physically and emotionally respond. Being able to see that a fearful response is not justified will allow you to fix it. How? By confronting what you fear over and over again without anything bad happening. Your mind sees there is nothing to fear. You're learning to get rid of a bad memory or thought by replacing it with a safe one. You might think this is a temporary fix, a mere mantra that helps you emotionally get over it, but it also *physically* helps you get over it! When you practice and practice, the feared stimulus no longer brings about feared responses because you have re-routed your brain's wiring. The connections physically change! The water pistol fight is no longer unfair, and reasoning now has a chance to regulate fear. Is this how you could overcome a tragic life? Is this how you can go from living in the dark and being so unhappy, to changing into a brightly-lit human? Yeah. That's exactly what happened to me! I learned to focus on the good rather than the bad by manually controlling my fear. As soon as a bad thought would come to mind, I would recognize the bad feeling and immediately flip it around in a more positive, peaceful direction, picturing something good in a different scenario. I just kept trying to lessen the worry in my life and I can't deny that because I did this, I was able to leave behind my life as a pessimist and continue on as an optimist. I get to experience happiness every day now! Don't you want to as well? Then start re-training NOW!!! It really works!

> BEING ABLE TO SEE THAT A FEARFUL RESPONSE IS NOT JUSTIFIED WILL ALLOW YOU TO FIX IT.

When we learn to do something and practice until it becomes a habit, like focusing on the good rather than the bad, our brain *literally* changes. I was using my newfound spirituality and positive outlook to fix my anxiety without knowing that I was actually *changing* my brain! If I had known, I could have gone more into depth by picturing these connections re-routing themselves. And yes, we

CAN physically change something inside of us by envisioning and believing in it. That's why it's good to know what you're doing on a scientific level as well as a spiritual one. When we give our minds the tools to fix problems and allow ourselves to be guided by faith, intuition and intention, we can transform into the beings we want to be. Our pitfalls, our emotions, our ways of thinking...are not permanent! We can change. *You*, the person reading this right now, can change!

> "Many psychologists are energized by the findings that we can change these deep-rooted distortions. Neither our genetic makeup nor our experiences should set the course of our life in stone. The world is full of stories of people overcoming adversity to lead happy and fulfilled lives, just as many have thrown away advantage and squandered their opportunities and talent. While our nature and our nurture certainly make it more likely that we will react in one way or another, the science suggests that there is nothing inevitable about this. By shifting our mindscape—the patterns of biases and distortions unique to us—we are able to shift the way we see the world."
>
> —Elaine Fox

There is indeed science in everything, including the functioning of the brain. But, there *are* other explanations or ways of understanding ourselves and the universe, other ways of healing and applying it...through faith...through spirituality...through intentions. Science tends to turn away from that kind of stuff because it's almost intangible; miracles can't be formulated! However, it's a very real part of life, something I'll get into later, so keep your mind open. When I talk about improving your health, it will benefit you to not only technically know what's going on, but to know on another level so you have more than one way to heal yourself.

LET GO OR BE DRAGGED

• •

If you're free, you're happy. Knowing that you're not stuck like this, that you have another way, is the beginning of freedom. Being aware of new things in life by keeping your mind open and malleable will allow you to access different strengths from within and change anything about yourself that you wish. Are you feeling optimistic yet?

Happiness develops from the way we experience life. It's a choice. It exudes from our souls and throughout our bodies when we give up fears, hate, and negativity. I came from a very dark place and emerged into the light, all by changing how I live my daily life. Seriously, I'm a different person now. Instead of letting everyday little things like worries or anger toward people control me, I now focus my mind on the present moment, release any negative feeling, and continue to see my uniquely crafted glass of past lessons, present blessings, and future accomplishments…half-full. These three steps will help you do the same:

1—Stay in the moment
2—Release
3—Remain optimistic

Let me tell you…allowing my mind to see things from a different perspective has been *soooo* freeing. If I ever start to worry, which I used to do very often, I tell myself that I'm being unreasonable and remember that there's a higher force working for me. This creates a happy scenario which dissolves the fearful one. It allows me to feel at peace and know that everything will be ok, that it's just my old fear brain talking. Or if someone says something rude to me, I view them as a misguided child who wasn't taught manners. I forgive and release, and then carry on with my day. It's really easy to negate negative thoughts with positive ones and release any feeling that you don't need to withhold. What's not easy is going through life being in a bad mood; it makes you emotionally and physically sick. My stress would cause me major headaches and anxiety. Think about it this way: if someone is physically harming you then you fight back, right? It's the same thing with your mind! The thoughts that are screwing with your emotions need to be stopped. How can you let a thought physically wear you down? It's silly if you think about it. Worries and fears are fake scenarios you create in your head. *Hello!* They're not happening, so why are you thinking about them? Giving your thoughts and emotions to something you don't want is basically praying for it and stressing yourself out like crazy! That's why you need to understand that your mind is a powerful thing that *will* cause distress to your body, if you allow it. It's important to take control and keep yourself mentally and physically healthy.

> YOUR MIND IS A POWERFUL THING THAT WILL CAUSE DISTRESS TO YOUR BODY, IF YOU ALLOW IT.

Switching negative mantras into positive ones brings forth the right scenarios to help you manifest what you *do* want, *and,* you'll learn to stop being so damn scared of things going wrong! Everything is ok in the moment that you're worrying, because it hasn't happened yet. Let me make it very clear: IT'S NOT HAPPENING. If it does, you'll deal with it then, and you'll be stronger because you didn't wear yourself out with stress. And chances are, if you're "praying" for the good outcome, you'll probably get it! Now that *I* control my mind, I feel I can take on anything! It's all about focusing on what you *do* want. Put your energy into everything good, everything you dream of. Focus on a healthy mindset and I promise your life will improve.

• •

In this book, I share not only what I've been through but where I went wrong and how you can avoid or come out of similar situations because I want you to see that change, no matter how bad your life is, is very possible, very easy IF YOU ALLOW IT. To the people with regret, who have been in or are in an abusive relationship, who have felt unloved, who have dealt with stress, who have fears, who have weight issues, anxieties, or who are just unhappy, I want you to hear me...

No matter what past feelings we hold, they are nothing but an association to a memory that is POOF! ...gone forever. MEMORIES AREN'T REAL; they're simply stored information or images. The only thing that *is* real is right now, the present moment. So, since our current mind-state determines our future, it's important to be optimistic. It's important to be free of negative emotional energy. It's IMPERATIVE to love yourself.

Sever the connection between memories and feelings when those feelings are holding you back in life. Demonstrate forgiveness, acceptance, love, gratitude, and practice. Practice! Practice! Practice! ... and you *will* take control of your life. Forgive whatever or whomever hurt you, accept the things you cannot change, love yourself, and be grateful for your experiences because they probably taught you lessons that may or may not be completely obvious to you yet. You're probably saying, "That's all easier said than done," right? Well when you take the first step toward change, everything else falls into place with MUCH more ease than expected. Anything you need will come to you because you're being guided by the greater good that is within you and all around you, and these floodgates of new, profound wisdom open up with every OH MY GOD moment that you realize that the impossible, just became possible. It's all about transcending boundaries. When you break free of the traditions and fears that no longer serve you, you're open to experiencing a whole new understanding and then, a whole new life. How do I know all this? I'm living it! There's just an indescribable joy each time you're awakened to the truth. Start releasing what's not needed within and watch as everything that *is* needed, **flows** into your life.

SUPERHUMAN

Summed up and ready for your taking, here it is:

THE SECRET TO FREEDOM: There is no one and nothing in this world that can give you real freedom from your troubles, but yourself. The warped reality in which you allow yourself to live is what keeps the secret to freedom from you, but you can change that. You can spin everything that's going wrong in your life, in a new direction, right now. Accept that no matter how badly you wish to obtain freedom in your life, in your heart, in your mind… you are only wasting time. Why? Because you already have it! We are all free beings already! It's our limitations that hold us captive because we let them. We BELIEVE in them. Beliefs are extremely powerful; they manifest into reality. When we recognize that the only things that *really* torture us are our own limiting, controlling, self-sabotaging thoughts, *we* can then control *them* by no longer giving them value. We can then be the talented, joyous, accomplished, FREE beings that we are! We can be happy…no matter what cards we've been dealt. Do you get it? Limits are lies. *You* are the truth. You set yourself free. Accepting limitation is saying to yourself, *My circumstances would never allow me to achieve my goal because I don't have the money, the connections, the opportunities, etc.* Opportunities come when we are open to them! When we're free from the lies! Catch my drift? When you believe there are no limitations, you can walk right through that brick wall of circumstance. I don't know how to explain it any better than experiencing the things that pop up once you "just let go;" the impossible you never thought could possibly happen, HAPPENING. The secret is having no doubts and unstoppable confidence, a complete belief that you are a free being right now who is capable of anything you desire. Stop wishing for a better life, **live** it! Freedom is not acquired, it's accepted. Accept that you are already free.

CHAPTER 8

RELAX! YOU'RE FINE

A re you still stressing? Just calm the fuck down. Breathe. Let the moment pass and realize …everything is OK. No matter what chaotic things happen to you, everything will be OK. OK? Release that bad feeling! It doesn't belong to you!

• •

First off, let me tell you something to put your worries, stresses, pains, and fears completely at ease this very moment. Are you ready for it? Here it is…EVERYTHING physical in this world is an illusion. Everything is temporary. Everything, except love. We are here to learn lessons of eternal love, not to be caught up in the physical because what we can see, hear, smell, taste, touch, and feel… does not last. That's exactly why it's all temporary…it's a **lesson** teaching us how to return "home" within ourselves. Home is love. We're here to experience pure, egoless love despite the drama, to love "the now" and understand that time is simply an illusion, to love ourselves, love others, and love our lives no matter who we are, what we have, or what has happened to us. When we can look past the illusion or temporary discomfort that comes from the physical, we set ourselves free with the truth. The truth is living peacefully, through love, NO MATTER WHAT HAPPENS. Unfortunately, because of an egotistical, existential standpoint, most of us are dying with fear. In a nutshell, it's nuts! We're all nuts and we don't even realize it. Peace a.k.a sanity, comes from being in love with the fact that you're alive, breathing, and **GRATEFUL**, no matter the circumstance.

• •

Now, we can get into "flow". To flow is to surrender your ego's fight against peace. It's the death of resistance and the birth of synchronicity. Letting things JUST BE as they are no matter how annoying or excruciating, is the key to inner peace. It's a return to love; it's allowing life to work itself out organically. Understanding that every little moment is an opportunity to change how we see the world, and acting and thinking in a positive way, is what allows us to flow in our crazy lives.

When I talk about positivity throughout this book, I don't mean that everything in life will be peachy or should be peachy. However, we can strive to keep a positive mindset. Being optimistic is what helps us overcome and achieve, but we are here to learn, and we can't learn the positive, we can't even recognize it, without the negative. We embrace our struggles and value both the good and bad, because we wouldn't appreciate the good without having experienced the bad. Would we be grateful for the sun if it wasn't for the rain? Training our minds to see that "rain" is there for a reason is how we learn to grow aware that EVERYTHING has importance. Everything is a lesson, and every circumstance is setting us up to choose a scenario. Our choices either come from resistance or from peace. When we are calm, loving, understanding, quiet, or grateful in a situation that would normally make us unhappy,

> **OUR CHOICES EITHER COME FROM RESISTANCE OR FROM PEACE.**

we enable happiness because we are at peace. That ultimately gives us more peace! More things to appreciate! Gratitude is powerful. Flow is an abundant synchronicity that is amplified when we are grateful and understanding in not so great situations. Something as small as someone cutting you off in traffic to many levels beyond that (even the worst things), are moments we either fight, or just let be. Think about it: would you rather fight to be right, or just be happy? Please note that I am NOT talking about any situation that involves fighting for your life or someone else's. In that case, FIGHT. What I'm talking about is letting stupid things go. You don't have to be positive all day, every day, in every situation, but it's not necessary to throw a dig at someone who wronged you. Let the universe handle that. Don't let the universe handle *you*.

• •

Let's look at the circumstance of someone cutting you off in traffic. Maybe you missed the green light because of it. Maybe you're a little bit behind in time. Stop being mad. Release your frustration. Let it go. Why? Being cut off could have just saved your life! Maybe the few seconds you were set back kept something terrible from happening. Fighting it by running the light or trying to get revenge may very well have led you to a bad situation. Do you ever think of that? Do you ever think that maybe there's some higher power trying to tell you something?

You can't rush or force life. You're exactly where you're supposed to be when you let things go and let the world work itself out. Once again, that doesn't mean always being positive. It means recognizing that it's ok to be open to the moment because there may be something of great value to learn from it.

When we embrace the moment by staying present in it and understand that everything happens for a reason, we are rewarding ourselves. What do I mean? An action or reaction is a choice and every choice leads to something else. Good choices lead to good things. Acting in any kind of negative way is self-punishment. The EGO is resisting. Resisting won't allow us to have peace because we're riding out negative feelings that only bring us to negative destinations. Accepting, releasing and allowing ourselves to **just be**...to just be present...to just be awake to the universe and understand that it will work things out *for us*, so long as we stay clear-headed, is peace. It's LOVE.

• •

Negative emotions, no matter how justifiable they feel, only hold us back. They're composed of FEAR. Fear is False Evidence Appearing Real. Love is Living One Vibrational Energy. I remember fighting with one of my boyfriends. We would usually yell back and forth, but one day while I was yelling, he must have "woken up" because he calmly said, "I know I have things to work on, which I will, but you're really upset because you don't feel good, not because of me, so you're taking it out on me."

I could have snapped back and said, "Go fuck yourself," but I didn't. He enlightened me and I felt stupid for yelling because he was right! No matter what someone else does, we control how we behave. We control how we feel. Letting someone get to us comes from something within us, not from the way they're acting. If you can understand that, you can understand that no one—nothing—has any control over you. It's all you. It's what you allow to be. That's why we need to be mindful of our *own* behaviors in order to change them for the better. We need to open up to one truth—one original vibration—and that is **love**.

• •

NOTE: Whenever you're feeling agitated, remember that the key to overall peace comes from being able stay calm and grounded in each situation, by remaining optimistic, or at least open-minded, which comes from recalling the power of love. IT COMES FROM

RELAX! YOU'RE FINE

DROPPING YOUR EGO!!! Remember that love is the only thing that truly exists and continues to exist. All of this is just an illusion! So, when you're getting upset, take a breath and allow yourself to *just be*.

• •

The key to becoming optimistic is to first be **aware** through **self-observation**, and to recognize each bad thought that enters your mind so that you can replace it with a good thought. Confront fears and in-the-moment emotions by changing the feelings you experience from negative to positive; look at things differently! If you worry, know that even if something bad were to happen, you could overcome it…you can overcome anything. In the meantime, why stress yourself out over something that's only in your mind? It's not reality! Choose to give *faith* control, not fear. Doing that will switch your overall vibration because you'll be allowing access to strength and love, enabling peace, which will cause your brain to change. It's understandable to have trouble with all of this at first because we live in a world with so much negativity around us, but it *can* be achieved. All it takes is practice and repetition.

> RECOGNIZE EACH BAD THOUGHT THAT ENTERS YOUR MIND THEN REPLACE IT WITH A GOOD THOUGHT.

• •

We're able to condition our minds like a person who masters a sport. Like the old adage, "Repetition is the mother of success." When we keep practicing, we keep improving. The same concept applies with interchanging and downplaying thoughts. Eventually, we become skilled at it.

I was an anxious person for a long time until I learned not to let bad thoughts affect me. As soon as they come, I automatically discard the negativity by releasing the fearful emotion before it takes any kind of harmful effect. Basically, I recognize the feeling of annoyance I am about to get from a bad thought, and immediately switch to a more positive mindset. I tell myself that things aren't bad after all. It began as something I had to be very conscious of doing. Now it's like my brain is a computer with virus protection that catches and deletes these pests even while the computer's off! It has made life *so* much easier because stress, worry, and fear were really bringing me down.

Use The Sedona Method™ too! Release the negative, even positive thoughts. *What is your NOW feeling? Could you welcome/allow that feeling? Could you let it go? Would you let it go? When?* Releasing makes negative emotions evaporate, and it allows positive emotions to bring bigger opportunities.

• •

Why not try some releasing at this very moment? Think about your emotional state right now, or just in general. What is your "now" mood? How is your day progressing? Could it possibly relate to your mood? Are you always in a bad mood? Do many bad things seem to happen to you but you can't understand why? YOU ARE SUBCONSCIOUSLY CREATING YOUR ENVIRONMENT. The energy you put out there moves into matter. The universe is matching you, energetically!

Remember, the present moment is painless. Any emotional pain you're experiencing is from a past event…even if the event was 2 seconds ago! Be mindful, stay awake through **self-observation**, be **optimistic**, and **release** any painful memory or current feeling that's affecting you! Just let go and you're free! Stop putting something off that is so simple yet so beneficial. Try it! What do you have to lose (besides a shitty feeling)? Nothing! What do you have to gain? Everything and anything!

RELAX! YOU'RE FINE

Did you release yet? If so, how do you feel? If you're feeling better already, great! If not, repeat until you are. Take the tool of letting shit go, everywhere with you, always. Use this exercise whenever and wherever you have an unwanted emotion. When you can imagine it leaving, you can feel it leaving, and then the emotion tied to that thought is gone …for good!

• •

Happy people stick out in this world. While I've never met a person who's in a good mood 24/7, some people make the most out of life, every single day. The importance of doing that is… you can only benefit from it! Where there's current discomfort, you'll find comfort in knowing that things will get better; seeing the brighter side of a cloudy day. Otherwise, you're stuck in that disgusting, hopeless feeling. Don't you want to just be happy instead of dwelling on what's wrong?

A woman I worked with, who is now a great friend, always told me stories about when she ran into a woman from down the hall who was the "Debbie" of all downers. When my friend said, "Hi, how are you?" the woman always had a negative response such as, "Terrible. I hate my job," or something along those lines. When the question was reciprocated, my friend always responded with, "Well, I woke up this morning, so I'm alive and I have my health" …one of those "awake-people" responses. After watching her friends being diagnosed with cancers and going through many things in her own life, she has no tolerance for complaining and *I get it*. We're too fortunate to be here to be sad!

It really hit me when I took a random class for credits. One day out of nowhere, my eccentric professor drew a glass on the chalkboard and colored half of it with a squiggly line. He said there are only two types of people in this world. One is a person who looks at the glass as half empty and the other who looks at it as half full. He said the people with the half full glass are always going to be happy no matter what. In that moment I remember thinking, *This guy is so crazy, and so right.* Life is what we make of it! When we focus on the negative, it does nothing but bring more negativity. When we focus on the positive, we're content.

• •

I've always wanted to relive the carefree feeling I had as a child...the feeling of complete freedom in mind and body with nothing but love and acceptance at heart. I've found that getting it back, requires change. And even though change may be scary, it's necessary to keep our lives moving forward. Otherwise, every day is just a repetition of our past.

While we as adults *can* become child-like and free, there's still a huge difference between us and children; we have responsibilities. We can definitely blame them for a lot of our unhappiness because they make us feel burdened.

Another major source of unhappiness many people experience is having a job they're not passionate about, or—let's be real—a job that they hate. It can diminish their quality of life because it's such a big part of it. Think about how much time we spend working in our lives. Don't you want to make your time worthwhile? Enjoyable? Fruitful? If your job makes you unhappy, either pursue what you really want to do or find a way to make the best of it, so you can be at peace. Make it less of a nuisance by setting personal goals. Write down what you want to achieve and when you will get there. This list will remind you that where you are now is only temporary and that your list of goals is waiting for you to scratch each one off as you accomplish it, something to work for in happy anticipation. Remember, life is what we make of it. You're never too old or too late to make something of your life. NEVER. Each moment we're alive is a blessing and an opportunity.

> "Man surprised me most about humanity. Because he sacrifices his health in order to make money. Then he sacrifices money

to recuperate his health. And then he is so anxious about the future that he does not enjoy the present; the result being that he does not live in the present or the future; he lives as if he is never going to die, and then dies having never really lived."

—James J. Lachard

Most people have self-limiting beliefs that their goals and dreams are unattainable. These doubts come from fear. Fear holds us back because when we believe in it, we give it power, making it real.

We don't have talents so we can let them go to waste! We're supposed to pursue what makes us happy! We're supposed to use our creative energy to make an impact in this life, in *our* lives. Anything you believe, you CAN achieve; the path you're following is created by your thoughts. Don't limit possibilities because the truth is, they're endless if you believe they are!

• •

How can we go through life without goals? How would we know where we're going and the steps it takes to get there? That's why it's important to not just think about where you want to be, but to plan how you will succeed.

• •

Here's how to achieve your goals:
1. Write down (or even draw) your goal(s) and be specific.
2. Create an honest timeline for when and how you will achieve them.
3. Be in total control. (Block out the opinions of others; this is your dream, no one else's!)
4. Be aware of any downsides or negative consequences, such as expenses and time away from your loved ones but don't let the obstacles stop you (even if it's something that seems impossible, just believe…the universe will find a way to make it happen).

5. Don't have any doubts!
6. Don't be afraid to just go for it! Many times, people end up regretting things they *didn't* do more than the things they *did* do.
7. Picture everything you want to happen, happening, but don't limit yourself to a vision; imagine the smells, feelings and sounds of your future accomplishment. (Your subconscious will use this visualization to create the reality.)
8. Don't revert to self-sabotaging actions or negative thinking.
9. Read/view your written goals often. (This reminds you of what you're striving for and plants the image in your mind of how you see your future, thereby creating it.)
10. Believe in yourself.
11. As you accomplish each thing on your list, check it off and be proud. Proceed with confidence; you're on your way!

• •

Please stop thinking you don't deserve success! You, just like anybody else, have the ability and the right to receive loads of money and happiness, if you do the right things to obtain them. What are the right things?

- Anything that uses creative energy
- Anything that is intended with love
- Anything that makes you genuinely happy
- Anything that makes anyone else genuinely happy
- Anything that will help others
- Anything that will better this world
- Anything that will make you a better person

The right things are not motivated by greed or negativity. Keep in mind that the **intent** in your goals should be to do something powerful, to contribute to love and healing in yourself, someone else, or this world. Money is not evil. I don't believe in evil; I believe in negative energy. Evil is a word used to describe negative energy *and* used to describe money, to make us subconsciously accept it as evil, which makes us fear money and struggle to obtain it. When you release that fear, accept that you deserve it, and do good things in the pursuit of obtaining it, money will come to you in abundance. Get it? Money has no control over you. As with other types of energy, *you* control how it affects you. *You* control whether your money is "evil."

• •

If you aren't budging from your hated job, find a way to be happy in your own mind. Don't let the work consume you. Take charge of how you feel. Set your mind at a place where you can be happy. The Declaration of Independence states, "We hold these truths to be self-evident, that all men are created equal, that they are endowed by their creator with certain unalienable Rights, that among these are Life, Liberty, and the pursuit of Happiness." The reason that it says "pursuit" of happiness is because while everyone is entitled to it, not everyone achieves it. It's all up to you to JUST BE …happy.

• •

MY SECRET? I care about everything, but I don't care about anything.

CHAPTER 9

KILLING THE EGO

There's one path in life. It goes in two directions—one way to love and the other to fear. We may zig zag, step off track, turn around, or backtrack, but we can't go in both directions at the same time. We must make a conscious effort to choose the direction we want our lives to go in. There is however, something that tends to pull us more toward fear. It's the ego.

• •

Sigmund Freud used the terms id, ego, and super-ego to describe the structure of the human psyche. The id controls our basic instincts: our needs, wants, pleasures, and sex drives. It wants instant gratification, causing us to be impulsive. The super-ego is the opposite. It's our conscience telling us how to act. It tempers our impulses by using the right and wrong we learned from our parents, caregivers, and teachers.

The ego is the middle man—the peacekeeper, but also the troublemaker. The ego tries to justify and carry out the id's impulses by making us believe something that may not be true, or good for us. It masks the id's drive by rationalizing its plan, then presenting the plan to us in a way which makes us act or think accordingly. For example, someone who is "always right" in arguments may feel they are right, and no one can tell them anything. They want to be right so badly that their ego justifies their feelings. They may suspect deep down that they're being irrational, but because their ego and id are so active, they'll "fight to the death" to convince you they're right. Their super-ego might attempt to say *you're wrong on this one* but because of the ego, to them their actions are rational.

Have you ever had a conversation with someone when you were in a relationship with someone else and felt like it was wrong or that your partner would be hurt by it? You find yourself going back and forth thinking, *Am I doing something wrong? But I'm just talking, it's harmless! If I'm hiding it though, it must be wrong.* Suddenly, you're like, *Fuck it, they've done this to me in the past so I'm not going to feel bad about it!* That right there, is your ego convincing you that your actions are justified. It's a loveless way of thinking because you believe it's ok to betray them because they did something like this to you. You're not only being loveless, you're living in the past! All that does is enable fear. It spins your world into a love-lacking, fear-filled circle that comes right back around to you. And guess what? Before you know it, your partner is betraying you again. It creates exactly what you don't want.

> **THE EGO IS WHERE OUR NEGATIVE FEELINGS, THOUGHTS, AND ACTIONS RESIDE.**

The ego is where our negative feelings, thoughts, and actions reside. Like a bad influence, the ego sees what we want and says *Go after that, do that, say that, get that. You can because...* and then the reasoning resonates because we believe it's our conscience talking when IT IS NOT. The ego doesn't allow, or delays our ability, to see reality because it creates a distorted way of thinking. Since we're not thinking realistically, we don't see reality; we see what our fooled minds want us to see. That's why it's so threatening to us! We are peaceful, loving, accepting, forgiving beings, and all the ego wants to do is keep us from that by creating a wall of fear.

• •

Love and fear are the only two true emotions. Everything else derives or branches off of them. Both cannot be present at the same time, just as we cannot truly smile when we're sad; it doesn't work! Unfortunately, FEAR RUNS OUR LIVES. It controls what we think and do because of what's empowering it …our ego. The ego's enemy, if you have not guessed it already, is **love**. When we invite love into our hearts, the ego resists it at first by making up excuses for why we don't need love or shouldn't have it. But if we're persistent, the ego surely dies.

To embrace love into your life, first accept all that is. Acceptance will miraculously call this source of light into you. Give up control; surrender and trust this mysterious universe. Relax into the moment without trying to force or worry about an outcome. You will begin to see everything you can improve. You will notice your faults and the faults of others, but not in the way you've always seen them. You will be able to understand from a new perspective, allowing you to deal with them gracefully. The solutions to your problems will be presented through your intuition and in "signs." Pay attention, they are not coincidences. They're given to you as opportunities to change, to grow, to have peace, to have synchronicity with the universe, or in other words, have things go the way they're intended. Synchronicity is harmony; we find it in the moments or days when everything seems to be going right. Don't get it? We FEAR what we don't understand, and that leaves us unbalanced and stuck in the dark. With pure love and acceptance of any given situation, we can *make* things go in our favor, simply by *making* good choices. The first choice is to let it be! It is what it is! It will be whatever it will be! LET GO OF THE CONTROL. Surrender the discomfort of not understanding because you're not supposed to understand! You're supposed to learn something about yourself in that moment. Get it now? With this welcoming of light comes more understanding, more compassion, more acceptance, and more love. Where does that lead you? To happiness!

Fear is responsible for every bad thought, every bad action, every bad manifestation, our regrets, our worries, and our mental and emotional blockages. Any negativity that we withhold is a spinoff of our fear-driven egos. It makes existence a struggle both internally and externally because of the false belief that we need to be guarded from everything in this world. When we guard ourselves, we fear the outside and that traps the fear *inside*. It takes over everything in us and everything around us, and we become bitter, sad people. THIS IS NOT HOW WE SHOULD BE. Loving, joyous, and peaceful is the original state of the human being because it's the original state of the soul!

• •

When functioning normally, the part of the brain which tells us to be fearful helps us decipher real threats and allows us to act on them. When overactive, we fear every little thing that poses as a threat, even if it isn't! Each of us must learn to separate the ego's input from our instinctual fear response. How? We must re-train our brain to realize we're being irrational when we fear a bad thought instead of a bad situation.

The tricky thing about the ego is that we don't "see" it so it makes us think we're right or justified when in fact, it's blowing smoke up our asses! The ego makes us fearful, prideful, defensive, EGOtistical beings, when we're supposed to be far from that! Anything outside of us having love for each other or ourselves, is unnatural. The problem is that to us, it feels natural to be guarded, and unnatural to be open. How do we break through that comfort zone? Again, we must **surrender**! You might think surrendering is about giving up and giving in. Waving the white flag. It's not! It allows us to open up to a **new**

awareness, a higher power which invites love into our lives. We're letting the moment be peaceful. We're letting go of stress, worries, fear, and anger so everything else can unfold the way it should. We're allowing love to take care of it, not our psyche. Do you get what I'm saying? Trust in the universe, not in your scared mind, and things will work out.

We can receive this divine consciousness that we deserve, that we are entitled to as human beings, which we've had in us all along… when we empty the space of the illusion-filled thoughts our ego has created. It's like when you clean out your closet. It may be temporarily, uncomfortably empty, but now you have space to fill it with a whole new wardrobe!

What happens when we surrender to love?
- it frees our past
- it allows us to enjoy the present
- it stops us from trying to grasp the future
- it releases any loveless thoughts
- it fills us with love
- it allows us to love one another
- it allows us to love ourselves
- it creates happiness
- it creates peace

How is it possible that love is powerful enough to create such bliss? I would respond, how is it possible that fear is powerful enough to destroy lives? Both are forms of energy and energy creates reality. Just because it's not visible doesn't mean it's not there; you can feel it! You can feel how both love and fear affect you. Love is warm and comfortable. Fear is cold and lonely.

Love is real. When you surround yourself with it and pull it from within, it radiates from your body. You become more appealing to others because you're exuding something beautiful. Being attractive is not only a physical thing; just like people are attracted to confident people, they're attracted to loving people. When you accept love into all areas of your life, you will notice others feeding off this energy. They may not be able to pinpoint exactly why, but they like you and are drawn to you.

Fear is a facade. It makes us look bad, when it's not even who we are! It's an illusion! Love is the only thing that is genuine and natural. Since we were originally created with nothing but love, the things that have instilled fear in us are man-made; they're inorganic. Just as a peach grown and sprayed with pesticides is still a peach, it's tainted with an unnatural substance. *Our* unnatural substance is the ego. Of course, we're not a peach; a peach can't rid itself of the pollutants it was grown with, but we can. We are able to, with time and effort, cut away the layers of fear trapped within us and expose the love underneath. Each layer that leaves us lightens our load.

• •

Close your eyes and imagine how it feels to carry a heavy purse or wallet. It's filled with the things you need to "protect" you, like make-up, hairbrushes, papers, receipts, business cards, etc. Now reach into it and take something out. Put the bag back on your shoulder or the wallet back in your pocket. Imagine that painful pull or that uncomfortable bulkiness dwindling. Do you feel lighter? If there's no obvious change, take something else out. You may feel lighter immediately or you may have to remove several more items. Either way, you're letting go, little by little, of the things you don't need but use to guard you (ego).

You may feel a little apprehensive or uneasy about letting go, but that's just your ego fighting with you (resistance). It knows you're killing it and the ego wants to live! Release it over and over, and eventually it won't bug you anymore! When we continue to let go of our fears and allow that space to fill up with love, we become lighter, happier beings. Everything we need in life is already within us. All other things are secondary.

KILLING THE EGO

We're all *so* defensive with the Berlin Walls we've built in front of our hearts to keep love out. It's frightening to let something unfamiliar into our lives. The ego's so afraid of love that it barricades itself by using us as shields. We are the only true weapons in the world! Our ammunition is the fear within us. When we attack each other, we are in reality, attacking *ourselves*.

The ego is a defense mechanism built into our personalities. It allows us to be so hurt (fearful) by insignificant things that we end up significantly hurting one another. It guards us from opportunities, success, love, and happiness, and contributes to the destruction of the human race, serving no real purpose at all! Ummm, *war*? Don't you want to put an end to this? Don't you want to stop being hateful and fearful? Don't you want to make things right for our future generations, for your children, and for yourself, right now? Well you can by tearing down *your* Berlin Wall. How? It's not easy, but the "wrecking ball" of love will certainly chip away at it with every conscious swing. We need more compassion for others. More acceptance. More love. The only way to get it is by defeating the ego.

> WHEN WE ATTACK EACH OTHER, WE ARE IN REALITY, ATTACKING OURSELVES.

Try letting your ego go for a minute and see how you feel. Start by bringing it out from the darkness, into the light, exposing it for what it is. Give it a gender, maybe even a face. Tell him or her, *I can see you and I know you're trying to protect me, but what you're doing is stopping me from being me, from enjoying my life*. Tell him or her, *Thank you for everything you've done for me, but now it's time to let you go*. Then welcome love. Ask it to come into your being. Tell it that you fully accept it and will allow it to guide you. When you keep inviting love, you'll experience more of it in your everyday life, allowing you to finally feel peace.

I can hear the pessimists saying, *This is some hippie shit, all this peace and love talk.* I can't control how you will receive this information. You are entitled to your opinion and you will be influenced to some degree by your inner resistance, and I don't have the power to change you. I can only hope you will see the truth for yourself by experiencing it, not by letting your ego decide this is make-believe because it's foreign to your current comprehension. I believe strongly in everything I know now because once you discover reality, the veil of fear no longer distorts your vision. Beliefs you've depended on drop out of sight because the freedom of love allows you to finally see the greatness you're entitled to, and capable of. Love is the truth and the truth will always set you free.

> LOVE IS THE TRUTH AND THE TRUTH WILL ALWAYS SET YOU FREE.

I feel sorrow for people who look down on these things. If they never give up their pessimistic attitude, they most likely won't get to experience such a profound appreciation and love for life. They may never see the true beauty of our human existence, at least not in this lifetime. We cannot judge them though, because each of us is on our own journey. Divine timing, divine order, and a person's own choices will allow what is meant to be, to be, but we can show others their options by simply being an example.

You beautiful but incredibly stubborn being… if you keep your mind and heart open, you will be *amazed* by what you'll discover.

• •

When you are guided by the light of love, life will work out beautifully, like a well-oiled wheel. When love is not present, your wheel will shriek and grind and struggle to go anywhere. Choose to welcome the light.

Now when you do invite love into your life, don't expect everything to be smooth sailing from that point. It will be stressful, even tumultuous at times, but please don't be afraid! This is part of elevating through healing. Any kind of detox, physical, spiritual, or emotional, will stir up whatever has disturbed you in the past and cause resistance. While it may be difficult at the time, it will be so rewarding after it passes. This is referred to as a "healing crisis." Things must get worse before they get better, right? When we break past the temporary low, we reach what feels like heaven. You'll experience many levels of this if you keep pushing through the tough parts. And never give up because the point at which you can take no more is usually the point where if you push through, success awaits you on the other side!

The most unloving thing about us is that we don't love ourselves, but we MUST love ourselves, no matter how un-loved we've felt in our lives, if we ever want to be happy. Why? Love is peaceful. Fear and hatred are chaotic; they bring nothing but emptiness into our hearts. True love for ourselves allows us to live in peace with others because there is no inner struggle. We have no horned version of ourselves sitting on our shoulders, telling us what to do; we **just know** what to do. The truth is, when we experience such a powerful force, there's no denying it. It's also hard to understand without experiencing it. But for some unexplainable reason, it defies all rules and limitations of this world. When we believe there are no limitations, guess what? There are none!

> "Our species is in trouble because we fight too much. We fight ourselves, each other, our planet, and God. Our fear-ridden ways are threatening our survival. A thoroughly loving person is like an evolutionary mutation, manifesting a being that puts love first and thus creates the context in which miracles occur."
>
> —Marianne Williamson

PART II
BIRTH OF THE SOUL

CHAPTER 10

WHO AM I?

"...We are but manifestations of a whole, a whole that by its very nature is both knowable and unknowable. All is essentially one. Every single thing is a manifestation of energy—one thing—that is continually transforming. It never stands still. Nothing is ever lost, just changed. And to know that is to know that it all couldn't possibly just happen to be here."
—*The Enigma of Energy*, Vidette Todaro-Franceschi (1999)

Come on! Everything we know that exists didn't just happen to be here! There's something out there, something that wants us to be what we're capable of being. It's time to stop everything and say, *I'm not doing the right things to become who I'm meant to be. I'm capable of more because I feel it. I feel that there's something much bigger and better for me than what I've limited myself to believe.*

• •

When you look at different species or creatures on this earth, do you see the similarities in all beings? We are all one. I believe we adapted to what our surrounding environment had to offer, making us look and act the way we do. Our ancestors developed into our genetic makeup and consciousness from what they were exposed to on the land (and sea).

• •

One day, I was in a pizza spot with my friend watching two police horses parked outside, eating hay. I've seen horses before but never studied them closely. When you look at those beautiful creatures, you will see similarities in their faces to human faces. Even with other animals and life-forms, certain characteristics or movements resemble other beings, like animals that look like insects or insects that look like leaves.

Nature and the forces of this universe have equipped us with everything we need to survive in our own ways. These instinctual and innate abilities and traits are unique to each species, yet all serve a purpose for survival and adaptability to this world. If used purposefully, all beings can live abundantly and in harmony, especially if humans are awakened to the spirituality of life. Whether human, animal, or plant, we're all connected to something higher, something divine. Humans have lost touch with this reality.

• •

Nature stays in constant communication with us. You can hear it if you quiet the chaos, stop blabbering about nonsense, and learn to listen to its messages. There is so much more to life than what we see. Being caught up in material things and petty problems has caused us to lose touch with the spiritual realm; we've lost touch with a big part of *ourselves*.

I've been learning about things that will eventually bring life back to where it needs to be—at peace and in harmony. Don't you think we should know about the afterlife and who we are? Don't you feel if we had more answers, everyone would feel more ease?

WHO AM I?

We're supposed to have this information. We're not supposed to have worries, fears, and sadness. We should be loving and joyful most of our lives!

• •

Now, I want to address unanswered questions about life and death. First, I'll get into who or what we are…

Using our senses to explain it won't cut it. Our physical being is merely the top layer. To us, experiencing life is mostly seeing, hearing, smelling, touching, and tasting, because we don't pay attention to the very core—the deepest layer. We're having a human experience; it's not what we *are*. It's not something we can see, hear, smell, touch, or taste. What's it? IT, is not something that must be known. It must be experienced from a deep level within us and around us. What is it? Our spirits—our true selves.

We are spiritual entities that have chosen physical forms to carry out a purpose. Many of us have lived *many* lives before and that information is encoded in our souls. The body is only temporary; the soul is forever. This is yet another life, another chance to fulfill our soul's reason for existence. This is hard to believe when all we see is bodies and faces, but the truth lies within us.

Why is it so difficult to see our true selves? I believe something has blinded us. Something changed a long time ago and it's destroying life; it's destroying our purpose.

• •

How can we believe in a spirit, if we don't understand what a spirit is? How can we believe it's a part of us? To put it simply, we *choose* not to believe in it. There's something in us that resists it, but another part that knows it's there. Think about these things… how can this be it? How can everything be here, be so beautiful and connected, and then when it dies, it's just gone? What put this here? What about the unexplainable things that happen in life, the miracles, phenomenon, coincidences, and spiritual encounters? What about the science of ENERGY!? We have a layer of us that is so beautiful, and when we don't allow ourselves that awareness, we are unfulfilled. Being unfulfilled is the same as being unhappy with yourself and with others. They say ignorance is bliss, but I call bullshit. How can you be happy when you're not seeing the beauty of your creation, or the beauty of someone or something else?

The CHOICE to focus on someone's faults, even our own, is the CHOICE to not see a soul. Not seeing someone's soul is not truly seeing them, and not truly seeing ourselves. Why? We're all the same! We all have souls! The soul is innocent and pure. Everything bad about someone developed from ego and conditioning, stemming from various levels of experience. If we only see what someone has become instead of understanding why they have become that way, we're limited by the sight we physically see and not using our insight of knowing and feeling. We're not being compassionate! Compassion is love. Love comes from the soul. If you're not acting in love, aren't you like the person you're judging? Where love is lacking, understanding is also, and all that comes from our screwed-up perspective on life, and our perspective of other living beings.

So how do we change our perspective? How do we acknowledge the soul? By learning! We must learn to open to a greater awareness, to control ourselves, love ourselves, heal ourselves, forgive ourselves, accept ourselves, get in tune with the earth, and get in tune with our inner-beings. It starts with accepting all that is and allowing freedom into our lives. When we do that, we're brought back to reality; we're grounded. Right now, people are floating by, missing out on the world around them and the world within them.

Isn't it sad how the world disregards life? We've been corrupted and are continuing to corrupt one another to the point that awareness of the soul is lost within us. All we see are fucked up humans walking around. We're blind to the food we eat, the things we say, the

WHO AM I?

things we do, and the control we let others have over us. This needs correction, now, immediately.

BECOMING AWARE OF THE SOUL

Our souls are much bigger and more powerful than our physical bodies. We gain this knowledge from humbleness and learning about the rewards that come from making decisions based on love...*and* by simply being present in life! It's standing still and quietly in nature; it's listening to the sounds around you. It's feeling the wind comb through your hair, and the warmth of the sun on your skin. It's the support of the sturdy earth beneath your feet...feeling peace resonate through you.

Alignment of the spiritual, physical, metaphysical, and existential certainties of our beings is a result of true awareness and choosing peace in that awareness. It comes from gaining knowledge, *understanding* that knowledge, and then "just knowing" from "just being." Just being is living in the present moment, not in the past and not in the future. We merge with the universe and live in peace by knowing that everything is as it should be and that everything will work out if we allow ourselves to be guided by love. Hardships and tragedies are only meant to inspire evolution in the current incarnation. If we let others, our egos, our misfortunes, or material things control how we move forward in the present, we're not allowing things to "flow" or play out as they should; we get stuck. Of course it's ok to strive for nice things, but we should make sure our intuition and positive intention are moving us towards a more meaningful goal through our pursuit of such things. We can help people along the way as we reach success and avoid being resentful, spiteful, or hateful. Because otherwise, what good is the reward? Do you get it?

> EVERYTHING IS AS IT SHOULD BE AND EVERYTHING WILL WORK OUT IF WE ALLOW OURSELVES TO BE GUIDED BY LOVE.

The loveless and meaningless way we live is resistance to the harmony we could have with the universe. It's why our world is so off kilter. It's why we're screwed up! Are you starting to see why life is so unreasonably uncomfortable? We make things hard for ourselves, like our "understanding" of death.

•••••••••••••••••••••••••••••

Do you want to know what happens after you die? Do you want to know if reincarnation is real? Read the book, *Many Lives, Many Masters*, by Brian L. Weiss, MD; it's a life-changer. I have never read anything else that made me cry in such a good, powerful way. Everything I've felt about life and death but wanted to know for sure was confirmed in this book. It provides comfort, reassurance, ANSWERS that people want to so desperately have. Perhaps you're a skeptic? Dr. Weiss was too. His patient, Catherine, changed that. When he brought her into a hypnotic state to try to ease her anxiety, he discovered the truth about the afterlife. She began to recall past-life experiences in such detail that even a professional like himself couldn't explain. Dr. Weiss couldn't deny the reality, even after using logic, his psychological expertise, and scientific studies. Catherine was telling stories, feelings, experiences, and detailed scenarios of lives she had lived before but could not have possibly dreamed in her current life. She also had profound voices of something or someone mystical channel through her at times.

Catherine's revelations blew Dr. Weiss away. He wondered, "Was this real? I found it difficult to doubt, in view of what she had just revealed, yet I struggled to believe. I was overcoming years of alternative programming. But in my head and my heart and my gut, I knew she was right. She was revealing truths."

A message came through in one of her sessions that really touched me. She was channeling the voice of a "Master" (an advanced spirit), "Patience and timing…everything comes when it must come. A life cannot be rushed, cannot be worked on a schedule as so many people want it to be. We must accept what comes to us at any given time, and not ask for more. But life is endless, so we never die; we were never really born. We just pass through different phases. There is no end. Humans have many dimensions. But time is not as we see time, but rather in lessons that are learned." Lessons… that's why we're here. Soul growth is our purpose for existence. We're here to *experience* the physical, to *master* the spiritual. To master enlightenment.

Many Lives, Many Masters unveils the jaw-dropping truth about reincarnation, but if you're looking for more, there's more available! See, *Real Reincarnation Stories* © 2014 RealReincarnationStories.com.[2] See also *20 Amazing Things Kids Have Said About Past Lives,* by Tara MacIsaac, Epoch Times October 31, 2013.[3]

• •

I've explained how we use our emotions to affect the things around us by transferring our mood into matter. There's far more to that…

Energy is an infinite constancy that can never be lost. It can, however, be moved, released, shifted, and changed. We're all energy, from our spirits down to our physical beings. It's how we construct that energy and use it in our lives that sets us on certain paths, but these pathways are variable.

People think what they do will change their soul. They fear what will happen in the afterlife because of what they've done in this one. However, what we do never changes who we truly are, it only makes us forget. God, or the infinite intelligence that's out there and all around us, loves us all unconditionally. He/she/it created us and knows it wasn't our fault that life turned out this way. ALL IS FORGIVEN IN THE AFTERLIFE. We're souls visiting here in human form to love, learn, give, and experience. We're not here to hate, to be judged, to be regretful, or to be fearful. Our human imprinted logic

---

2 http://realreincarnationstories.com/stories#sthash.aWJDmjPg.dpbs
3 http://m.theepochtimes.com/n3/337315-10-things-kids-have-said-about-past-lives/

arouses those negative feelings in us; they're not comparable to what we authentically are.

> SOME SOULS ARE HERE MAINLY TO BE GIVERS, SOME MAINLY TO EXPERIENCE, AND SOME TO MASTER LESSONS.

Some souls are here mainly to be givers, some mainly to experience, and some to master lessons. These lessons are karmic debts which a soul can hold onto through many lifetimes. These debts need to be paid to make things right for the next time around (next life). Otherwise, that new life will most likely be the same or harder than the ones before. Why? The soul is striving for growth. The universe keeps presenting opportunities for growth until the opportunities are taken. The collective consciousness of nature wants peace for us so we can level up our awareness and express what we truly are…fully loving energies. We reach that enlightenment through lessons of hardships that teach us to rebuild ourselves even stronger. We become strong in the sense of wisdom and love. We're meant to use our forces to harmonize with the universe and every living thing by learning to change anything inharmonious in our lives. Each experience becomes a tool to fix our mistakes. When we fix our mistakes, we can help the rest of the world fix theirs.

Everything is a lesson to be learned. Unless we wake up and make good for our wrongs by changing course, we may have to work through hardships in yet another life *and* in this life, until we get it right. It's all about progression. Lessons allow for progression because they give us chances to change.

• •

Picture a soul moving from body to body, awaiting a spiritual awakening. If they don't "wake up" in that life, at death the soul can carry the wrongs that were never made right and the emotional memories that person held into the next body. If in that life they are awakened, their spiritual awareness transcends into the physical world and the soul's mission is closer to completion, allowing that person to finally live their life more peacefully and harmoniously. We can't experience peace and harmony when we fear the unknown and the fear of what we've done wrong, stops us from doing right. That guilt—that feeling of unworthiness—makes us neglect our souls and follow our emotions. It's why we continue to make bad choices! Fear of death was designed to scare us and keep us in check (like the ego), but all it does it create *more* fear and then more hardship.

Desperation causes humans to live in a materialistic, fearful, unjust world *of our own creating* because it's easier to push life aside than to truly live it. Here's the secret: it's NOT easier! Living loveless is a burden on our souls as well as those we affect. When we realize we're all loved, we can love ourselves and understand that anything we've done in the past is nothing in the now. It's what we do and what we are aware of in the present moment that will deliver us from this unnatural, fearful way of thinking and living.

Remember, you're a creation of this universe. The wrong you've done is a glitch in the system. It's not permanent! You're not a bad person! You are forgiven; you are loved by someone or something more powerful than you can understand. When you change your perception of yourself by accepting this love, you can then wake up from the awful dream you've been living. Be the best person you can be, right now. Love is there for you if you allow it.

• •

NOTE: I am repeatedly mentioning "waking up," or having an "awakening," because when you "wake up," you really wake the fuck up! You see life the way it REALLY is. It's like someone flips a switch that you never knew was there, and sanity turns on. Seriously look at us… humans think so poorly and do such crazy shit! WE'RE SCREWED UP!!! You know things are bad and it's not because of anything but HUMAN BEINGS. We're supposed to be Earth's caretakers, but we destroy it instead. We destroy ourselves! When you let your pride, ego, anger, sadness, doubt, negative thinking, and negative behavior go right out the window, you've cleaned house. You're open to new possibilities of success, love, hope, peace, and happiness. You go from being part of the problem to part of the solution. Let's change, people! Let's be genuinely happy and gloriously uninhibited! Let's really *live* in this life. All it takes is the flip of a switch. Flip your whole mindset!

• •

The more I am connected to this lifestyle, eating healthy foods and practicing peace and love, the more I'm able to feel connected to something authentic. I'm working from "the inside out," clearing everything that's blocking the sense of life I couldn't see before. I'm grounded yet flying *so* high. My body is aligning with my spirit and the universe, and I can feel it! Now do you see why I feel like a **Superhuman**? I've never been a religious person, so this is something new yet so profound. We lost these capabilities somewhere down the line, the connection to another part of ourselves, another part of this world.

• •

Scientists believe that a long, long time ago, we had access to 12 strands of DNA as opposed to the two that we access now.[4] With those extra strands functioning, human beings had multidimensional consciousness, the power to heal themselves, psychic abilities, and communicated with spirits. They had no illnesses and lived in harmony. Sounds like a fairy tale, right? It's very real and may come back; people are experiencing it.

Science has labeled 97% of our DNA "junk DNA" because we don't use it.[5] We're finding out now that some people can access other

---

4 http://humansarefree.com/2011/04/amazing-scientists-our-dna-is-mutating.html
5 http://myscienceacademy.org/2013/01/23/scientists-finally-present-evidence-on-expanding-dna-strands/

WHO AM I?

parts of their brains. Some children have this access at birth. They have abilities beyond scientific explanation like clairvoyance, which allows them to predict things, and telekinesis, which allows them to move objects with their minds. People may pass that off as phenomena, but it's how life *should* be.

Not convinced yet? Doesn't it seem strange that we're all so unaware about what's next for us, yet there are numerous stories about contact with the afterlife? Isn't there something unnatural about the way humans live? We go through our lives dealing with so much sadness and then die from terrible sickness and disease. Something about that never added up for me.

Here's the truth: someone or something, somewhere down the line, interfered. We lost touch with who we really are, souls who travel to this earth. At the end of a life, if a soul doesn't or can't fulfill its purpose, it leaves the life-form and travels elsewhere to complete its mission; some people think the soul moves to a parallel universe. Some believe we are existing in parallel universes simultaneously, right now! Déjà vu? Maybe we're blindly participating in a race of time to see who saves the world! Who knows? What we do know is that *this ain't it*. There's a bigger purpose for us than to exist in this miraculous, infinite world thinking and living small, while destroying everything we need to keep us here. We are turned away from the truth about our souls and capabilities on purpose. We're suppressed for a reason, a heinous, corrupt reason.

> WE LOST TOUCH WITH WHO WE REALLY ARE, SOULS WHO TRAVEL TO THIS EARTH.

This all comes back to "waking up." When someone is awakened, they are **aware**; they start to understand the soul and become one with it. When you become one with your soul, you're able to spot all the things that are not meant for this world, all the things that are destructive to who you are. I don't want to frighten you, but things are far more crooked than we perceive. Those in power who have sought control over something that doesn't belong to them, *life*, have unfortunately been successful in limiting humans. By placing a veil of fear and sickness over us, they prevent us from reaching our full potential and impacting this world for the better. It's scary to have this knowledge, yet at the same time, it's so beautiful because those who are understanding are coming together to change it all. Can you feel your soul? Are you starting to understand who you are and what you can do?

• •

Our souls are infinite entities of light that braid into our bodies at the time of incarnation and leave at death. They use us as hosts to complete something, to fulfill a purpose. That purpose plus the history or information of our soul is in a part of our brain that we don't access. It doesn't make sense that we only use 10% of it and have no use for the other areas. We just haven't been able to tap into it or understand it because we lost that connection (or it was taken away). It may have been the food we began to eat or perhaps someone interfered with it, or both, but we're starting to get back in tune with that part of the brain. We're at a point where life and morality are being put to the test, and the spiritual world is guiding us.

> **OUR SOULS ARE INFINITE ENTITIES OF LIGHT THAT BRAID INTO OUR BODIES AT INCARNATION AND LEAVE AT DEATH.**

Science is messing with life by cloning and doing unnatural things. Media and the people in power are shoving more of our own our fears down our throats to control us and make money from us. They're also instilling made up fears that manifest into our physical beings and can literally kill us. I believe the higher intelligence of the universe recognizes this and wants us to change. It *needs* us to change.

WHO AM I?

• •

Things on earth are so bad that people think it's the end of the world, when I believe it's the beginning of a new one. This is an opportunity for rebirth, a transition into the next evolutionary step of our existence. The spiritual realm is working at an extraordinarily high level to be remembered by the human mind that has been systematically dumbed down, and that's why more of us are getting in touch with ourselves. More of us are waking up! We're eating healthier, juicing, fasting, meditating, and searching for more natural and spiritual ways of healing instead of using allopathic medicine…and it's working!

To dig deeper into it, we're all being pulled by a force, vibration, or energy that's trying to change us, but since our bodies can't make sense of it, we're subconsciously resisting and feeling ill. Many people are having little spurts of depression mixed with moments of bliss, flu-like symptoms, changes in sleep patterns, and many other things that tend to go away quickly because nothing's wrong! It's our egos fighting against what's happening! The human mind, as it is now, can't comprehend what is happening, so it must make an excuse for why we're feeling this way. In other words, the ego tricks the mind and the mind subconsciously creates ailments in the body. All physical ailments develop from thought before they develop physically. This force is working to level out the spiritual world with the physical world and we're experiencing a major shift in energy, confusion, and a stirring up of fear so it can be released and resolved. Love wants to guide us, but like everything else intended with love, the ego works hard to resist. Do you feel it, on any level? If so, embrace it. You're changing.

• •

Those who are "waking up" are probably starting to understand life and death a lot more now. You're probably coming to peace with it. For those of you who are not, who fear death or have lost a loved one, understand that nothing is ever lost. Everything and everyone is made of energy and energy cannot be destroyed; it's infinite. Someone who has died is still a part of this universe. Your loved one still exists. Their soul will continue its journey and their energy will always be part of yours, as yours is a part of theirs. Understandably, the thing that hurts the most is not being able to see them, to talk to them, or to touch them, but they're still there.

Since we are matter (which is slowed-down energy), when we die, our soul which is also energy, is no longer confined to the slowed-down mass that is our body, and we become everything and anything. We become nature. I believe spirits give you signs like dropping feathers or bringing birds to you. Have you ever experienced that or felt someone's presence?

The human mind takes the hit for the loss because what we don't understand creates confusion; it creates pain. Our souls know the truth but since we're not consciously or "logically" aware of them, we often don't access that information, leaving us with little to no comfort. But as much pain as we have and as much as we want to hold onto those we've lost, we must allow their souls to move on. We must wish them love on their journey and let them go. Holding on is a selfish human desire. They're fine, and they want *us* to be fine. They want us to move on, to be happy, and celebrate life. We can always keep their memory, but we should let them go, for them and for us. This is what I meant when I asked, *Don't you think we should have more answers?* We hurt because we fear what we don't know. Fear is like a mirage of water in the desert because we're so thirsty for the truth that what we think is real ends up being only an illusion.

Fear is a distraction from all that is bad. Love is a concentration of all that is good. Once again, let love and ONLY love guide you, because there is so much you're not seeing right now. There's so, so, so much more to this thing we call life.

WHO AM I?

We desperately seek the truth from abstract sources when all along, it lies within us and around us. If only everyone could understand that we are joyful, loving, peaceful beings in our true nature and what separates us from that is the ego. When we allow pure love into our lives, we become closer to our spirituality, bringing a new perspective on life and death, eliminating the ego, and banishing our fears. Love opens our eyes to see each other more spiritually than physically, and there is no higher state of awareness than truly understanding ourselves.

> WHEN WE ALLOW PURE LOVE INTO OUR LIVES, WE BECOME CLOSER TO OUR SPIRITUALITY.

Those who have died are being cycled into a new life, a new start. Their energy, the love from their pure state of being which emerges if not on this earth then at death, is very **alive**. They appear in the clouds, the flowers, the wind, and the tiny bird sitting on your windowsill. Choosing to see them is choosing to believe in the beauty of this world. Our egotistical minds don't want that; they want us to continue being hurt and blinded from this beauty, confusing us with "what ifs" about the unknown. Allow yourself to believe, to know, to be free.

I remember sitting in the kitchen talking to my grandma about my uncle, her son, who had recently passed. She said that after his death, she was talking out loud to him when two doves appeared in her backyard. Right after she said that, for some inexplicable reason, I got up and looked out the front door. I said, "Grandma come here!" We each shed joyful tears as we watched two doves walk around the front yard. Doves are a symbol of love and peace and are also said to be messengers. Life gives us signs all the time. Choosing to see them is choosing to see the beauty of this world. What do you want to see?

SUPERHUMAN

• •

We don't understand so many things about the universe. What I've shared may sound totally crazy, but I believe huge revelations are coming soon. The things I've talked about will begin to happen and these changes will advance our minds. Keep yourself open to the possibility that *anything* is possible. While the changes might be colossal or mind-blowing, they'll only be better for us. How do I know? I've harmonized what I've learned about this universe with what I feel is the truth, by trusting my intuition, by trusting the power of love, and by having faith. When we all have this new awareness, we'll be able to do more and make life more joyful.

• •

You could sit in front of your TV, play on your phone, feel things, hear things, smell things, TASTE things (we all know how easy it is to get sucked in front of the TV with food), but at some point, you will realize that you're wasting time. You'll realize you're putting off that phone call to mend a relationship, putting off forgiving someone, putting off truly feeling, experiencing, and thinking. You're putting off love. Is that living? Human beings are smart and capable of great things yet limited by such nonsense. This is not life; this is not how it's supposed to be. There's more than the physical aspect of existence. We have our five senses, but we constantly use those senses in ways that block off *other* senses. We can "feel" ourselves, "feel" others, and "feel" the magic that coincides around us and resides inside of us. Yes, magic. I think of energy as magic. They are tiny things in constant motion that make up our physical structure and everything around us even though we can't see them. With our thoughts and actions, we can move them, change them, transfer them, spread them, transform things with them, and create things with them; we make miracles happen! We're so scared of life and so scared to be real with ourselves that we don't tap into this magic. We hold onto emotions, we

WHO AM I?

bury ourselves in feelings, we cover it all up with make-up, clothes, personas, job titles, and other things that don't matter. It all stems from our programming to fear death. When we fear death, we do everything we can to stop thinking about it and thinking about who and what we are. We constantly focus on physical senses and feed our egos.

Don't you think that's what "they" want? Why would those in power want us to be metaphysical, powerful beings who don't fear death? I'll tell you why ...they couldn't suppress our visions, dreams, capabilities, or truths. THEY COULDN'T CONTROL US AND PROFIT OFF US. We shut off death and we shut off thinking about what else there could be. We'd rather be blindly comfortable in the moment instead of beautifully **knowing** who and what we are, experiencing things the way they really are, feeling the powers that we have, and understanding how to control life and not letting life control us. The things we let waste our time and poison our minds like television, smart phones, video games, etc. program us to limit our true potential. We're wasting the real moments! These things are only a distraction from **living**, from releasing our emotions, from being our authentic, magical selves. Yes, you are magic! If that didn't go over your head, then you're hearing the alarm. It's time to start waking up. Believe me when I tell you, YOU ARE CAPABLE OF ANYTHING. YOU ARE LIMITLESS. All you need to do is open your eyes.

• •

So, beautiful, limitless soul… if I told you I have more secrets to life would you believe me? Well I do! You can take it or leave it but I'm putting them all out there. I'm giving you a rare opportunity to change the way you see and live life for the better, forever! When we are unaware of truths, we live in a box placed over us by lies and misconceptions. Most people are afraid to even peek outside it! They're comfortable living within the confines of systematic programming.

SUPERHUMAN

These truths have been hidden from us for so long, and now that they're in plain sight, people are hiding from *them!* Is this you? Or are you ready to embrace true existence? For the last few years, I've not only looked, but jumped outside the box, and what I've seen is absolutely amazing! I discovered that everything we believe and everything we think we know isn't real! You probably said, *what!?* There has been a HUGE veil over our eyes.

Food, water, and energy are the keys to life. Do you know that water can react to words and emotions? Are you aware that your intention alters it? Did you know that the foods we eat everyday are killing us and keeping horrible ailments alive? Or that cancer can be cured naturally…mindfully? How about the fact that you can change everything in your life by changing your attitude? Or, that you are electric? What about changing your eye color? Did you know that was possible? I've found the answers to these questions and many more by studying the power of raw and living foods. How? Once you make the first step toward change, everything flows to you.

• •

There's so much outside of our basic knowledge that we don't know or understand. We are all living our lives in the hardest and most devastating way. Want the truth? Two main things are ruining our lives: the way we think and the way we eat. Our separation from God, the spiritual world, our souls, and the creation of illness, disease, and negativity come from the fears banged into our brains, and the poisons hidden in our foods. We ultimately destroy ourselves by choosing to stay in our comfort zones of circumstance and poor health instead of choosing to be loving and healthy. However, it is possible to change it all around. I was an average, unhealthy, unhappy person, but I transformed into a **Superhuman,** and so can you.

CHAPTER 11

THE RAW TRUTH

● ●

How am I alive? Poor eating habits came with me into this world like a genetic disease that grew worse the more I experienced emotional turmoil. Not only did I have terrible self-discipline, but I ate terrible food! All the odds were against me, but I overcame. Learning the **truth** about life and taking the initiative to change saved me.

● ●

I was breastfed until I was about two because I refused to eat any kind of food. My mom was concerned, but the doctor said so long as I had her milk, I had all the nutrients I needed.

When I was a little older, I refused to eat almost anything besides Reese's Peanut Butter Cups® (I'm not even joking, that's almost all I ate). My mom tried and tried but I refused to eat normal food. The doctor told her, "She'll eat when she's hungry."

As time went by, I consumed more of a variety but still nothing healthy. I barely ate fruit and feared vegetables. If I ever tried them, they had to be smothered in cheese. That's when the flame from my love affair with Reese's® dwindled, when the creamy, salty, succulent taste of cheese became my obsession. Isn't it crazy how our senses take hold of us?

• •

During my pre-teen years, I was hooked on McDonalds™. The Happy Meals collection of toys drew me in before the food captured me like crack. I eventually worked up to three or four CHEESEburgers and four- to six-piece nuggets…in one sitting! That's a lot for anyone.

About this time, I started gaining weight. My brother had constantly made fun of me for being too skinny and now for getting heavier! Young girls are extremely susceptible to weight comments, whether they're skinny or fat. It's a time for self-realization, and any little doubt clogs the mind. It affected me for sure, so I ate and ate.

• •

NOTE: Remember, other's opinions really have nothing to do with you. Know who *you* are (self-awareness) and that's all that should matter.

• •

Fat is not how I would have described myself, but I was clearly overweight. I always had a small waist but huge thighs and butt. My largest weight gain left me at 180lbs (I'm 5'4"). I felt uncomfortable in my own skin. It's hard to find outfits and feel like you look good when you're not happy with your body. I was down on myself.

Around the age of 20, I slowly started to **awaken**. Before, life had been a continuous head game; my mental and emotional state had never let me carry out an ambitious plan long enough to level up from my circumstances. The truth is, that wasn't my fault. It's not *your* fault. It's not our fault…that we doubt ourselves! It's learned behavior! Suppressive behavior turns fear into a reality that controls our dreams, when we're not even aware we're "sleeping." But guess what? It's changeable! We can wake up and win at this game called life! The thing that changed for me was feeling, *so deeply*, the "rock-bottom" that people talk about, a complete surrender after all the fighting I had done within myself. Suddenly everything was different, and I was finally ready to cut the bullshit and get to work.

• •

Before I continue…

I believe that "waking up" is something anyone can do, possibly even someone with a mental illness. I'm big into psychology. I've been observing and analyzing human behavior for a long time. It may sound weird, but I look at people as computers, robots. We have a main control center (the brain) which changes according to how we program it (knowledge). It sends signals throughout the body to make parts of the body move or warn us of a problem. We contract viruses which change our systems and cause anything from a malfunction (changes in behavior, thoughts, or health), to a crash (death). We even have "buttons" (meridians), which when touched, can initiate healing on different areas and organs of our bodies. Kind of cool, kind of creepy, right? But it's true! The way people think and behave is from being programmed and hacked, and I look at those "crazy moments" as glitches in the system …malfunctions! Why can't it be fixed? I believe it can. Remember re-training the mind or neuroplasticity? Some of us just need a lot of re-programming! That's not a reflection on them, it's a reflection of the things they went through and were given in this life. I don't believe in bad people. I believe in screwed up people. I believe what we were passed down genetically, combined with what we physically and mentally put on, in, and around our bodies, either hurts or heals our brains. Knowledge and my own experiences tell me this is true.

I can't imagine going back to living, thinking, and behaving the way I did before I had this major life change, before I WOKE THE FUCK UP. Back then, I was a puppet of society because I didn't know that **real life** *existed. No one does when they're sleeping or mentally ill. It's like not knowing that you're trapped in your own body. Only the people who have shifted to the other side of "being" will understand. That's the point of this*

SUPERHUMAN

book. I want EVERYONE to understand. I want EVERYONE to wake up, **live***, and cherish life on this earth. People do terrible things, but they're broken. They may see glimpses of a different way of life but can't help but fall victim to their psyche, the control center of human behavior. No one deserves to be in constant psychological pain; it's torture. I saw my brother go through it every day of his life and it destroyed not only him, but my family. Do you know someone like this? Regardless of what they do, we should always direct love toward them because when we hate, we keep healing from taking place in them, and in ourselves. When we can understand that about people, we can stop hating. We can start loving and healing.*

I understand mental illness now and I can't agree that the mentally ill are a lost cause. It starts with what we consume and how we let others influence our perception of life. Behavior is learned. "Food" is tainted. Whenever I eat poorly now, I can feel my sanity slipping away. It comes back as soon as I practice healthy habits again. I don't believe in permanent health damage. I believe that nature has all the cures, and healing begins when we root ourselves back into the soil from which we came. Is it possible for you to heal yourself and become a healthy, normal person? Yes, if you're willing to do the work and receive help from others. Have faith in yourself and the abilities of your mind. Remember, we're not limited to our physical structure. Our bodies are just our vehicles. We are capable of anything.

• •

Too busy living the fast life, I never took a moment to stop and see where I was. I had filled my world with drugs, alcohol, unhealthy food, headaches, anger, sadness, and regret. I came to the point where I just wanted to live, and by live, I mean be happy! I wanted to wake up from my bad dream and experience every moment with clarity. So, what did I do? I stopped feeling sorry for myself. I stopped holding on to anger. I searched deep within and realized to truly be happy, I needed to make some major changes. Nothing I had done

THE RAW TRUTH

before was bringing me closer to my goal, so I knew it was time to "play the opposite game," to live on the other end of the spectrum. **First step**, I would change my attitude and be free of the past by forgiving and letting go. **Next step**, I would change how I treated my body.

• •

Improving my eating habits was a major goal in my pursuit of happiness. When I was emotional, I ate. When I ate, I gained weight. When I gained weight, I was unhappy. It was one big circle. Sound familiar? Many people go through this and it's no way to live. *Desperate* for a plan, I began my research.

While searching for the healthiest diet, I came across two words that would change my life forever: RAW FOOD. I had never heard of it before; it was something so different yet so real. After reading only a few lines, I was instantly sold. I'm in no way a gullible person; this was true resonation and recognition of truth. My inner voice said, *This is right!* From then on, I never doubted this way of living; it all makes sense! It makes perfect, logical, undeniable sense.

Here's the deal: We must eat foods designed specifically for our species. This is the key to unlocking our human potential. We are living in a strategically designed system which is specifically, deliberately, and forcefully organized to dumb us down and wear us down for profit. I started "waking up" to some truths before I became knowledgeable about raw and living foods but eating them took me on a journey that I'll never abandon, nor would I want to. I can't be fooled again because now I understand. I understand the way life works, I understand why it works that way, and I won't accept being brainwashed ever again! Everything your body absorbs, EVERYTHING, food, water,

> **WE MUST EAT FOODS DESIGNED SPECIFICALLY FOR OUR SPECIES.**

emotions, and observations will affect your overall wellbeing. These inputs make you who you are in everyday life, in every situation. They make you think, feel, and behave according to their positive or negative influences. Day in, day out…THEY CONTROL YOUR HAPPINESS. However, it doesn't *have* to be that way! Your health and happiness is YOUR CHOICE. YOU can **control** what you literally and figuratively feed your body and take charge of how you consciously live your life.

> WHEN YOU REALIZE WHAT HUMANS ARE, WHAT YOU ARE, LOVING YOURSELF AND OTHERS IS INEVITABLE.

A raw food diet woke me up, without a doubt. It opened my soul from the inside out. It made me **aware** of the fallacies we as humans are forced to believe all our lives, yet it also made me humble and at ease. Humble? At ease? How, when I'm learning all these lies? So much truth poured into me that I began to overflow with self-love, which washed away my ego. When you realize what humans are, what *you* are, loving yourself and others is inevitable. I wasn't offended by society's restraints; fuck being angry, I was motivated. I began to feel a purpose, a drive. I felt good about myself despite the bad! It lit a fire under my ass and all I wanted to do was add to the number of people who were like me out there, working diligently to take back our freedom. Above all, it made me feel unstoppable and I want everyone to feel that way. I want people to know that the stuff we think is simply going in one end and coming out the other, either makes or breaks us. People say, *You are what you eat*, right? Well, if you eat dead food, you're basically dying, and if you eat living food, you feel alive! You look alive! YOU ARE ALIVE. Your spiritual senses heighten. Your abilities come to the surface. So yea, in a sense, you become what you consume. Who tricked us into thinking we need to eat cooked dead animals, overly processed, artificial shit, when we are living, breathing organisms who need life to survive? These are the questions you start asking when you're on a

THE RAW TRUTH

journey of enlightenment. You discover who you are and who you are not. You start to feel your problems aren't that bad, and the things in your past that you once couldn't get over, are so much easier to overcome. You make more and more positive changes in your life because what you absorb controls your happiness; it controls how you feel, think, and act, your conscious existence, and your right to know who you truly are. When you control what you allow to enter your space, you control everything else. When you know who you are, *and I don't mean that in a personal sense, I mean who WE are because we are all one, and we are all prodigious fucking beings*, you can then live out your life the way you choose, not the way others have chosen for you. Choose or have it chosen for you. I choose raw; I choose awareness; I choose health. **I choose life**. You?

· ·

When humans occupy the correct ecological niche, they become powerful, robust, yet peaceful, happy beings. If we can achieve that from eating the right foods, why do we eat the wrong ones? It's lack of awareness, a big cover-up of the truth. Here's the truth: Living food contains enzyme-rich nutrients supplied from the earth to help us not only survive but to tthhrriivvee. Enzymes make you feel *good*. They are needed to feed oxygen to our cells and they break food down to convert it to energy. Just like we need oxygen to breathe, so do our cells. When they don't have enough, they die, aiding in the creation of disease.

All living food is raw but not all raw food is living. The circulating enzymes categorize food as alive. Non-living, raw food is sometimes sprouted to make it come to life, but it's never chemically changed. Raw food is just that, raw, not cooked. Raw food may also be dried, either sun-dried or dehydrated. There's controversy about dehydration temperature though; some say 105 degrees, others say 115, but the lower the heat, the more enzymes stay intact. When food is cooked, it kills the natural vibration. Most, if not all the living enzymes are destroyed; it becomes dead food. Dead food is slow to digest, less nutritious, and not meant to be eaten all the time.

Low and high vibrational foods taste and feel very different in our bodies. Raw and living, HIGH VIBRATIONAL foods, are vital to our wellbeing, supplying us with vitamins, minerals, enzymes, and proper alkalinity. We're alive, so doesn't it make sense to put food that's "alive" into our bodies? It grows on this earth ready to eat, and ready to nourish us. Proper nourishment is the key to stopping and reversing physical degeneration! The raw food diet is grounded in science and in plain old common sense. We lost clarity of that. We sold our souls for convenience. We abandoned our health. Processed foods with preservatives and *who knows what else*, are slowly killing humanity! Many people don't want to hear it or don't want to believe it, so they just turn their heads and take another bite. Are you one of them? Which is open: your mouth or your mind?

• •

There will always be people who don't believe. There will always be people who don't want *you* to believe. Regarding the raw diet, I understand the concerns because anything that has to do with health is serious. When it comes to the raw food movement or a raw food lifestyle, like any kind of life-changing or altering premise, there will be scammers. There are some very well-known and trusted "gurus" out there who are doing the world harm by being in the spotlight. They'll sell you a dream riddled with bad intentions and walk away with a clear conscience. Raw food is not bad, but sometimes not so good people tie themselves to something good and it eventually gets a bad rap. That adds to the fears of unsure people, making it harder to adopt in society. My intention in sharing this information is purely loving. I want others to "wake up" and *literally* wake up, to feel amazing, to truly experience life. "Sleeping" people don't know what they're missing because they find comfort in their captivity. "Awakened" people learn the truth by pushing through to set themselves

THE RAW TRUTH

free. I'm just one of those people who have learned, and I want to share. I want to open the door and allow you to walk through it.

I know what this lifestyle does to the human body, mind, and spirit. I know what it does to MY mind, body, and spirit, so no one can tell me otherwise. When you've seen medical proof that you are healthy, when every part of you functions as it should, when every cell in your body is celebrating, then trust me, you're not hearing shit from anyone about health. I live like I have never lived before. I feel like I have never felt before. Why would I believe anyone trying to discredit this? Why would *you* believe anyone trying to discredit this? I'll tell you why…because *you* haven't experienced it yet! *They* have not experienced it! So I get it! I can't honor an opinion if those offering the opinion haven't done the work for themselves.

> IN OUR AGE OF FAST FOOD AND HEALTHCARE, WE NEED TO DECIDE IF WE SUPPORT LIFE OR DISEASE.

I can only deliver the message to those who can hear it. If you can hear me and you really want to understand, do the work, because right now you're probably like Rip Van Winkle, sleeping, aging, and one day, later in life, you'll wake up to disarray around you. I can't wake anyone up; that's their job. I can, however, tell you one of my own fairytales. It goes a little like this: Once upon a time, after some deep cleansing and a lot of clean eating, a human being named Kate felt like a magical, mystical unicorn sliding down rainbows, galloping through sunny meadows, beaming with light! True story. The end.

> "The highest form of ignorance is when you reject something you don't know anything about."
> —Wayne Dyer

It's unbelievable how we can ignore what we do to ourselves when we're reminded of it every day when we face ourselves in the mirror. How we can we be so neglectful, enabling the chronic pains and illnesses that can so easily be alleviated? In our age of fast food and healthcare, we need to decide if we support life or disease. Do we support the positive, re-growth and re-birth of humanity, or the negative, continuous corruption of life?

Do you realize that we are the only species that doesn't eat a raw diet? The raw diet that fits *our* biological structure. We are so smart when it comes to creating convenience for ourselves but so dumb when it comes to common sense. Stop believing that we were meant to burn the dead carcasses of tortured animals, call it a burger, and then throw it on some overly processed bread along with moldy animal secretions from a suffering animal which we label as "cheese." It's disgusting and disturbing.

> **NOURISHMENT FROM THE EARTH ALLOWS US TO BE LIGHT IN OUR PHYSICAL FORM.**

If you support life, if you support *your* life, it's time to wake up! Nourishment from the earth allows us to be light in our physical form which brings us closer to spirituality, closer to God (whoever/ whatever/ he/she/it is), and closer to happiness. By light, I don't just mean our weight. I mean light in the sense that we don't have poisons, chemicals, metals, harmful organisms, etc. living inside us, weighing our life-force down.

The more natural our bodies are, the more synchronized we are with nature, with the universe, with our true selves, the more WE CAN LIVE LONG, LONG LIVES. The "foods" and "medications" we consume slowly kill us physically, mentally, emotionally, and spiritually and keep us from the truth. The media, technology, and material items are there for distraction, to dumb us down. Raw foods, herbs, nature, and **love** ARE OUR TRUTH, the truth that was meant for our bodies and our souls. Free your mind, clean your gut, clear your conscience, nourish your body, cherish life, *all life* … and you will return home.

THE RAW TRUTH

Life is about balance. Through conscious behavior, we balance our physical body, our metaphysical body, and our mind. Think about the shift I talked about: "The Awakening." More and more people are finding balance and encouraging the shift. Increasing our awareness of heaven and earth will drastically change this planet for the better. Welcome and congratulations to all the people who *are* "waking up." We need more of you. And since you're reading this book, I can bet you've probably already got one foot out of bed!

• •

Now let's get down to it! If you're interested in eating the healthiest way possible and becoming the healthiest being you possibly can, there are some things you need to know. First, when beginning a raw food lifestyle, you must do some cleansing! I can't stress enough the importance of DETOXIFICATION. From your physical body to your highest energy frequency, there are blockages that must be cleared. In the physical sense, these blockages stop nutrients from taking full effect or reaching the proper areas of the body. In the spiritual sense, they block connection or communication between the energy fields around the physical body, and the multidimensional consciousness (your spirit and the spiritual world) by disrupting the mind (the "understanding" center). Following me? The stuff we poison ourselves with is why we're unhappy, unhealthy, and unspiritual! Raw food mends some of the connections and breaks through some of the blockages, but YOU have work to do first. You can detoxify before *or* while eating raw, but either way, a detox will greatly benefit you. It helps the process go much faster and smoother with a lot less resistance. Resistance makes it easier for us to fall back into our old ways, so we want to have the strength to push through that.

Eliminating all the bad stuff in our bodies will give us back something we've been robbed of our whole lives: our natural, healthy, happy, human bodies—a natural, healthy, happy, human EXPERIENCE. When we remove the toxins, chemicals, medications, drugs, "foods," dyes, perfumes, preservatives, GMOs, metals, and anything else foreign that changes the structure and information in our cells, our bodies start regenerating clean, healthy cells that do what they're supposed to do! What do you think happens when our bodies are constantly attacked by harmful things? Unnatural changes are forced upon us, and that affects how we function, eventually wearing us down until we die. You think living until 80 or 100 is a long time? We're meant to live *way* longer, if not forever. You just said *yeah right*, didn't you? When our cells are fed the correct information, not only physical information from food but information from our thoughts, they function efficiently, keeping our systems flushed, hydrated and nourished. That allows our bodies to keep regenerating. Do you think about what's really going on inside you? Eating a GMO-filled, non-organic CHEESEBURGER is like saying "Whatever self, fuck you! I don't care about you," on so many levels.

> "Carrel's experiment convinced many biologists to accept immortality as an intrinsic property of all cells, not just the cell line through which genetic material is passed to offspring, called the germ line. Consequently, the phenomenon of cellular aging was regarded not as an intrinsic characteristic, but was attributed to external factors such as the accumulation of waste products within the cell."[6]

We have poisoned our bodies with toxins from years of eating unnatural and unhealthy "foods." Our lowered immune systems have made it easy for not just the food to affect us, but for airborne toxins to as well. These toxins exist in our skin, our blood, our organs, our brains, and throughout our bodies and minds. When we eliminate something that we've been consuming for years, the body goes

---

6 Jiang, Lijing, "Alexis Carrel's Immortal Chick Heart Tissue Cultures (1912-1946)". Embryo Project Encyclopedia (2012-07-03) ISSN: 1940-5030, http://embryo.asu.edu/handle/10776/3937

through physical withdrawals, like someone coming off a heavy drug. The symptoms may or may not be as severe as that, depending on the levels of detox you do, but you will have withdrawal and you should be prepared for it.

I don't want to scare you, but it's not easy switching to a raw diet. You will have physical withdrawals, but the toughest obstacles are the emotional and psychological ones. When you clean yourself from the inside out, you get closer to your true nature. Everything in between that and who you are now surfaces, which causes resistance. What do I mean? You will fight to hold onto the emotions, to the things you've learned, and to the person you've become, because your ego doesn't want to let go of the familiar. But, once you allow yourself to release what no longer serves you, you become spiritually awakened, connecting to the earth and something much higher. You become a whole new person! The new you is a better you with a clearer understanding of the world, but it's still a major life change that will call for mental strength. That's why mental and emotional preparation, knowledge, and self-awareness are so important! Raw foods and detoxification will advance your healing journey like Nitrous Oxide boosts a car in a race, so I want you to be ready for it.

> HOW COULD PUTTING MAN-MADE SUBSTANCES INTO OUR BODIES NOT CHANGE US?

Are you still thinking, *How can food change who I am?* Think about the chemicals (and who knows what else) that are on and in your food, or the fact that a lot of "food" isn't even real! We're natural things that came from the earth, another natural thing. How could putting man-made substances into our bodies *not* change us? They absolutely do and that's why people are sick (mentally and physically).

If you want to move forward with a raw lifestyle, you MUST first be mentally prepared. Then, you MUST detox.

SUPERHUMAN

Mental Preparation: (see also chapter three for help with setting goals)
1. **Love** yourself, then share love with others
2. **Forgive** yourself and forgive others
3. Express **gratitude** for EVERYTHING life has to offer
4. Dig deep into past experiences, then **release** all emotional energy (The Sedona Method™)
5. Continue to release any unwanted emotions
6. Figure out who you are (**self-awareness**)
7. Discover reality (AWARENESS of **the truth**)
8. Get a game plan to stay on track
9. Do not let the opinions of others influence you (even some doctors will be against a raw diet, fasting, or detoxification, but unless you have a medical concern, make your own choice)
10. **Accept** the things you cannot change
11. **Change** the things you can
12. Replace any negative thoughts or feelings with positive ones
13. Remind yourself that you are strong and can get through anything
14. Be proud because you're doing something amazing
15. Remind yourself often that you are about to become a cleaner, better, happier, healthier person, and these obstacles (withdrawals or negativity) are only little hurdles on your way to the finish line
16. Don't give up! Have faith in yourself, not fear! **Fear = lack of persistence**

• •

"There is no such thing as failure. There are only results."
—Anthony Robbins

Are you mentally prepared? Are you ready to detox? There are many kinds of and levels to detoxifying yourself. Most of the toxins are in our colons, in the layers of impacted mucus, also known as mucoid plaque. This matter is the colon's response to protect itself from threatening foods and toxins. While it's a defense mechanism,

THE RAW TRUTH

it also blocks the colon walls from digesting nutrients efficiently. As time goes on, it thickens, creating more and more toxicity which makes its way into the bloodstream. I don't want to totally gross you out, but there are parasites in there too. Yes, we all have organisms and parasites inside us. Illness occurs when our bodies become a "breeding or feeding ground" for these parasites to thrive. They don't like healthy hosts! However, this is a part of life. Everything wants to live and needs to eat to do that. We don't want them eating us, and we also don't want to strengthen them with fear or hate. What do I mean by that? Negative energy empowers the things we don't want to exist, even the seemingly horrific creatures inside us! It's the same with disease. Basically, if we've fought something with a negative emotion, we've in the end, fought ourselves. We're not learning and giving meaning to what it brought us; we're not embracing it with love, no matter how bad it is. Remember, we need to value the negative things in our lives as well as the positive ones so we can change something in ourselves. If we want to expel something out of us or out of our lives, we must deal with it gracefully.

• •

What cleanses should you start with so toxins can be eliminated smoothly, with the fewest problems? Liver, kidney, parasite, and colon. Don't forget to do the "mind cleanse" first! The colon should be cleansed before and after the others. Why before? It's the last stop so if that's cleaned out, the others are going to work better. Why after? Again, it's the last stop, so after the toxins are released from the other cleanses, they'll need a final flush. I cannot stress enough that you should get your mind right before anything else, so when things get tough and you have that closed-minded person in your ear you will be able to stay strong.

> GET YOUR MIND RIGHT BEFORE ANYTHING ELSE, SO WHEN THINGS GET TOUGH YOU WILL STAY STRONG.

Make sure you know what you're doing and that you're doing it in a safe manner. Cleansing can be harmful if it's not done correctly.

• •

The things we put on our bodies, in our bodies, and in our minds completely change us and make us unhappy and unhealthy, ultimately distorting reality. It's very sad. Life isn't as we see it and that can be hard to digest. It's unsettling to know that the things we've grown up on and enjoy are silent killers skewing our view of the world, taking us down physically and mentally, mostly for big business' financial gain. What's uplifting is knowing that we can change it.

Detoxification and these extraordinary, edible gifts from the earth are the truth and the reality that many of us are unfortunately not seeing, a reality that allows us to live happily and robustly. I can tell you a million times that you need to be prepared mentally, but being fully prepared comes from awareness and determination, knowing the truth and stopping at nothing to achieve it.

• •

Mental preparation is not simply telling yourself to be ready and to be positive; it *is* being ready with a supported, positive mindset. With knowledge, detoxification, and a good, strong mental attitude, we can clear out what's not needed in our bodies, and in our lives! When we've accomplished that, everything else will run smoothly and efficiently and our bodies can absorb the most nutrients from living foods and eliminate any new threats quickly. Cleansing will stir up toxins which will cause withdrawals or a "healing crisis." YEARS of foods, chemicals, medications, organisms, BELIEFS, and who knows what else are stored inside you and when you release them, you're re-introducing these toxins back into your body before they make their way out. Just think though, how *amazing* you will feel when it's finally out of you. After my cleansing, I could feel that my body was clean inside, all the way up through my skin! Not to

THE RAW TRUTH

mention my enlightenment from spiritually "waking up!" It's indescribable! Sometimes things get worse before they get better, and in the case of detox, the good will far outweigh the bad.

• •

NOTE: Another thing you can and probably *should* do during or right after your colon cleanse is to get a colonic. I'll discuss this later.

• •

For our bodies to absorb nutrients efficiently, we need to clear the "plaque" inside us. A cleanse that does the trick is a mixture of Psyllium Husk and Calcium Bentonite Clay. There are many colon cleanses on the market but be knowledgeable about what you buy. Some don't use Psyllium and Bentonite clay as the active ingredients, and that may be better for some people. Figure out which cleanse is right for you and how long you should do it.

Psyllium Husk and Calcium Bentonite Clay Cleanse:

1 rounded tsp. Certified Organic, Whole Husk Psyllium
1 tbsp. Liquid Calcium Bentonite Clay

Mix quickly with warm water and drink immediately. Follow with another glass of warm water. In the morning, add fresh squeezed lemon juice to the water for extra cleansing. Repeat 2-3 times a day and drink warm water throughout the day. If you're eating on this cleanse, wait to eat at least an hour before taking the mixture and at least an hour after.

*Don't do this cleanse for too long. If you're unsure if it's right for you, do your research and/or check with your doctor. You want your body to be able to work naturally and not depend on forced movement. There are many colon cleanses you can pick from. Do your research and pay attention to ingredients.

SUPERHUMAN

• •

Now, the topic of ORGANIC food. It's such an important part of the raw lifestyle. It's important to all ways of eating, period. People will try to debate that and say that it's not better for you, but they're WRONG. I can taste the difference. I can smell it. I can feel it! Ask anyone who eats this way, and they'll tell you the same.

To me, the most telling evidence is that organic produce tastes pure and delicious. Conventional produce is likely to be genetically modified or engineered, sprayed with chemicals, and grown in "treated" soil. This pollutes the food and the earth. It's unnatural, harmful, and disturbing. Farmers are now spending big bucks to convert their farms into organic. More people are becoming aware and buying organic produce and now organic meats. A little organic food for thought: Doctors often recommend an organic diet to cancer patients. Surely that shows that conventional foods are doing some harm, yes? Yes! Choose organic! Especially post-cleanse because you don't want to re-introduce toxins after you're cleaned out, do you?

• •

There are three major mistakes people make with food. They don't know **when** to eat, **how much** to eat, and most importantly **what** to eat. "When" should not be the standard breakfast, lunch, and dinner; three meals a day. Eating frequently is key. Of course, you can have meals, but if you want your body to properly digest and use energy appropriately, small, frequent portions are necessary. Our systems want simplicity! Snacking every few hours throughout the day will speed up the metabolism and keep the body lean. Not to mention it's fun! I enjoy eating all day long. Who wouldn't?

"How much" is important. If you're eating entire meals every few hours, you *will not* be lean (not to mention your grocery bill will be out of this world). The body wants small portions! They'll digest quickly but keep you satisfied for a few hours until you consume the next portion.

THE RAW TRUTH

Now, the most vital part is what to eat. Eat whole, raw, and organic foods. Look for Certified Organic, 100% Organic, or USDA Organic. AVOID GMO's! AVOID PRESERVATIVES! Other foods may digest quickly if you eat them in small portions but they're not keeping you healthy. The body needs and craves pure, nutritious food. But nutrients as we know them, aren't the extent of it. Let me blow your mind… food is not only nutrition, it's information; it influences the functioning of our cells. When we eat pure food from nature, our cells work as they should, keeping us healthy and regenerating whenever something foreign is introduced to our bodies. What do you think the information from genetically modified, artificial, FAKE foods are telling our cells? What do you think they're doing to our organs? The truth is quite scary, and most of us have been tricked into thinking these types of foods are OK to eat. They're not!!! When we feed our systems properly, they thank us by taking care of things on and in our bodies, including our mind. The longer we eat poorly, the less human we become, because this "new information" is taking over our body and changing the coding of our DNA. This is not make-believe, it's science! No matter what you've eaten in the past, you can start to regenerate now. You can start to look and feel better, NOW. I'm living proof!

Ask yourself, what do I eat daily? What are my eating habits? If you're making any of the "when," "how much," or "what" mistakes, you need a new game plan! Mine began by switching to raw. As I went along, I learned how much of it my body wanted and needed, and when I needed to eat.

• •

Since I've been experimenting with raw foods, I've discovered amazing secrets. It's the fountain of youth! It can save lives! Raw and

> WHEN WE EAT PURE FOOD FROM NATURE, OUR CELLS WORK AS THEY SHOULD.

living food can help cure and prevent cancer as well as many other diseases and ailments. From what I've learned, I believe it can cure them all. I'm telling you this from my own knowledge and belief... WE CAN ALL HEAL. Fuck anybody who said, "This can't be cured or healed or mended because..." Think and believe that it CAN! NOTHING in this life is set in stone. Stone is only matter, and matter is only energy.

My health and appearance has improved after eating this way. This is not just my own opinion; everyone I encounter is amazed and they all want to know how I did it. Weight loss is a common struggle, and everyone is searching for the secret. It's not like I lost a drastic amount of weight, I just exude health now and it's noticeable. On top of that, people assume I'm much younger than I am. Not only do I look younger, but I feel it! I didn't know feeling this good ALL THE TIME was even possible! Every part of me is working at top efficiency because of FOOD. Oh what a world it would be if everyone *knew* the benefits; how radiant they look, how alive they feel, how happy it makes them. Don't you want to experience that? You can! Don't you want to stay young and vibrant? You can! Don't you want to get off medication and restore your health? YOU CAN!

• •

Is medication helping us or is it secretly killing us? I know how I feel. How do you feel? If I'm ever unwell or if my loved one has an issue, I will research a natural remedy first; medication is the last resort. People always trust their doctor, but they don't realize that a lot of doctors' education is paid for by drug companies.[7] While your doctor may be honest and have the best intentions, they're influenced by people

---

7 *Doctors with links to drug companies influence treatment guidelines,* http://www.jsonline.com/features/health/doctors-with-links-to-drug-companies-influence-treatment-guidelines-ki7pjr6-184041791.html. *Drug Companies & Doctors: A Story of Corruption,* http://www.nybooks.com/articles/archives/2009/jan/15/drug-companies-doctorsa-story-of-corruption/?pagination=false

THE RAW TRUTH

who want to keep you ill so they can make money off you. They want you to have issues so you will buy their drugs. Drugs can be harmful, prescription or not. I'm sure you've laughed while shaking your head at the commercials that first tell you how the medicine will help one thing but then spill a mile-long list of side effects. The most alarming are the ones that include death. Is it worth it to risk your life for a little relief? No! That's insanity! What's not insane is finding a natural cure or remedy with minor to no side effects, something that comes from the earth and will not harm you. Medicine is found in nature.

> "When diet is wrong, medicine is of no use. When diet is correct, medicine is of no need."
>
> —Ayurvedic proverb

The book *The Raw Lifestyle* includes stories from doctors and regular people who are living proof that raw food heals. When I hear people talk about their ailments or being diagnosed with cancer, I want to shout to them, "It can be cured!" However, I do not and cannot push that information on anyone. I can only give it to those who want it and want to put it to the test. You can find evidence and many testimonials in books and on the internet. Take a look!

I was talking to my cousin Ashley one day and she told me about a lady she knows whose son was cured of cancer by a holistic doctor. What was it that the doctor prescribed for him? Chemically engineered medication? No! Holistic or Naturopathic doctors use herbs and natural remedies in combination with a plant-based diet, and focus on healing the patient's whole being, not just their physical ailments. Most of the time, they're seen as taboo, but only by the ignorant. While they may not have MD after their names, their practices are growing for a reason. Some people lack knowledge of the subject, so they don't understand it, but others completely write it off without knowing anything about it. Holistic practitioners (I include spiritual healers and energy healers here too) are the people who should take over our healthcare. They need to restore the damage we've done to ourselves!

Eating healthy, natural things from the earth can only do good things for us, right? Right! What else are they there for? To make the world look pretty? They do, but that's not their purpose! They exist to nourish our bodies and to make us as strong as we can be. When I eat raw foods, I feel **alive**. The enzymes or vibration in food give us energy and make us feel good. Some can even cause a euphoric feeling; I've experienced it.

• •

Another form of natural remedy that works wonders (ESPECIALLY in conjunction with a raw diet) is the use of oils. They become effective through inhalation, topical use, external use, or internal use, each having their own application and healing purpose. I've been experimenting with different oils and I'm relatively new to it. However, one I absolutely live by is oil of oregano. When everyone around me has a cold or the flu, I'm germ free! Whenever a, co-worker, friend, or family member is sick I tell them to try it, and the reaction is always the same: "Tastes horrible but I feel better already!" It's a potent miracle in a bottle! Be sure to buy the real deal, not the over-diluted kind you find in the grocery store. Everyone should have it in their medicine cabinet. It's amazing. It's a secret remedy that few people know about and I can't understand why this isn't among the first things doctors prescribe. Instead, they recommend antibiotics. Before you take another antibiotic, do some research.

Another is Egyptian Black Seed Oil (*Nigella Sativa*). I'm using it to hopefully cure my asthma. It's a remedy that's been used for thousands of years (maybe more) and is rumored to be the cure for all diseases. Who knows? Maybe it is!

"Nature itself is the best physician."

—Hippocrates

THE RAW TRUTH

Raw, whole foods really are medicine. Everything we put into our bodies is either killing or healing us.

Did you know we should consume mostly fruit? Humans are fruitarians or frugivores, even though many people think we're vegetarians. Fruit has a higher vibration than vegetables. Their enzymes not only give us energy and feed our blood oxygen, but they also aid in the digestive process…and they're full of fiber! It's harder for us to break down plants. Eating fruit is simple, nutritious, and healing; our bodies love it! Also, the sugar is GOOD sugar, not the processed, store-bought kind. People always tell me it's bad that I eat so much fruit because of the sugar in it. What about the sugar in almost every kind of processed food? People put sugar on and in many other foods too. Where's the logic in that? There is none! It's simply a lack of understanding.

• •

Fruit is full of antioxidants, which are important for keeping the Lymphatic System running smoothly. The Lymphatic System uses vessels to carry lymph fluid throughout the body. One of the lymphatic system's primary functions is to carry toxins through our organs to remove them from the body. The major organs that do this are the kidneys and epidermis, or skin.

Think of each of the cells in your body as a tiny little person. They need oxygen and nutrients to keep them alive and they also need to excrete toxins and acids, or waste, like us using the bathroom. The fluid that's surrounding them is what brings them nutrients and oxygen, but it's also what carries out the toxins. If the fluid isn't constantly being flushed or is working inefficiently, the waste surrounding the cells will poison them. This is where sickness and disease can occur. It is imperative that we keep our Lymphatic system running in top shape. If we're backed up with toxins, we're killing ourselves. Stop committing cellular suicide! Take care of yourself.

• •

SUPERHUMAN

Green juices are excellent for us because not only are they chlorophyll-rich, but also because the enzymes are readily accessible. There's no need for our system to break down the vegetable because we have a shortcut to the nutrients. These enzymes are excellent at attacking dead or bad cells and creating new, healthy ones. Greens also help restore the natural function of the pineal gland—our spiritual connection center!

One amazing juice is Wheatgrass. It only takes one or two ounces per day to do wonders and has even been said to cure cancer. Wheatgrass is filled with beneficial vitamins and minerals. It also works as a cleansing agent or internal detergent carrying toxins, metals, and many other harmful things out of the body. It has a long list of benefits, including the building of blood cells. The chlorophyll in it is nearly identical to the hemoglobin in our red blood cells. As pungent as it is, wheatgrass is your friend. It fights for you, attacking then expelling the damage done over years of unhealthy habits!

• •

Another of nature's miracle medicines is a very controversial one. It's…the herb! Chronic! Mary Jane! Ganja! MARIJUANA! More evidence is surfacing about its amazing benefits and uses. There's proof that it can treat, even cure cancer[8], along with having positive effects on autism[9] …AND SO MANY OTHER THINGS.

---

8 http://patients4medicalmarijuana.wordpress.com/2010/01/04/marijuana-cures-cancer-us-government-has-known-since-1974/. *Harvard Study says Marijuana Cures Cancer,* http://www.endalldisease.com/harvard-study-says-marijuana-cures-cancer/, http://www.scientificfactsofpot.com/. *Marijuana And Cancer: Scientists Find Cannabis Compound Stops Metastasis In Aggressive Cancers* by Robin Wilkey, *Huffington Post,* http://www.huffingtonpost.com/2012/09/19/marijuana-and-cancer_n_1898208.html

9 *Marijuana cannabinoids found to help combat autism* by Ethan A. Huff, Oct. 6th, 2012, http://www.naturalnews.com/037445_marijuana_cannabinoids_autism.html. *A "Cure" for Autism—Medical Marijuana,* http://marijuana-cannabis.tumblr.com/post/16826260087/medical-marijuana-cure-for-autism. *Ryan's Story: Medical Marijuana And Autism* by Natasha Zouves, Jan 12th, 2012, http://www.neontommy.com/news/2012/01/ryan-s-story-medical-marijuana-and-autism

THE RAW TRUTH

A controversial news report told the story of a woman named Hester-Perez who was giving her autistic son pot brownies.[10] Her son Joey was emaciated to the point that she believed he was going to die. He was also so out of control with his aggressive and dangerous behaviors that she was desperate to try anything. When she gave him pot brownies, he gained an appetite and calmed down almost immediately. She claims it saved her son's life.

Some things in life cannot be doubted, like one tearful yet uplifting story about a father who cured his cancer-stricken, two-year-old son who was dying right before his eyes, with Hash oil.[11] The father ordered the doctors to take his son off chemo, which had been making him sick to the point that he couldn't eat. The father then secretly began putting Hash oil into his son's feeding tube. The child almost immediately had an appetite and eventually was completely cancer free!

Another story is about a man who had been through several procedures and chemotherapy to rid himself of cancer.[12] Nothing worked, and it kept spreading until he went behind his doctor's back and began treating himself with Hash oil. His cancer… gone! People are even curing their skin cancer by applying it topically. It can be used internally and externally with the same results. INCREDIBLE.

There are many other stories of people who will testify that marijuana is beneficial, not detrimental; even some doctors and politicians support it. You can find a lot of information on the internet about the benefits of marijuana. Look it up, you'll be amazed.

---

10 *Mother Gives Son Marijuana to Treat His Autism* by Joseph Brownstein, Nov. 23rd 2009, http://abcnews.go.com/GMA/AutismNews/mother-son-marijuana-treat-autism/story?id=9153881, http://www.ksdk.com/video/1056602972001/0/Mom-treating-sons-autism-with-pot-brownies
11 Dad Gives 2-Year-Old THC Oil to Fight Brain Cancer, Son Now Cancer Free, http://www.youtube.com/watch?v=8rWZtnY_Tp4
12 *Cannabis oil cured my cancer* by Jeff Ditchfield, http://norml-uk.org/2012/08/cannabis-can-cure-cancer/

SUPERHUMAN

• •

How does weed cure cancer? There are receptors in the brain and body which interact with cannabinoids, the structurally related compounds found in THC (Tetrahydrocannabinol). Scientists have labeled these receptors, which are found in the brain and in the immune system, CB1 and CB2. CB1 receptors are copious in the brain and throughout the major organs. CB2 receptors are found in the immune system. When the cannabinoids bind with these receptors, they send messages that make the cancer cells self-destruct.[13] In the Youtube video *Proof Marijuana CURES Cancer*, you can watch cancer cells die when they're presented with cannabinoids; what happens is unbelievable. Why has this not replaced horrific chemotherapy treatments or invasive surgeries? Why are people still dying of cancer? Why are CHILDREN SUFFERING? Honestly, it makes me sick.

Many years ago, people had access to an abundance of medications with Cannabis as the main ingredient.[14] People used it to treat all kinds of problems. Whoever is responsible for taking this away and covering it up is responsible for the pain and death of many people.

• •

While no one has died from an overdose of marijuana, it still has a few destructive side effects. People who are prone to mental illness, such as schizophrenia, may have an onset after using marijuana. It may also cause anxiety, depression, or slow reaction time, and what you're smoking it in can be harmful too. Since a small percentage of people have reactions from it, it shouldn't be used by everyone. However, we can't deny that it can save lives.

---

13 *Proof Marijuana CURES Cancer,* http://www.youtube.com/watch?v=9cUC8tjoB_0
14 *MEDICAL CANNABIS A SHORT GRAPHICAL HISTORY ITS GOLDEN AGE,* http://antiquecannabisbook.com/chap2B/GoldenAge/GoldenAge.htm

THE RAW TRUTH

Marijuana is an herb, a cure. It is on this earth to heal, not to hurt. Do you want to know what doesn't heal and what definitely hurts? Alcohol...it even kills! It's a legal, man-made DRUG that's easily accessed. Yet weed, a PLANT from the earth, is illegal. *What!?*

Marijuana can be used medicinally, and it also makes people more tranquil. Now this is a no brainer: If you had to choose whether to live in a society where everybody drank alcohol or where everybody smoked weed, which would you pick? Think about it this way: When's the last time you heard a story or watched a movie depicting a violent pothead?...I'm waiting. An alcoholic? All the time! I believe that if people knew more about weed and weren't so afraid of it, and if it were LEGAL, they'd stop abusing alcohol.

> MARIJUANA IS AN HERB, A CURE. IT IS ON THIS EARTH TO HEAL, NOT TO HURT.

I used to abuse it. I was a reckless teen who got a kick out of the things I did and said when I was drunk, especially when my friends relived my blacked-out activities the next day. While it may be fun to get drunk, many bad things can easily happen and often do. Not to mention the internal harm we're doing!

If you drink, think about why you're drinking. Are you trying to run away from an emotion? If it's to escape reality, you will never truly accomplish that. You need to find a solution within you, not drown yourself in a substance that's poisoning your insides!

The main problem with *my* drinking was that I drank liquor, heavily. Most kids were beer drinkers, but I couldn't stand it; I had to have the hard stuff. Strangely, while everyone else was getting sick, I rarely did. I can count on one hand the number of times I've thrown up from drinking. I think my liver is one giant, soaking-wet sponge, because where did all that alcohol go over the years? I'm now working on wringing it out by detoxifying myself.

SUPERHUMAN

• •

We are so screwed up as a society. I hope to change minds and lifestyles. Fast food restaurants are around every corner, but raw food restaurants are scarce. There's a liquor store and bar on every block yet weed is a black-market item and medical marijuana dispensaries are being shut down. It doesn't make sense! While I understand the argument that weed is a gateway drug, I *don't* agree. The only reason it may lead someone to other drugs is because it's labeled as a stigma. When someone feels they're doing something bad already, there's a "fuck it" effect, and they think, *Well, I might as well do other bad things.* In reality, it isn't bad because it isn't a drug![15]

The biggest gateway drug is alcohol. When people drink and are presented with drugs, they are more likely to do them. I've seen it numerous times from the people I least expected. When you're high, you're satisfied with that feeling and don't need anything else, and you're also more aware of what you're doing.

I may have experimented, but abusing drugs never appealed to me. I smoked weed for years before I ever tried anything else. I did try other drugs because of my own personal issues, but certainly not because I smoked weed! However, I'm not saying that it's ok to abuse marijuana since it's an herb. Like anything else, too much is not good for you. I learned that from smoking the way I did. I'm now restoring my lungs through detoxification as well.

• •

Marijuana will be legal soon, I know it. The truth can't be hidden forever! Free recreational use will be great, but the best part is that it will save lives! It will help so many people overcome their suffering. Look into it! Don't deny the truth because you were told to believe

---

15 http://www.huffingtonpost.com/kevin-armento/why-marijuana-is-not-a-dr_b_571531.html

THE RAW TRUTH

otherwise. Let the agreements that society has forced upon you go and open yourself to a bigger awareness!

• •

Weight issues are another major problem. There are far more obese people than malnourished people in the world![16] Did you know that? It shows that we're gluttonous; there's no reason *anyone* should be starving. However, it's not all our fault because we have so much temptation around us. It seems impossible to be healthy, and the desire to be skinny is so harmful because we go to drastic measures to achieve it.

Many people have weight fluctuations throughout their lives because they can never achieve or maintain weight loss. I've experienced it all. When I was young, I would take weight loss pills and do all kinds of harmful things to my body. I would drop pounds for a certain amount of time but then I'd gain it all back. As a result, I was more miserable than ever. Can you relate? If so, are you ready to fix the problem? Here's how…

Living a raw food lifestyle will not only bring you to your ideal weight but it will maintain it. Notice I said *it* will maintain your weight, not you. That's right; the food does most of the work. According to *The Raw Food Lifestyle*, "5,000 calories of raw food is 1,000 percent better for you than 2,000 calories of the standard American diet" (SAD). You can eliminate exercise (which I don't recommend *AT ALL*) and still be thin. You can eat all the raw food you can fit to fill you up, and still barely gain a thing. I've never had that "problem" before. My problem was always not being able to lose weight. I was fluctuating between 150-175lbs for several years prior to eating raw. Not only was I eating unhealthy foods, but I ate too much of them, and lacked the proper mental state to keep the weight from returning!

---

16 *World now has 'more people dying from obesity than malnutrition,'* http://metro.co.uk/2011/09/22/world-now-has-more-people-dying-from-obesity-than-malnutrition-160264/

Constantly being let down every time the scale went up, was what sparked my desire to change. I asked myself, *Am I ever going to stay at a weight that makes me happy and when in my life will that be?* I felt I was wasting away precious years and wanted to put a stop to it immediately. What about you? Are you with me?

Here's *my* formula for physical health **success**:
1. Figure out what it is in your past that's holding you back in life, making you overeat or eat unhealthy foods
2. Let it go (forgiveness, acceptance, love, gratitude, and lots of releasing!)
3. Thoroughly research raw food
4. Detoxify
5. Eat raw
6. Live life with love and be happy!

My results: I now stay between 130 and 140lbs and couldn't be more satisfied. I feel amazing, have extreme energy, and I'm no longer dealing with the stress that comes from weight management. I feel like a **SUPERHUMAN**. Some people call this the Raw Food Diet and it will allow you to diet in a productive and safe way, but it's more than that…it's a lifestyle! You must own it!

Every time you're about to take an unnecessary bite of food, ask yourself, *What's driving me to eat more than my body needs?* Is it boredom? Is it a lack of self-control? Is it an emotional issue? When you pinpoint the problem, you can work on a solution.

If you overeat when you're bored, find something else to enjoy to occupy your time. Don't sit around because you'll become antsy and

THE RAW TRUTH

eat before you're consciously aware of what you're doing! If you lack self-control when it comes to eating, find a way to calm your mind and body. One terrific way to do that is yoga. Take a class or meditate on your own for a little each day; it will teach you discipline. Or, if you eat when you're emotional, figure out what's making you that way. Work on letting it go, forgiving, and moving past it.

When you know what's causing you to overeat, you'll become more conscious of when you're overeating. After that, be more conscious of *what* you're eating so that you can eat the right kind of food as well. What's the best way to do it?

1. Clear your mind. Let go of the past, your guilt, regret, anger, or sadness.
2. Know your intolerances, allergies, and state of health (some people need to be monitored by a doctor when changing their diet).
3. Do plenty of research.
4. When you're ready, gradually eliminate unhealthy foods and begin to incorporate healthy foods.
5. When your diet has become mostly plant based, organic, whole, and raw, stay focused! SEE, FEEL, and BELIEVE in the results!

• •

If you do experiment with raw food and switch back to the SAD, *you'll feel it.* The times I've fallen off track, I noticed that everything was a disturbance. Everything was irritating and edgy, and life didn't flow. When I eat raw, I'm peaceful and spiritual. If I slip, it seems like my world falls apart. My mood changes, I feel achy, my skin doesn't look good, I gain weight quickly, I'm anxious, I'm not happy, and I just don't feel right! It's like my body is saying *What are you doing to me!?* There's no grey area either. I feel amazing when I eat well and terrible when I eat badly. Have you dieted at some point in your life and then cheated on that diet? You probably felt not only physically bad but guilty too, right? Your body knows what it wants. It wants to be healthy, but your stubborn pleasure-seeking mind wants you to indulge. I'm not perfect; even though I know how life-changing raw food is and how destructive processed food is, sometimes I still struggle to make the right choices. However, I don't look at my setbacks as failures. I learn and grow from them and don't sit around wishing I could have my lifestyle back, I take it!

• •

There's no easy way to give up junk food. It's almost impossible to ignore the aroma of cooked foods. What *is* possible is to make a personal choice. Each of us has one main freedom in life. That's freedom of the mind. Setting goals starts with re-setting your brain. It's work because you must re-learn, but the lesson is worth it.

Choosing to do something different is powerful. If you understand how important raw foods are for your health, you'll do what you need to do to make the change. Knowledge only has power when you put it into action.

"In general, mankind, since the improvement in cookery, eats twice as much as nature requires."
—Benjamin Franklin

People hear about eating raw food and think, *Well, I can't be happy eating carrots and celery all day.* It's not like that! We can make so many things with raw food and there are so many raw foods available. I've whipped up some of the most amazing dishes from raw cookbooks and my own experimentation! I've made "alfredo sauce with pasta," "lasagna," "Caesar salad," "pizza," "cheeseburgers," "loaded nachos," "pecan pie," "fudge" …the list goes on and on! I've even created my own recipe for "eggplant rollatini," and let me tell you, it's fucking delicious.

Many raw dishes taste like the real thing…sometimes better because the taste is so pure! How are they made? They're self-processed nut and plant-based recipes that are not cooked. If they're made correctly, they contain a special ingredient…**good intention**. Have you ever seen "love" listed as an ingredient? That's not to be cute. It's real! When a person applies positive energy to whatever they're making, the consumer will benefit. When you eat raw, you FEEL how good the food is for you. There's also no "stuffed" feeling, only a satisfied one, and you have an insane amount of energy!

• •

I was a junk food junkie. I loved everything bad for me, so it was a hard transition to raw. Now that I'm on track, I'm hooked. Now, I crave raw food! I wake up with a desire to fill myself with fresh fruit. I feel the nourishment and energy from my daily Wheatgrass shot. I anxiously anticipate the delicious dish I'll have for dinner. I indulge in guilt-less, raw chocolate. The food I eat is amazing. Not only is it delicious but it's good for me. How do I know? I can see and feel it!

• •

Where do *you* begin?
1. Do your research. (Look up anything and everything about raw food.)
2. Make your personal conclusion. (Continue the journey if you're a believer.)
3. Eat fruit for breakfast. (You can eat fruit throughout the day, but it must be consumed on an empty stomach, not mixed with other foods because fruit digests in the small intestine.)
4. Drink lots of pure, good-intention-infused water. (Half of your body weight in ounces i.e.: 130lb person would drink about 8 glasses of water a day. Divide 130 by 2 then divide that number by 8.)
5. Snack on raw nuts, raw seeds, or sun-dried fruits throughout the day.
6. Purchase a raw cookbook. (The tools you'll need the most are a blender and/or food processor)

7. Plan the meals you want for the week and how much money you'll need for all the ingredients. (Check the availability of ingredients since some are seasonal. If raw meals are available to buy in your area, that's even easier!)
8. Have raw snacks on hand so you don't resort to unhealthy foods.
9. Pay attention to your body's wants and needs. (The more you eat raw, the easier this is.)
10. Release your emotions whenever you want to eat unhealthy foods. (The Sedona Method™)
11. Be happy, be healthy, and enjoy yourself!

• •

Now that I'm a raw foodie, life has become clear. Life has become spiritual! Why? The cleanliness of your body affects the brain and senses (not just physical senses); your pineal gland will decalcify. When we consume unnatural things, the "third eye" (pineal gland) calcifies, blocking that "sense." Now that I have more clarity, my intuition and interpretation of life are almost magical. It's like existing on a different plane of consciousness. You may think this is crazy, but I don't use logic anymore to make decisions. I've discredited my old "type A" personality because in the end, it doesn't work! It destroys our focus on enjoying life, learning lessons, and following our soul's divine path, in divine time. My gut *indescribably* allows me to know the right answer in every one of life's *what should I do* moments. Besides **just knowing** the right answer, something incredible always seems to happen when I follow my intuition: affirmation and reward. And the "signs!" There's no denying the "signs" that appear before my eyes whenever I ask the universe for assurance! Try trusting your gut. Try asking the universe for a sign. See where life takes you.

> TRY TRUSTING YOUR GUT. TRY ASKING THE UNIVERSE FOR A SIGN. SEE WHERE LIFE TAKES YOU.

THE RAW TRUTH

Intuition is an internal compass. When you realize it's there, it points you in the right direction. If you let it guide you in every decision you make, it can drastically improve your life.

• •

I've always been able to predict things, and people are amazed by it. The ability has only grown stronger as I've become healthier. Some are more intuitive than others just as some are healthier than others despite their bad eating habits, but there's always room for growth. When I was so unhealthy, some of that ability was blocked. Now that I'm cleaning out the blockage, it's growing stronger. What's going on in the gut surely affects the brain!

When your body is healthy so is your mind and your clarity. It's like when you bring a filthy car to the carwash. As soon as it's clean you can see out of every window, whereas before you could only see through the little area your windshield wipers cleaned. This mental clarity will help you make choices, allowing your mind to expand in different directions, to see other possibilities and not have a one-track mind. I always stay true to myself and believe in the things I *feel* are real because as much as my eyes, ears, and brain tell me something is true, my gut doesn't lie. Intuition is a powerful thing. Use it!

• •

The more in depth I've become with this way of life, the more I'm aware of other unhealthy practices. Since I'm so conscious of what I put *in* my body, I've become more conscious of what I put *on* it too! Our skin is the largest organ, absorbing about 60% of what we put on it. We bring the chemical world into our natural biology when we apply unnatural things to our skin. I now use all natural, organic, non-GMO, chemical-free, and synthetic-fragrance-free shampoos, deodorants, soaps, creams, and make-up (household cleaners and detergents as well). They can be found at many health food stores and online.

SUPERHUMAN

I put Castor oil on my scars and scabs instead of medicated creams. It works by finding the damaged or uneven cells, and then rebuilds and restores them. I rub it in, allowing the friction from my hand to heat it up; this works it into the skin better.

Castor oil also has other beneficial uses, such as Castor oil packs. This is a homemade pack that makes the oil seep through your skin, allowing your organs to function better. It's good for someone who's constipated or just wants to give their system a boost.

You will need:
- wool or cotton flannel cloth
- oven-warmed castor oil
- heating pad
- plastic wrap
- towel
- patience

Soak the cloth with the warmed castor oil, cover it in plastic wrap, and place the heating pad in between a towel, on top of the plastic wrapped cloth, over the right side of your abdomen as you are lying flat on your back. Stay still for about an hour.

Another thing I put on my skin is extra virgin, raw coconut oil. I eat it too because it has amazing health benefits, especially for the brain. While it's a food, it's also good for external use (not to mention it smells delicious!). It leaves my skin feeling lightly moisturized and soft.

I also use Calcium Bentonite Clay, both internally and externally. When it's applied to the skin, it draws out toxins, heavy metals, and dirt. It's also said to be amazing for circulation, Varicose veins, cysts, cancer, acne, skin tags, skin conditions, insect bites, wounds, viruses, burns, and many, many other things. I like to use it as a mask; it leaves my skin so soft and clear. Internally, it detoxifies the digestive system, liver, and colon, while also absorbing heavy metals and toxins. There are *numerous* benefits and you can learn all about this clay at http://www.aboutclay.com/clay_info.htm. It's miraculous! I recommend keeping it on hand.

• •

NOTE TO ALL PERFUME/COLOGNE WEARERS: Perfumes are chemical warfare! The second you smell a chemical, it has entered your bloodstream. What do you think it's doing when you put it directly on your body? If you're not concerned about what it's doing to you, think about the people around you! Some know they're sensitive to perfumes because they are affected physically with migraines or allergic reactions, while others have no idea that your choice to douse yourself in poison has caused them to feel sick. Is your own scent that repulsive that you have to cover yourself in chemicals? I don't think so. Take a shower, you'll be fine. While perfumes are repulsive for some and nice for others, this is not a joke, it's harmful! STOP using it.

• •

Did you know you can brush your skin? Just like we brush our hair, we can brush our skin too. It removes dead skin cells, toxins, scars, and helps with circulation. I use a 100% natural skin brush, starting from my feet, working my way up to my heart. This circulates the blood that sometimes becomes stagnant in the lower body, bringing it back up to the heart to be re-circulated. When I use the skin brush before or after a shower, it feels like my skin is breathing, a very refreshing sensation.

For my hair I use natural, organic shampoos and conditioners, but I also do treatments with castor oil, coconut oil, black seed oil, neem seed oil, or aloe vera. I apply it to my scalp, brushing it down into my hair, and leaving it in for about an hour or so before I shower. They condition the hair and scalp like hot oil treatments. I've noticed an improvement in the quality of my hair since doing this.

As you can see, there are many aspects of this lifestyle that go beyond eating.

Some other ways that I clear toxins from my body are through massage and colonics. Massage releases the toxins that are trapped in scar tissue or knots, as we know them.

Colonics pull toxins from your colon and can be extremely beneficial to your health. Disease starts in the colon. As we consume "food" over the years, the food attaches to the walls of our colon and the toxins from it aren't being removed; they stay behind and poison the body. Some studies say the average person carries 5-25lbs of impacted fecal matter, while others say 5-40lbs. Consuming red meat (and probably any meat) adds to the problem. It doesn't pass through our bodies as efficiently as it does for carnivores who have smooth, short insides. We're not designed to eat flesh! Breads, dairy, CHEESES, sugars, and other processed "foods" also contribute to the impaction of fecal matter.

Cheese is something I grew up on and *loved* to eat. If anything seems impossible for you to give up, think about me giving up cheese. I still miss it but will never touch it again. On the bright side, raw nut cheeses are just as tasty!

You're probably wondering why cheese is so bad. Dairy is POISON![17] It causes mucus to build up and harden inside us. Our nation is sadly misinformed because we think we need to drink milk for calcium. On the contrary, it's damaging our bodies! We can get calcium from other sources. We're not meant to consume the milk of animals.

---

17 *The Poison of Dairy Products,* http://www.materia-training.com/en/articles/poison-dairy-products. Who is Dr Morse? Part One, http://www.youtube.com/watch?v=87uWGAiv88o

THE RAW TRUTH

If your diet includes dairy, it would be in your best interest to stop consuming it now and maybe even get a colonic.

• •

What exactly is a colonic? It's a water filtration system also called colon hydrotherapy, which sends purified water into your colon while pulling out harmful waste and toxins (it's a more advanced enema). The more treatments you have, the more likely deeper, impacted fecal matter can be reached by the water.

Some people recommend that we get colonics on a regular basis or go through a series of them in a short time. I don't necessarily agree with that. If we overdo *anything*, it can be harmful to us, especially when it comes to the functioning of our bodies. You don't want to mess up the peristalsis of your colon or intestines! DO NOT OVERDO IT; your body takes care of this naturally. Think of a colonic as a little boost you can use *occasionally*.

• •

So far, I've had six or seven colonics spaced out over a few years. I had heard about celebrities doing them and was intrigued because they're often the people who are let in on health secrets. I've also noticed a lot of famous people are vegetarians, vegans, or raw foodies. It's because they meet so many people, people with knowledge and secrets to health. Us average Joe's aren't health conscious because our peers aren't. We don't normally receive information like that unless we're seeking it …or it's seeking us.

I was nervous going in for my first colonic, as I didn't know what to expect. From then on, it has been a piece of cake! It's interesting to see how it works, being able to watch your body getting cleaned out. Are you squeamish? It's not bad at all!

• •

SUPERHUMAN

One time I was waiting for my colonic when an elderly woman walked out from hers. Her son, who was the biggest skeptic, was sitting in the waiting room. The look on his face was like *you're all nuts, what am I doing here?* I was eavesdropping on her conversation with the technician. She was telling him she couldn't believe how good she felt and that her doctor *and* her son forbid her from doing it, but she knew it was going to help her. Her son was understandably concerned about her, that's his elderly mother, but her doctor had her on all these medications that were making her constipated and very ill, yet he was telling her that getting a colonic would be harmful. I'm aware of this kind of ignorance, but I have never heard it come directly from someone's mouth. Who does that, especially to a sweet little old lady? As she spoke, she was shaking her head, realizing how wrong her doctor was... a person she entrusted with her life! It was great to see her son become a believer that day too! His face brightened after hearing her say how good she felt.

I would suggest for anyone, young or old, to research colonics. If you feel comfortable with it, get one done; it will benefit your health in many ways.

• •

Some benefits I've experienced from this lifestyle:
SKIN—clearer, smoother, look younger, wounds heal better and faster, "glowing"
EYE COLOR—clearer, lighter, shinier, "sparkling"
HAIR COLOR/TEXTURE—thicker, stronger, lighter in color, healthier, shinier, grows faster
NAILS—grows faster, stronger
PAINS—fewer headaches, no backaches, TMJ relief
MIND—relaxed, clearer thoughts, easier to control thoughts & emotions, intuitive abilities
STOMACH—no pains, alkaline pH, easy and fast digestion, frequent elimination

THE RAW TRUTH

HEALTH—immaculate, no allergies, no sickness, feel good
MIND and BODY—in sync (mental and physical), no stress, no pains, not affected as much by the negativity of others
MOOD—happy, carefree, feel powerful
SLEEP—no longer an insomniac! Wake up feeling refreshed
CONSCIOUSNESS—wide "awake"

Some challenges of this lifestyle:
- *food temptations*
- *negative energy from others*
- *lack of support or encouragement*
- *commercials, advertisements*
- *food and restaurants everywhere*
- *lack of availability of raw food or raw restaurants*
- *being "awakened" to some shocking truths*

Some Thoughts
- *If you can change your mind, you can change how your body feels. Choosing healthy food is the next step. When you feel the positive effects of eating healthy, you want more, therefore you stick with healthy foods which create positive thoughts.*
- *When you start to feel down, bad, or discouraged, your mind allows your body to feel the same way, so the unhealthy eating begins. If you can switch those thoughts to positive ones, you can overcome the cycle of eating and feeling bad.*
- *It's not an easy struggle but the victory is rewarding.*

To achieve complete happiness, your body not only needs to be healthy, but your mind does as well. Here are additional tools to build a healthy mind:

Health beyond eating…
- smile frequently
- say thank you often
- hug your loved ones, and tell them you love them

SUPERHUMAN

- ignore the faults of others
- think positive thoughts and positive things will happen
- release emotional energy
- trust your intuition
- watch a funny movie
- laugh often
- love continuously
- forgive
- seek to understand
- avoid TV, computers, and technology
- stay away from the microwave ...literally!
- avoid perfumes, colognes, and fragrances
- listen to upbeat music
- spend time outdoors
- take in nature's scenery
- exercise
- listen to the wind
- go to the beach, listen and watch silently
- smell the fresh air
- sit in the grass, breathe deeply and slowly
- find a place to sit and relax that makes you feel whole and happy
- concentrate on every sense while at your peaceful spot
- meditate
- override every negative thought with a positive one
- practice breathing exercises
- take a walk
- swim
- spend time (no fighting) with loved ones, friends, or pets
- keep good people around you
- ignore any negative (people, energy, feelings, news)
- don't watch the news often or EVER! Most of it is fake! You will hear anything that's important from others.

CHAPTER 12

REAL EYES REALIZE REAL LIES

Some of the physical benefits I have experienced from eating raw are:
- clearer skin and complexion
- softer skin
- smoother skin
- a more rested appearance
- a more youthful appearance
- prettier and healthier appearance (genetics are enhanced)
- healthier hair
- thicker nails
- lightening of dark circles under eyes
- clearer eyes
- **lighter colored eyes**

Eye color change is possible. My eyes are literally changing. They're currently in the hazel stage where sometimes they look light brown, sometimes amber, sometimes they're a mix of brown and green, and sometimes they look green. Lighting does affect the color, but my nutrient intake and the cleanliness of my body do too.

Before I started eating raw, my eyes were dark brown. Pictures from when I was young indicate I had some color in them. After my first few months of eating raw, I noticed them change. Studying them closely in the mirror, I could see tiny slivers of green. At a normal distance, they were still brown. I had read about this happening to people who switched to raw food, but I was amazed to see it happening to *me*. I thought, *I have something real here that so many people would love to know.* Not only can you change your mind and body inside and out from eating raw food, but you can have bright eyes. If your eyes are already light, you can make them clearer and brighter.

• •

Some studies say there are only two true eye colors: brown and blue. Others say that all babies are born with blue eyes. Then there's the theory that we all originated from brown eyes. I don't have a solid answer to any of that. I also don't have a preference. All colors are beautiful. But, any newborn I've been around starts out with dark blue eyes that almost look black, and either turn darker or lighter as they get older. Blue and brown are the only true colors? *Hmmm,* I don't know …if my brown eyes are changing, why can't anyone else's? We all originated from brown eyes? I think it's actually blue.

> IF MY BROWN EYES ARE CHANGING, WHY CAN'T ANYONE ELSE'S?

My theory is that the expression of our parents and ancestors' genes are brought out in us as we are brought into this world. I don't mean the dominant and recessive genes that determine the color. It's more complex, the gene color's origin. I believe it has to do with how well our parents and ancestors were able to care for themselves. If certain nutritional needs weren't met because of lack of supply due

REAL EYES REALIZE REAL LIES

to weather conditions, location, personal choice, or whatever, their bodies adapted, and it's shown through the eyes. It's expressed quickly as we are exposed to our environment and our family's "traditional foods." Since color emerges as a child ages (quickly or over a period of time), these genes may be expressed or suppressed because of predisposition and current nourishment and environment. I believe color mutation is predetermined but not irrevocable, and not enabled until we enable it. Basically, what our parents, their parents, and so on did to their bodies trickled down into our DNA, changing certain genes which either get expressed or suppressed, starting as early as our mother's intake of nutrients and the environmental factors while we were in the womb. This would mean the expression of certain genes could set off things in our bodies that we didn't even cause ourselves. I believe, from experience and observation, that when we have raw foods, herbs, proper water, good energy, and by releasing all the crap we hold onto (literally and figuratively), over time we can restore the original blueprint of our DNA and restore the color of our eyes. Can I be wrong about this? Sure! Anything's possible; my mind is always open. Do I believe I'm wrong? No.

    A variation of this theory is referenced in the book *Rainy Brain, Sunny Brain*. Renato Paro, head of the Biosystems Science and Engineering faculty at the Swiss Federal Institute of Technology in Zurich, conducted an experiment where he briefly increased the temperature of the fluid around the embryos of white-eyed fruit flies from 25 degrees Celsius to 37 degrees. These flies, which genetically have white eyes, when hatched had red eyes. Several generations later, even after interbreeding them with white-eyed flies, red-eyed flies still hatched!

    I believe we're all supposed to have light eyes. The mutation of healthy genes, or the affect from environmental and nutritional changes that were passed down to us, are expressed in our bodies, reflecting through our eyes. Also understand that the things *we* do and eat *also* affect color, because just like I'm changing my eyes from dark to light through nutrition, I've seen others' eyes turn from light to dark through poor eating.

Ethnic groups who have predominately brown eyes may have developed them as a result of the food in their environment many years ago. Maybe they didn't get the same nutrients as some other nationalities with predominately light eyes did. Maybe now since we have easy access to all kinds of nutrients, this change is possible for *everyone?* I don't know. However, I've studied and experimented with raw foods and the results don't lie. When I eat strictly raw, my eyes get lighter and lighter. When I incorporate cooked foods, they start to get darker. Feel free to challenge me on this! Challenge yourself!

• •

Have you ever seen someone with green or blue eyes and an orangey-brown center around the pupil? Or blue eyes with a green center around the pupil? There are many color combinations; we usually classify them as mixed or hazel.

When two or more colors within the iris "mix" due to the surrounding lights and hues, the eyes can appear to change in color. That's why someone with blue eyes can sometimes look like they have green eyes and vice versa. They really have blue eyes. When a person with brown eyes sees color in their irises, do they really have blue eyes? Some studies will say no, if the eye is considered mostly brown. Is this definitive? I'm not convinced.

• •

Open a women's magazine and look at the close-ups of the models. The pictures are always so clear that you can see the details in their irises. I never noticed this before. Now when I'm skimming through, I can't help but study each one of their eyes because it's so amazing. You'll see many "hazel" or mixed eyes with spots or marks in them.

Certain marks or discolorations in the original color of the iris can reveal potential health concerns or genetic susceptibilities. The

REAL EYES REALIZE REAL LIES

practice that studies information in the iris and pupil is called Iridology. Each person has a unique pattern of characteristics, fiber structures, and colors in their eyes. An iridologist interprets these fibers, colors, and markings to assess a person's state of health, potential state of health, and genetic predispositions on a physical, emotional, *and* sometimes, spiritual level. They can see what's going on inside the body by mapping out each area according to an Iridology chart, and locating possible illnesses, emotional imbalances, or psychological issues. Look at your eyes closely in the mirror. Do you see little lines and shapes? Colors?

> **CERTAIN MARKS OR DISCOLORATIONS CAN REVEAL POTENTIAL HEALTH CONCERNS.**

I compared an Iridology chart with my own eyes. I could find my lungs (asthma) and other small internal issues I had. These areas were a different color. I was amazed! With this new excitement, I took a picture of my mom's eyes, which in Iridology terms are biliary (hazel). I compared them with the chart and mapped out areas of darkness or discoloration. Then, I asked her if she had any problems with this or that. Her answer was yes to all my questions. Every internal issue she had was shown in her eyes. It was incredible.

There is so much more to Iridology than just looking into a mirror and comparing your eyes with a map. After years of self-study, I finally took a course to become certified, and I found out that there is A LOT to learn and know when studying a set of eyes. An iris chart is only an approximation, so the study should be left up to a professional. However, there's no harm in looking!

• •

I learned something as a "fact" in Iridology that I can't fully support. While I may be wrong about this, I believe it's possible for brown eyes to turn blue. In Iridology, it's understood that a true brown eye cannot turn blue. It's said that a biliary or "mixed eye" can because it is considered, in my own words, "clouded" from an internal system that's toxified, sluggish, acidic, etc. But my question is, why is a biliary eye, which has similar constitution subtypes to a blue eye, able to turn blue, yet a brown eye, which has similar constitution subtypes to a biliary eye, not able to turn biliary? It makes me think that everyone's eyes are blue or even a very light color, and the current colors shown are in different stages of "cloud."

Constitution subtypes are characteristics in Iridology that define things that most people with that eye color may physically or emotionally experience. For instance, a person with blue eyes usually has a more acidic system which affects their lymphatic system, causing "drainage" issues that can lead to allergies, intolerances, joint problems, etc. Brown or hematogenic types tend to have blood anomalies as well as digestive issues. The biliary type is in the middle, sharing characteristics of both. Even brown types can have similar characteristics to blue, like sluggish lymphatic systems. What does that say to you? To me, it says that it's too coincidental, to be just a coincidence! It seems like that's how it is now but wasn't meant to be that way or isn't what it could be. Are you following me? What about people who have one brown eye and one blue? Do they have two separate systems inside? No way! Or what about people with MPD (Multiple Personality Disorder) who have not only sudden eye color change, but different markings on their skin as they change into "different people?" The "different people" are different personalities to someone on the outside, but to the one experiencing it, they may **feel** they literally become the "person." The agreements they have about themselves as each "person" can change them physically. Why? Beliefs manifest! When they change, so does their belief system and whatever those beliefs embody. Our mind influences our health. One common example is when we get upset. We may feel physical pain in our stomach.

Skeptical? Not sure your thoughts are influencing your body? Not convinced we can change our health through our beliefs and emotions?

REAL EYES REALIZE REAL LIES

Not buying it that our eye color may have a lot to do with our subconscious? Well, how about this: The study of the effect the mind has on health is called Psychoneuroimmunology. Yes, SCIENCE is involved with a form of manifestation. Mind-body unity IS A REAL THING!

In my opinion, we could mentally change our health, appearance, and physical nature on the spot if we weren't as consciously fucked as we are now! Can we dig deeper into this eye color thing and consider that maybe we don't have all the facts yet? I honestly believe we all share the same eye color, but our eyes are reflecting different stages of health from inheritance, nutritional intake, environment, and current mental state. If I'm wrong, I'll accept that, but I'll never go against my own gut feelings no matter how credible a "fact" is. It's up to me and only me to prove myself wrong. You don't "awaken" by continuing to believe what others tell you is true. However, whether a brown eye can turn blue is not the message here. The point is, there's a significant change in the eye when mental or physical health has improved, which is not something to be overlooked. (And yes, the pun was intended.)

• •

In the days before x-rays and tests, how could people possibly know what was wrong with them? Were we created to make machines to find out what's wrong but in the meantime, suffer or even die? No! God, or our creator, gave us a window! The eyes may be the windows to the soul, but they're also windows to our health—physical *and* emotional health!

Just a quick note: emotional wellbeing is *definitely* revealed in the eyes and you've most likely seen it for yourself. Maybe you knew someone was angry despite their calm demeanor because their eyes gave it away. Way back, when I saw the eerie look in Emilio's eyes, he was revealing the state of his mental health. It's not something I can describe exactly except to say there was a noticeable change, like a severe stare.

SUPERHUMAN

We can certainly see the reflection of a person's mental health and emotion in their eyes, but it's not just the iris that shows this. Look up pictures of serial killers; you'll notice similar, intense eyes or stares. Look up pictures of pedophiles too. Their eyes tend to have similar characteristics, especially in the eyelids. I've studied this a lot over the years because of my interest in mental health and iridology, and what I've observed is fascinating. I'm not saying that everyone who has eyes like these descriptions are pedophiles or serial killers, but there's something interesting about the similarities.

• •

The further I take my raw lifestyle, the lighter my eyes get. In the light, they can look green. While green is not a true eye color, it's amazing to see the color change in different stages.

It's extraordinary that I'm able to change my eye color, but the most incredible change is my health. I've never **felt better** or **more alive** in all my years on this earth. I wake up every morning feeling brand new, ready to start the day. I lay my head on my pillow at night and fall right to sleep, resting well with peaceful dreams. Having been an insomniac since I was a toddler, this was a major feat. If it worked for me, it can certainly work for you!

• •

After *years* and *years* of belly aches, body aches, headaches, and just plain feeling like shit, my body has forgiven me for all the disrespect and damage I've done to it and is now rewarding me for taking care of it. We habitually groom ourselves on the outside, but the inside is neglected. It makes no sense! *I* made no sense! I ate bad and then felt bad; need I say more? As time goes by, we're only making ourselves sicker and weaker by eating poorly, even if we can't physically see the damage! Groom your insides as well as your outsides and watch how your body and mind say, *Ahhhhhh,* THANK YOU.

• •

REAL EYES REALIZE REAL LIES

There's nothing more important than taking care of *yourself* first. One might say, *Well, taking care of my loved one is.* While I understand that, you need to be in top shape so you can be there for them. That's why they say if the oxygen masks ever fall in a plane, put yours on first so that you can help the next person. You're of no use to someone else if you can't help yourself. Put your oxygen mask on now!

> YOU'RE OF NO USE TO SOMEONE ELSE IF YOU CAN'T HELP YOURSELF.

Health is especially important for parents to understand. Your children did not ask to be brought into this world. It's your responsibility to take care of yourselves so you can be here for them. I believe choosing to have children is a selfish act in the first place. I'm not saying it's wrong to have kids or that anyone who has a kid is selfish, but let's be real, it's not the kids you're doing it for…they don't exist yet! There are a lot of good reasons not to have children. For one, it's not necessary. We have cycles of unhappy people unintentionally showing other beings the way to unhappiness. I understand when people marry, they may want to start a family, but many times people are longing to fulfill something in themselves, hoping children will bring them the love or happiness they're missing within, or in their relationship. Those are big expectations for a tiny, vulnerable being. I wish more people would feel the same way and just concentrate on creating more purpose and meaning in *their* lives, and in the lives of those already on this planet. It's sad that so many parents are caught up in their own stuff that they don't realize how they affect their kids in the moment *or* in the long run. Do you see why taking care of yourself first is so important?

If you have children, it's imperative to treat, feed, and teach them with love. A child can't decide whether it wants to be created, so it's fully the parents' responsibility to nurture the child, along with themselves.

SUPERHUMAN

• •

This brings me back to the topic about the color of babies' eyes, changing. When my cousin's baby was born, he had dark blue eyes. They looked very dark, but I saw a hint of light hit them. I knew they were going to turn light; his mother has very light blue eyes. Color is a result of genetics plus nutritional and environmental factors. My cousin takes care of herself, eats healthy foods, and breastfeeds her son. Breast milk is important because the baby is consuming the mother's nutrients along with other beneficial things (assuming she's healthy). Formula is not meant for a baby's body. That's why her son has bright, blue eyes like hers.

My friend's baby's eyes were also a dark blue when he was born. She has light green, mixed eyes. Her postpartum diet is irrelevant since she didn't breastfeed. The baby's stomach never adapted to formulas; they were always switching them. He's now four years old, eats the SAD, and his eyes have gone from dark blue, to mixed, to dark.

I also watched eye color change in babies I would babysit. When I first started, the first child was one and a half and had colorful light green/blue/brown eyes. Her baby pictures indicate that her eyes had been blue. She's now four years old and has much darker green/brown eyes (mostly brown). The same thing happened with the second child as well as the third. I paid close attention to third because I was expecting it to happen. At a few weeks old, her blue eyes gradually began to darken. They started to get a white cloud around the pupil that grew darker over time, eventually covering the iris. By the time she was one, her eyes were a green/brown color. The mother has bright blue eyes. They fed the baby formula (do research on formula) and the other kids ate a lot of microwaved foods (do research on microwaves), fast foods, processed foods, meats, and cheeses. The baby had stomach issues from the formula and they were all sick often. I'm not discrediting the mother; she loved her kids and tried to feed them healthier foods too, like vegetables and fresh fruit. And

REAL EYES REALIZE REAL LIES

yes, I know children are often sick, but I feel this is not the way it's supposed to be!

The immune system weakens over time as more unnatural, unhealthy things are consumed. No one should feel guilty for this because society has deemed it OK for so many years. Come on, how are we supposed to believe "food" is really poison when it's dressed up in fancy packaging and slick slogans? Why would these "foods" be sold and advertised everywhere if they're that harmful to us? It's all control! Control over humanity by destroying bodies and minds, by destroying lives through manipulation of a human weakness we call CONVENIENCE. Children are no exception to the game. You may think to yourself, *It's not that serious,* but it *is* that serious! We've adapted to consuming replicas of nature created by people we don't know, entrusting that the most important things we need in life—foods—can be man-made into something that they're not supposed to be. Food can either be medicine or malignancy. People don't know they're not only harming themselves, they're harming their kids! While it's perfectly ok to make mistakes in life, what's not ok is to consciously, continuously ignore what the human body needs. Are you ignoring it?

> THE IMMUNE SYSTEM WEAKENS OVER TIME AS MORE UNNATURAL, UNHEALTHY THINGS ARE CONSUMED.

• •

I've observed other people's eye color change. A few of my friends who have adopted drastically healthier eating lifestyles, have all had some color change in their irises as well. I've noticed their dark eyes now have slight green tints to them. So, I made my own conclusion: The food we eat is killing us! Unless we do something to change it, it will eventually make humans obsolete…and our eyes are trying to warn us! The good news is that this can all be reversed. I'm doing it

SUPERHUMAN

after 20+ years of TERRIBLE eating. My life changed because of **raw food**. I'm living proof that it works; it's in the raw pudding!

• •

1/24/12

It was last night, January 23, 2012 when I saw the real change. I was at a friend's wake, so I had been crying. When I went to the bathroom to clean my face, I looked in the mirror and saw these predominately green eyes staring at me. I've read about how tears bring out the color in your eyes, but tears had never brought it out like this before. It was a breakthrough in my hard work in a time of such sadness. I couldn't be excited because I felt so down. I was nervous though ...nervous that people who knew I had brown eyes would be seeing this. I was talking to a friend who knew me well but hadn't seen me in years. He was staring intensely at my irises. The look on his face said it all.

Today, since I'm not crying, there isn't much green. However, when I look in the mirror in the sunlight...lots of green! Not as much as last night, but still a lot. It's exciting to know that everything I stayed strong in believing is paying off. It's not just the color that makes me happy; it's also my health. If I was doing all this just to have light eyes, I probably would have struggled more, but the fact that it goes hand in hand with being healthy, is such a reward.

• •

I don't want to sound insensitive if you have food allergies or reasons why you can't go all or mostly raw or make you feel hopeless. I'm an extremist. Once I discover the truth about something, I skyrocket in that direction, and I know not everyone does that. However, we all have things we need to heal and there's a starting point for everyone. We're all works in progress. My point in ALL of this is for you to understand that; get a glimpse past the smokescreen and see that there

REAL EYES REALIZE REAL LIES

are things we believe to be true, BIG things, IMPORTANT things, that are *so* very wrong, so you can wake up! So you can change! The "food" we believe is acceptable to eat is a lie that is so twisted that I would be doing a disservice if I didn't share what I know. A raw food diet can **heal**; it could mean the difference between life and death to someone. Why would I keep that to myself?

Allergies, diseases, ailments, imbalances, and intolerances come from things deep within us, whether they be physical, emotional, or both. That's why detoxification, releasing, and eliminating the undercover poisons we eat and mentally accept daily is so crucial. Cleansing our bodies and incorporating healthy foods into our diet can be a starting point for anyone. Cutting out meat can be a starting point for anyone. Working on *emotions* can be a starting point for anyone. Simply being open minded can be a starting point for anyone! It's up to each of us to personally decide where and with what, we wish to start. But we must start somewhere!

CHAPTER 13

BEAUTY AND THE BEASTS

Going raw made me a vegan. Of course, I wasn't going to start eating raw meat, but that wasn't what completely turned me off. First, I learned how *terrible* meat is for the human body, mind, *and* soul. Then I learned how—I don't even have a word for it—it is for the animals. I didn't know what they went through and I would imagine many people don't. What most see is an unintelligent being that is supposedly below them on the food chain. Well, it's like this… A person can look like they're fine, walking around every day with a smile or relaxed face, when they are carrying deep pain or emotions. It's the same with animals. They may look fine or unintelligent, but is it possible that humans can't read them correctly? The horrifying truth that humans don't seem to play connect-the-dots with, is that they're NOT different from us. They feel emotions. They feel pain. They love. They fear. They protect. They want to live. They scream out and struggle before they're killed. They don't want to die.

You don't seem to think that you're chewing and digesting something that once breathed the air you do, something that could look you in the eyes, feel the way you do, emotionally and physically, something that was able to bond with you. You don't think about or even know the terror that animal went through: the torture, the sadness, and the pain. It seems so normal because you grew up that way. But it doesn't make it right, no matter how many people are on the bandwagon. Remember our agreements? This is yet another one instilled in us. It's another psychologically programmed, socially accepted, false belief, making us fear something bad will happen or that we will have to face some truths if we resist, so our minds don't even question it. Our brains shut off and our mouths open. *I* always thought it was normal, but now I'm passionate about *not* consuming flesh. Plain and simple, it's disgusting; not only is it unnatural and unhealthy for humans but it's **wrong** for us to kill animals! Even a child can tell you that![18] *Guess what boys and girls?* We don't need to eat them to survive.

> NOT ONLY IS IT UNNATURAL AND UNHEALTHY FOR HUMANS BUT IT'S WRONG FOR US TO KILL ANIMALS!

Animals are being raised, tortured, and killed in the most inhumane ways; it's barbaric. They feel emotional and physical pain just like we do. What gives humans the right to harm another being that wants to live peacefully? False entitlement. Murder is murder, torture is torture, and it doesn't change that fact because you pay someone else to do it. Think about the furry pets you have in your home. Would you let them be treated the way the food that's on your plate was treated? There's no difference!

• •

It deeply saddens me that people mistreat animals. Since I was young, I've had a special bond with them. Not only do they trust me, but I pick up their emotions empathetically, through energy.

When I was little, I swore my cousin's German Shepherd would talk to me. Not verbally, but spiritually. I could just sense how she

---

18 http://www.youtube.com/watch?v=CHABgTqqrz0

BEAUTY AND THE BEASTS

was feeling. As kids, we have powers that we lose or become less in touch with as we get older. One of them is being in tune with animals. Emotion is one of the first things children pick up on or notice. Even as an adult, I feel emotions from the animals I encounter. They give off a great deal of energy, which is how they communicate in nature.

While animals may not be able to talk or do everything we do, they're not below us. Animals are better than us because they follow the laws of nature and abide by their purpose on this earth; we destroy it. Be kind to them.

"Until one has loved an animal, a part of one's soul remains unawakened."

—Anatole France

Have you heard about pets that mourned their owners' deaths? What about animals saving people's lives? A collie named Max saved his owner's life by sniffing a lump that had been undetected.[19] The owner, Maureen, said that Max had been nudging at her breast and then acting very sad which was unusual for him. He helped her discover the lump which saved her life.

There are many other reported cases of animals "calling out" health issues. They're smart creatures with heightened senses and strong intuition. They can do amazing stuff. A cat named Oscar[20] was adopted from an animal shelter and brought to live in a nursing and rehabilitation center. Oscar wasn't a people-friendly cat, as he liked to keep to himself. However, he had the ability or power to sense when a patient was about to die. The staff would find him sleeping in bed with the patient who was "on their way out," sometimes predicting the impending death before any of the staff. To some, Oscar was an

---

19 http://www.dailymail.co.uk/news/article-1156683/Saved-dog-tor-Pet-collie-sniffed-owner-breast-cancer.html
20 http://www.telegraph.co.uk/news/newstopics/howaboutthat/7129952/Cat-predicts-50-deaths-in-RI-nursing-home.html#mm_hash, http://www.rd.com/advice/pets/the-cat-who-could-predict-death/

angel because he stayed with their loved ones as they took their final breaths. I would agree he is an angel; he's here to do work.

Just because Oscar is an animal, just because any animal is an animal and not a human, doesn't mean they're any less important than you or me! Tell me, where does one draw the fine line that says which animals are ok to kill? Look deeply into their eyes …that will tell you everything.

We are animals, animals are us! WE ARE ALL ONE. Look at monkeys! Look at pigs! Pigs are intelligent and behave like dogs! So do goats! Cows! I can go on and on because they're all beautiful, loving creatures and the truth is, that humans are the savages. Mankind has become the biggest threat to itself, because by eating other beings we're destroying them, our health, our wildlife, our true nature of compassion, peace, and ultimately, our ecosystem. We're ruining the planet! Did you realize that? Maybe it's time you see the truth.

• •

The unmeasured loyalty and love that animals have for people is beautiful. Animals, *period*, are beautiful. They have emotions like we do! They feel joy and pain. If you don't believe me, read the story of two elephants who were re-united after 22 years at an elephant sanctuary.[21]

This is what the Elephant Sanctuary co-founder, Carol Buckley, said:

> "Jenny came into the barn for the first time since Shirley's arrival at around 7:00 p.m. There was an immediate urgency in Jenny's behavior. She wanted to get close to Shirley who was divided by two stalls. Once Shirley was allowed into the adjacent stall the interaction between her and Jenny became quite intense. Jenny wanted to get into the stall with Shirley desperately. She became agitated, banging on the gate and

---

21 http://www.elephants.com/shirley/shirleyPhotos2.php

BEAUTY AND THE BEASTS

trying to climb through and over. …After several minutes of touching and exploring each other, Shirley started to ROAR and I mean ROAR—Jenny joined in immediately. The interaction was dramatic, to say the least, with both elephants trying to climb in with each other and frantically touching each other through the bars. I have never experienced anything even close to this depth of emotion."

• •

I had a cat when I was little that was unlike any cat my family has ever had, *and believe me, we've had a lot of cats*. He was like a dog trapped in a cat's body because he was so loyal and liked to go for walks on a leash! He literally came running into my life one day. I remember his little white-tipped paws trotting down the backstreet and into our yard. His name was Max.

Max became my best friend as he was always by my side, being a comfort in the hard times every kid has, *even though everyone thinks kids don't have troubles*. I'll never forget what he did one day. I had been fighting with my parents and felt they didn't understand my point of view, so I got into the shower to drown my tears. I sat down in the tub with my arms wrapped around my knees when I noticed the shower curtain move to the side. Max popped his little head through, then jumped in and stood in front of me, looking into my eyes and meowing. He *hated* water, as most cats do, but he completely tossed his innate fear aside to comfort me. My tears subsided as I sat in amazement, staring at the water pounding down on his furry body. I felt such a deep love from not only the action but the look in his eyes, that it has touched me forever. Max's soul was incredible, and I'll never forget him.

> THE UNMEASURED LOYALTY AND LOVE THAT ANIMALS HAVE FOR PEOPLE IS BEAUTIFUL.

SUPERHUMAN

Doesn't this tell you something about animals—that they're far more than four-legged creatures that walk this earth? They're here to live in harmony with us, not to be looked down upon, and not to be smothered with cheese and sauces to satisfy our selfish taste buds.

> "The earth we abuse and the living things we kill will, in the end, take their revenge; for exploiting their presence we are diminishing our future."
>
> —Marya Mannes

We are not designed to eat meat. Look in the mirror at your teeth. They are not meant for ripping flesh. They're meant to grind seeds, nuts, etc. Our insides aren't meant to digest flesh either. It takes a long time for it to go through our system and then it builds up in our colon. Red meats are the worst; they put our red blood cells at a state of high alert. ALL meat is highly acidic (well under 7 pH). Our pH's are meant to be alkaline (above 7 pH). When we feed our bodies acidic things, mucus forms as the body's defense to protect us, but it does much more harm than good.

And chickens. We're genetically manipulating them to be deformed and develop in half the time it takes to grow naturally. How can that be good for us? How is that fair to these animals? The whole thing is out of hand especially since it's unnecessary for people to eat this way. The main argument is that they *need their protein*. Do you *need* all the *other* harmful things in meat too? What you really NEED is your **health**. What you *really, really* NEED is to salvage this planet. The excuse that humans can only get protein from animal flesh is just that, an excuse; we can get it from many other sources.

> WHAT WE REALLY NEED IS OUR HEALTH. WHAT WE REALLY, REALLY NEED IS TO SALVAGE THIS PLANET.

• •

BEAUTY AND THE BEASTS

Here are some excellent sources of plant-based protein:
- Leafy Greens
- Nuts
- Seeds
- Beans
- Nut butters
- Quinoa
- Avocado
- Spirulina
- Chlorella
- Fruits
- Raw Hemp powder
- Nutritional Yeast

• •

Dairy is *not* cruelty free. The things they do to these MOTHERS is callous. Ripping their babies away from them, probing and prodding them, hooking them up to machines, molesting them repeatedly for their milk while they mourn the loss of their babies. Yes, they mourn. And the babies? It's insane. Feminists who consume dairy make me shake my head. They're so informed and righteous about women's rights, but what about an intelligent animal that goes through far worse than what human women go through?

Eggs are also not cruelty free. Besides the mistreatment of the chickens, the male chicks are often discarded alive or outright killed in a disgusting way. What the fuck has this world come to that there is such disregard for life? Just like our ignorant, iniquitous enslavement of people, one day we're going to look back at the pain and horror we forced on these beautiful, innocent creatures. I'm not sorry if this bothers you because it should bother everyone. I'm only sorry for the animals—sorry I can't make it stop, but I'll do anything in my power to make a change. You can make a change right now, by no longer being a part of it.

SUPERHUMAN

• •

If you're not going to do it for the animals, do it for ALL OF US. FOR THE PLANET. FOR OUR ECOSYSTEM. Wake up people! Eating meat is killing our chances for survival! Are you aware of how much of our land and resources go into our destructive lifestyle? It's ridiculous that people fear all the threats to mankind except the biggest, most ignored, most damaging one …OURSELVES. Our selfish, ignorant, uncompassionate selves.

> "Nothing will benefit human health and increase the chances for survival of life on Earth as much as the evolution to a vegetarian diet."
> —Attributed to Albert Einstein

I used to eat meat, never thinking about it. No one does. Why would you when you're not taught **real** things in school or in life? Why would you when the poor animal's face isn't staring back at you from your dinner plate? It's out of sight, out of mind. But now you know what you're doing, or you will know soon. Now that I'm aware, I won't go back. I don't even desire meat; it's repulsive to me now. If you don't think you can possibly give it up, cut it out gradually and substitute other ingredients in a healthy, proper way. You too will eventually be disgusted by it (and healthier than you've ever been in your meat-eating life). The idea of it will make your stomach turn, not just when you're chewing it. Why? Once we are free from it, we **feel** the truth; our bodies let us know we were never meant to have it.

A healthy, plant-based diet will make you look and feel better, all around. Every vegan I've talked with says the same thing: it's the best thing they've ever done; they only regret not doing it sooner.

• •

BEAUTY AND THE BEASTS

Here's the shocker: yes, I'm vegan and yes, I do purchase meat. I'm conflicted because it's what my dog needs to eat, yet I wish I could give it to him with absolute certainty that there was no cruelty involved. I also wish I could feed him something else instead and confidently know he will have a long, healthy life. He, like me, is living the raw lifestyle, but along with plant matter, his diet consists of raw meat and raw bones, and I can't deny that *he* was designed to eat it. The proof is in his mouth and in his digestive tract. His sharp teeth and strong jaw muscles were meant for ripping flesh and chewing through bone. His jaws can only move on a vertical axis (up and down motion) to chomp meat, as opposed to humans or horses who grind their food. His stomach acidity is strong enough to fight bacteria, to digest flesh and raw bone, and his short digestive track eliminates it quickly. Am I not thinking about the animals that died to feed him? Of course, I am, but it's what he needs to thrive. I don't like seeing animals in the wild kill other animals either, but it's a part of life. Wolves hunt their food. Dogs are basically wolves; their insides are almost identical. What's different about canines today is their physical appearance.

> NO LIFE, NO MATTER HOW BIG OR SMALL, SHOULD GO UNRECOGNIZED.

My dog can't go out in the woods and hunt his prey so it's up to me to supply him with the best and most nutritious food. That's the dilemma with being a vegan yet having an animal in your home. Nature designed animals to be wild, but humans designed this world to work for human convenience; it's an unsuccessful life for them out there. I buy meat and animal products that are raised and killed in the most humane ways (understandably, no life taken is humane). I also say a prayer of love and gratitude for that animal's soul before feeding my dog, because no life, no matter how big or small, should go unrecognized.

SUPERHUMAN

• •

It's important to know what you're doing when feeding your pet raw and feeding yourself raw. I figured out how to feed him through the internet, books, and his body. There are ways it can be harmful if it's not done correctly. Do your research not only on what to feed your animal but also on why it's important. Then, find a knowledgeable, holistic vet who can advise you how to properly feed your dog or cat a raw diet.

• •

My dog is a big reason I remain "raw," and my love for him is why he remains "raw." I want to be healthy for myself but for him too. His presence has not only made me a better person but drastically calmed my fears after something that happened to me, haunted me…

I was home alone one night. Music was blasting, the stove was fired up, but I kept hearing something at the door. I thought it was the cats outside trying to claw their way to my food, but after it continued, something inside me said, *That's not the cats* (intuition). That's when I crept over, out of view, like I was James Bond on a mission. When I got to the door a guy popped up and ran out!

This person obviously saw me cooking and heard the music, so he thought he had the perfect opportunity to do harm, and in a way, he accomplished it. I was terrified; I couldn't sleep. I sat up most nights in my bed hugging my knees because every little noise made me jump.

The fear tortured me every day. I couldn't take it; I needed a diversion. I decided that diversion would be going to live with my grandma in Florida—something I had always planned to do but never did because I feared leaving my parents alone with my brother.

I stayed with her for about a month, but my thoughts continually tormented me. One night I couldn't sleep, so I turned the TV on to see a special about kids who were killers. One kid walked in his

BEAUTY AND THE BEASTS

house, shot his dad in the head, and then murdered his mother. I lost it. I was already freaked out about leaving my parents on top of being scared someone was going to break in! That was it for me.

• •

Returning to New York after my stay in Florida was a breath of fresh air as bitter cold as it was outside. I was overjoyed to see my parents, even though I had a tremendous amount of guilt for leaving my grandma. It broke my heart because I know how badly she wanted me to stay, but I also knew I couldn't run. I needed to take control of my fear. So, I got a dog—a big one. I needed the protection, the peace of mind, and the ability to finally get a good night's sleep, but it wasn't just about that. I have ALWAYS wanted a dog to care for and love. This felt like the right time.

He changed my life. He showed me a lot about myself—what I had to offer and what needed work. He took my mind off a lot of things that I didn't need to be focusing on because I became consumed with caring for him. He took away a lot of my fears. As he grew, he became more and more of a handful, but I loved the responsibility.

The dog behavior books that I read all said that the main factor in good training is **positive reinforcement**. So that's how I trained him! I would praise him with words, touch, treats, and ignore the negative behavior. It worked because he grew into such a sweet, yet courageous dog. I taught him not to be afraid of things, just as I would raise a child. When there was something that frightened him, I'd explain what was going on and touch him, so he felt my ease. A skittish dog can be a dangerous dog, as many bite out of fear. This applies to children as well (not usually the biting but the defensiveness they develop from being scared). It's a tough world out there and they need to be prepared for it, but kids just like dogs need reasoning, understanding, and lots of love to repel fear. Are you emotionally preparing your kids or pets in a positive way? They mimic your behaviors, feelings, and attitudes by watching how you deal in everyday situations. Show them love and guidance, not worries and fears.

• •

Feeding our animals properly is a major part of their care. We should understand their bodies just as we understand our own. Reasonably, people worry about giving their pet raw meat and bones, but most of their worries are just fabrications passed on from people who are misinformed or uneducated. When it comes to fears, we tend to follow the myths and ignore the facts. If you want to know the truth, do your own research! Here's a little food for thought: Would you eat dry cereal every day for every meal? What do you think dog food is like? It was designed to save money and time, but in the long run, it costs us more money on vet bills and the worst part is that it costs our loved ones their lives. It's not good for them! Don't let the wet food fool you either; it's *all* bad. It wasn't meant for their systems.

Before I got my dog, I knew I was going to feed him a raw diet. It was just a matter of when to switch his food. Everyone, *including my old vet,* told me the all-natural puppy food he was on was good for him, so I decided to keep feeding him that until he got a little older. But one day, I was in the bookstore skimming through some raw food books when I landed on a page that detailed how harmful dog food was, even the all-natural brands, some of which are among the worst! I learned that the companies can change the ingredients and don't even have to disclose that information! It was funny (not ha-ha funny) because I had noticed his food was suddenly a different color than it had been, and he wasn't gobbling it up like he always did. I was also shocked to learn that veterinary schools are sponsored by these food companies, which plays into the conspiracy that

> WE SHOULD UNDERSTAND OUR PETS' BODIES JUST AS WE UNDERSTAND OUR OWN.

they're trying to keep your dog just healthy enough to survive but sick enough that they constantly need vet care, like *our* healthcare; it's all a big business.

After I learned this, I slid in the question to my now former vet, asking her how she feels about feeding raw. Her demeanor completely changed. She was always kind of rude, talking down to her clients, but she pepped right up in a personable way saying, "Oh I think it's great; however, you never know, and you don't want to take a chance, ya know?" It was almost like she was saying, *Shit, if she feeds him raw, he's going to be healthy and that means less money for me!* Feeling very uneasy and in a way betrayed from it all, I began to panic. I thought, *I need to take him off this immediately.*

My dog was about seven or eight months old when I introduced him to raw meat and raw bones (supplements and greens as well). His health is good, and I don't doubt this way of feeding. Two people very close to me unfortunately let those myths—those FEARS—get to them. They've also doubted the way *I* eat and let me tell you, that's going to be something you experience whenever you make major life changes to better yourself. The people closest to you sometimes will worry about and judge you more than they offer their support. Stay strong.

CHAPTER 14

WHO'S GOT YOUR BACK?

Just when you think you're on top of the world, bat in hand, ready to swing...life throws you another curveball. You look around and realize no one's cheering for you. What do you do? Drown in the silence or seize an opportunity for growth by rooting for yourself?

• •

If you decide to take on a raw-vegan lifestyle or even just a vegan lifestyle, most likely you'll have very little support. People don't "get it" so they don't accept it. Some will ridicule your choice, some will debate it, and some will look at you like you have ten heads. If you're lucky, you'll have at least one good person in your corner.

Don't let me scare you though! There *are* some who will praise you, acknowledging your willpower, your drive, and the thing that matters the most, the love you have for yourself! When you eat well, you feel good and you look good, and if that's true, then it *must* make SENSE to eat this way, *doesn't it? Common sense? Hello?? Anyone???*

It won't stop there. When you eat well and your body and mind change, the things around you will change. The way you see life, your perspective, *will* change. You'll feel a deeper purpose for your existence which may cause you to make life altering decisions, sometimes detaching from certain people, jobs, or commitments. If not your diet, *this* will most likely unsettle others. Sadly, you're likely to have very little support when you decide to make major changes that will better your life. But look at it this way: people are barely rooting for themselves so how can you expect them to be your cheerleader? Not being mentally prepared for that is how dreams get shut down.

• •

If we tune into them, the fears others put on us are like loud noises that drown out the voice of our intuition. Most people think a dream is just that—a dream, not reality. They think it's not something that can ever be accomplished because there are too many responsibilities and obstacles for it to be anything but fantasy. But, whether you believe your dream is attainable or not, you at least owe it to yourself to find out! Notice I said *owe it to yourself*; that's right, you owe it to nobody but you.

• •

A little advice: Don't tell anyone your next move, especially people who you don't think will have your back 100 percent. Why? The way they react to your news or ideas, even in the slightest unsettling way, can stop you from reaching your goal, or at the least, can delay it. The path you were originally, passionately, and positively creating and **choosing** can easily be rerouted by negative input from others (whether they meant to do that or not). The way they made you feel can deviate that path because you manifest with your feelings, so if your feelings are influenced by *other's* feelings, what do you think is going to happen to your creation? Be mindful of this, even if you think you can shake it off and stay on course.

Becoming a vegan is *not easy to keep secret* because people see what you eat. Becoming your most powerful self by creating the life you

WHO'S GOT YOUR BACK?

dream of …very easy to keep from the wrong people. You don't need recognition or reward from anyone but yourself. Kill the ego.

• •

When you've arrived at a crossroads and want to follow your dreams but have a familiar voice saying *I can't do this. What will others think? How can I possibly accomplish this?* Then it's time to stop listening and start doing. If you want to create a life of meaning, purpose, abundance, and happiness then do it! It's not as hard as your programmed mind wants you to believe! Doubting your capability and listening to those fearful, pestering voices (the ones in your head *and* the ones around you) WILL LEAVE YOU STUCK. When you ignore them and do whatever it takes, starting with setting your mind on what you desire, you'll find that everything you need will come to you and obstacles will fall to the side.

For me, it started with a desire that I believed in strongly. I built it with confidence and trust, then solidified it with no doubts. I haven't completed my dream yet, but the people, opportunities, and things I thought were impossible *to even get a glimpse of miles down the road*, keep crossing right in front of me with each kind, confident, passionate, **faithful** step I take. It's all because I didn't listen to anyone's fears! Not even my own! I quit my job along the way which was one of the scariest things I could have done. We need to make money, but sometimes we come to the crossroads and know that if we stay where we are, we're stuck and cannot possibly move on without making sacrifices. I just knew; I felt it. I couldn't fully accomplish what I needed to without leaving the place that bombarded me with negativity and drained all my energy—energy that I needed to be using elsewhere! We can make money in other ways, by doing the things we enjoy; we don't have

> I DIDN'T LISTEN TO ANYONE'S FEARS! NOT EVEN MY OWN!

to stick to familiarity! While I'm not telling you to quit your job, sometimes it's necessary to take leaps to overcome the fears holding us back. Familiarity is indeed something that holds us back from success in many aspects of life. It's comfortable for *us* to stay put, but it's also comfortable for others, like our families who worry about us. Sometimes, the people who love and support us the most don't have our backs when it comes to things they can't understand, but you and only you feel that feeling deep down inside (not the voices) and **know** what's right for your life; NO ONE ELSE DOES. If you're ready to embrace your dreams, you can't listen to the opinions, the threats, the demands, the FEARS of others.

• •

What's up with all the negativity? What the ego doesn't understand it must defend against, which creates fear. That fear is presented through other's opinions of *your* lifestyle, based on their agreements of what one's lifestyle should be. Because they don't understand it, it's foreign, something their ego wants to reject. Be aware that you'll probably also encounter jealousy from people who feel as if "they could never do it" (which is their self-limiting doubt).

> STAY STRONG, EMBRACING IT ALL WITH LOVE AND ACCEPTANCE.

Remember why you're doing this. Stay strong, embracing it all with love and acceptance. Outsmart temptation and any outside influences. Just because the pizza commercial is taunting you, it doesn't mean you have to let it win! Just because your father shot down your idea, it doesn't mean he's right! I know how hard it is; I've been there. But with every defeat over the allure of temptation or the gift of love you present to others in the moment of their fears, you're growing something very powerful within yourself. When you look back, you

WHO'S GOT YOUR BACK?

will realize **your choices** created the success and new opportunities in your life, not the influence of others!

• •

Sadly, many people don't know their worth; they think they're not important, that they have no place in life, that they're not wanted, needed, loved, or cared for. However, everyone is born with purpose. Everyone is unique. Everyone is **loved** because energy *is* **love**. EVERYTHING IS LOVE. We are created with it. We are made of it. The day we are brought into the world a great deal of energy is introduced. Our energy contributes to not just the happenings of our life, but all the lives we encounter; it's important. Yes, it has its ebbs and flows, and ups and downs, but it never becomes anything less than what it is. It's the ego which hijacks our purely loving selves, our energy, and drives us down a road of self-hate that leads to self-destruction. What influences the ego? Unfortunately, other people do. When we can strip away the picture the ego has falsely painted of us, we can see who and what we are and then embrace it.

Life as we are aware of it in our current state of human consciousness makes us unloving, or I should say, love-lacking. Lack of love tortures us for years and years, and some of us die slow deaths, while others wake up and live. Those who stop listening to everyone and everything around them discover truth and use it for their betterment. I'm excited to say that people are now waking up in numbers and quickly. Why? This is a time for great transformation in not just us but in the whole world. It's a shift in global consciousness. Why are so many still sleeping? Why do some wake up and others don't? Even in the darkest of times, there's always a light available. Some people know it's there, while others don't. The ones who do may not choose to flip the switch. They are paralyzed with fear—fear of navigating the unknown darkness to find the light. Others have no clue a switch even exists. They believe life put them where they are, and blindly suffer through it. Yes, you will have to suffer through some things as a physical being because you feel pain, but it should only be temporary because it's only meant to be temporary. Pain is weakness leaving the body, right? Once you release it, what happens? You grow stronger; you learn from it. When you learn you can get through it every single time, you learn to appreciate the lesson that it's teaching you. You learn to appreciate the darkness, as much as the light. That my friend, is called waking up. If you're waking up, be grateful, feel blessed, be happy, and most importantly, be you, not who your ego convinced you to be, and not who others convinced your ego to be. Your divine purpose will guide you to abundance as soon as you start "walking the walk and talking the talk."

• •

Not only is the ego influenced by others, but we're mentally programmed by society to follow the rules, to shut down our uniqueness, to be molded to a structured existence, to obey fear; to be kept *nicely in check*. They want us in check for what purpose? It's for the extremely wealthy "power players" of the world to continue to profit from our cognitive dissonance! We create a caricature of ourselves in our own mind, along with a projection of the world that is manifested by misinformation. They want us to cooperatively follow along with the way they run this world, so they pull the wool over our eyes. It all starts in our homes with the programmed elders we're taught to obey—the ones who don't even realize they're setting us up to fail in a society that wants us to fail. When you start waking up and changing the system, the lack of support is real. Be ready for it.

• •

I was a victim of structured programming. I knew there were strange coincidences in my life, but I was never taught to believe in signs, let alone taught what they were. I knew one thing though: some felt *very* strange and very important. There was something significant about them.

WHO'S GOT YOUR BACK?

Those "strange coincidences" were all telling me the same thing: *Hold on through all the bullshit you're going through …there's meaning to all of this.* I remember one especially, not only because of how it felt at the time, but because I still have it. What is it? Don't laugh… it's a fortune from a fortune cookie! Fortune cookies weren't just pieces of paper with someone else's wisdom on them; they were clear messages to me at that time in my life. One of the first few I saved was one of the most powerful ones, because it resonated in my soul and in my circumstances. It read, "You are imbued with extraordinary vitality." I was. I am. I've escaped death multiple times. I've made it through trauma. I am here at this moment writing this, determined, and I was there at that moment reading it, determined. It was more than, *This fits what's going on in my life*; it was, *This is important, Kate, pay attention*. It wasn't coincidence. It was, *There's a reason for your vitality and this piece of paper is trying to tell you*. Are you saying, *Nah, it was a coincidence*? There's no such thing, but I won't try to convince you of that. However, if you do question coincidence, here are two I just pulled out as I was looking for the other one. **I know**, I'm supposed to share them with you. This may resonate with you right now. The first one reads, "Some people dream of worthy accomplishments while others stay awake and do them." The other, "Enjoy life. This is not a dress rehearsal." If you've **felt** this, PLEASE don't be afraid to walk in the dark alone. That simple light switch, *which exists in EVERYONE'S darkness*, will illuminate everything in your life once **you** take the necessary steps to find it. There's nothing to fear.

> STOP BEING SCARED TO DO THINGS! WHEN YOU HAVE AN OPPORTUNITY, TAKE IT.

What does this all mean? Stop being scared to do things! Don't let the bullshit in your life stop you from everything you can do. Don't let others stop you! When you have an opportunity, take it. When something feels good to you, believe it. When something feels bad to you, believe that too. Don't hold onto *any* feelings; stay present. Do good things for *you*; it's not selfish. It's selfish not to do good things for yourself. Believe you are powerful, because you are! Believe that you can have and do anything; you have a beating heart, contracting and expanding lungs, and a magnificent mind that is ALL YOUR OWN. Take action. Stop letting time pass and be the person you were before all the shit screwed with your head. Show them…no…show *yourself* what you're capable of. Live like new energy just brought into the world, because at any given moment, you have a chance to be renewed and reborn. You are energy—transformable, transmutable, and absolutely fucking amazing. Remember that.

• •

Want to engage your wildest dreams? Be authentic, be you, do you. Fuck everyone else! I find so much truth when I am real with myself, others, and my own thoughts, as hard as that is sometimes. Being real can easily rub people the wrong way, and you can even make yourself uncomfortable. That's the point though. You never want to be too comfortable. You never want to live to make others comfortable. You want to do what keeps you growing. If you follow people, you are submitting to their ideas, their wants, and their desires; it's stunting who you are and who you're supposed to become. That's why the universe, the law of attraction, manifestation will bring you every hardship it can until you snap out of it and realize you can easily be the captain, not the co-pilot, in total control of your destination.

> I FIND SO MUCH TRUTH WHEN I AM REAL WITH MYSELF, OTHERS, AND MY OWN THOUGHTS.

Loving and bettering yourself creates a ripple that travels through your water as well as through those who drink from it, so don't ever feel guilty for doing good things for yourself. Remember, we affect those around us. When you're living your best life, you'll show others

WHO'S GOT YOUR BACK?

how to do the same. The starting point is self-awareness. Find out who you are, accept yourself, and begin to heal through self-love. Then you can build your life the way YOU want it!

• •

I am an empathic person who takes on other peoples' feelings, which may be who you are too. I've learned to distinguish which feelings are mine and which are theirs, release that shit and carry on with my plan. Release, release, release. Aaaand action!

• •

Understand that people don't have all the facts. They only have their opinions, their programmed thought processes, and their troubled emotions, and you have your dream! YOUR dream—it's up to you to make it come alive! Believe in it wholeheartedly, because if you don't, who will?

Don't let lack of support bring you down, and don't try to change anyone's mind or be angry with them for something they don't understand. Let sleeping people lie! We all need to shut up, relax into who we are and what we feel is true, keep our fears away from others, and keep others' fears away from us. We don't need to be so opinionated and judgmental! We need to **love**, period. It's our responsibility to listen to our intuition and ride with that. No one has the right to another person's brain. When it comes to decisions, we can relax in the moment and act according to our intuition. We should know what we're feeling is *our* true nature, and not the way someone else made us feel.

• •

Living with my parents was my biggest challenge when I began my raw lifestyle. Not only did I not have their support, but they had junk food everywhere! They didn't understand how and why I live this way, so they didn't respect it. They were worried because I did "extreme" things (extreme to them) like cleanses and fasts, but I never heard an, *I'm proud of you for taking better care of yourself.* Isn't it better that I'm eating natural food instead of filling myself with junk? I don't understand why people don't see how tremendous this lifestyle is! How can you doubt the benefits of healthy food? If you research it and still don't believe, I don't believe *you!* You're lying to yourself! More and more news is coming out that tells people to eat more fruits and veggies and the benefits of healthy food on the body. There's no difference except that the raw lifestyle is a more advanced, complete concept of that.

Temptations are everywhere... fears are everywhere... and it makes everything that much harder! What you must to do is keep your mind focused. You decide if you use that discipline inside you. The way you choose, good or bad, will affect you. If I had continued the way I was eating, I believe I would have come down with some terrible ailment. There was probably something brewing inside me, but now I'm inadvertently treating it.

If I had continued to see life the way I did, living in a world of circumstance, I would never have been able to see the beauty that I see now. It's everywhere I look because I'm creating it; I'm matching it. You can too.

● ●

Would you like to stop worrying? Would you like to live in the moment and enjoy it? Would you like to be healthy? These things are possible for you if you accept that you deserve them, listen to your intuition only, and acknowledge their possibility.

People tend to develop more health issues and take more medication as they get older. While it's true that their declining health is because of the food they eat, the beliefs they're stuck in also contribute. They believe, *This pill will help me,* and *I can keep eating like this.* They don't *truly* see the correlation between health and food, because if they *really* did, they probably wouldn't eat the way they

WHO'S GOT YOUR BACK?

do! They wouldn't believe that their only option is medication, and THEY WOULD MAKE BETTER LIFE CHOICES. That, however, is a part of the structured programming that uses fear as a tactic to stop us from waking up and discovering that herbs, food, clean water, and a healing mindset are all we need to be healthy. We've relied on medications for so long that it's scary to think that these "powerful" people in the world have such control over our wellness, that they want us sick enough to make money but well enough to stay alive. Hey, a dead person is not worth anything and neither is a healthy one! This is only one of the many truths you will discover once you begin to "wake up." Do you see why some of those "sleeping people" would rather stay asleep? Very understandable, right? Acceptable? Not for me; I want to know it all. I want to know how to protect myself and how to heal this world. How about you?

> OUR BODIES HEAL THEMSELVES (AND FEEL FANTASTIC) WHEN WE TREAT THEM RIGHT.

The truth is, if you never make that major life change to be healthy, the crap you've accumulated will most likely be the cause of your demise. Wouldn't you rather change today and turn it all around? Wouldn't you rather enjoy life and be happy? We are meant to live long, healthy, happy lives, without all these ailments! Our bodies heal themselves (and feel *fantastic*) when we treat them right. It's what we're supposed to do!

"Let food be thy medicine and medicine be thy food."
—Hippocrates

ATTENTION: We're not meant to be on this earth to die; we're here to **live**! Do you have kids because you want them to grow old and die? No, you have kids to enjoy them and for them to enjoy life! Children are doomed from birth with all the garbage people feed their mouths and minds. We need to change and make this a new world instead of sitting around fearing the end of it! Nourish yourself, nourish your children, nourish your animals, nourish the earth. Support change.

> "To cherish what remains of the Earth and to foster its renewal is our only legitimate hope of survival."
> —Wendell Berry

Remember how I said you're lucky if you have at least one person in your corner? Well call me Rocky and him Mickey, but his name is Chris. He understands my lifestyle choice. He's supported me through this and I'm grateful.

Chris and I became friends years ago. We've always had a bond or connection that allowed us to get along so well with each other. When I introduced him to this way of life, he immediately took to it, never doubting me. Chris not only supports my eating habits but *everything* I do. He's seen how everything I'm passionate about transcends into reality, and his encouragement has helped me tremendously. In return, this lifestyle has helped him tremendously.

• •

After the summer ended, Chris decided he wanted to jump on board with me. He's been overweight all his life and finally had enough. He said after seeing my transition he wanted in on it too. Knowing I have the knowledge and experience, he left it in my hands to help him achieve his goal.

I set him on a strict regimen of eating raw and living foods and exercising. On October 2, his starting weight was 328 pounds, standing at 5'10" tall. By January 13, he weighed 259 pounds! Not only is he down 69 pounds, he gained a great amount of muscle, just in three months! Along with rapidly losing weight, Chris says he feels so much healthier.

WHO'S GOT YOUR BACK?

In the beginning, as a coffee drinker who was working 12-hour days, he thought he wouldn't have the energy to get through the day. I promised him the sugar from the fruit he ate in the morning would give him that energy. The raw food he would eat throughout the day would too. He admitted that everything I told him would happen did happen. Every time he moves another belt notch, he feels proud and it makes me happy. It's also exciting because I'm seeing someone else transform into a **Superhuman**! He's changing his life and he's going to be at a place he's never been *very* soon.

• •

While I'm sharing everything, I should also tell you I've given up sex. Not that I was promiscuous, but I decided one day that I needed to void it completely for a while. I wanted to concentrate for once, so I could accomplish my goals.

Every time I was in a relationship, they became my priority because they made me theirs. Then when we became intimate with each other and I was cheated on or lied to, my world would turn upside down and I couldn't focus on anything important. My life would come to a halt. Now I'm making up for wasted time by going for my goals, not worrying about a guy, and it feels amazing!

• •

While sex is pleasurable and keeps you healthy, it can be damaging if it's not done with the right person. Who is the right person? Love must be the motivation, not their ego. When the ego is involved, sex is loveless, and somebody usually gets hurt. So, since it's such an intimate act and people often catch feelings from it, it should be done with someone trustworthy.

Your body is your temple! If you're taking chances with it and being destructive with your health *and* emotions, you're destroying what you live in, your soul's home! Since I've learned to love myself and focus intently on my goals for the first time, I'll wait for the right person and time before I have sex again. It's part of the self-love and discipline that came with this lifestyle change. It's a personal choice and everyone has a right to their own choices. Just remember, every choice you make leads you to something else. Choose wisely.

• •

I've obviously made mistakes in my life with eating and jumping into things like sex and relationships, and while they taught me great lessons, they also took away a big chunk of my childhood. Having sex is an especially big decision for kids to make, even though they may not realize it in the moment. I want young girls to know that they have their whole lives to experience things. Sex is better when you're older because you've acquired more knowledge by then and can make clearer choices. You only have one chance in your life to be a kid. Enjoy it and wait to have adult experiences later. Your patience will become a virtue.

If you're already involved with someone, make sure they have your best intentions at heart. Know for certain they're the person you want to give yourself to because you are giving more than your body; you're giving your mind and your energy, which will influence everything in your life.

• •

The biggest lesson here: always support yourself, your beliefs, and your gut feelings, even if no one else does!

PART III
LIFE

CHAPTER 15

NATURAL BORN HEALERS

The Healing Power of Water, by Masaru Emoto, is a "must read" for everyone. YES, *everyone*; if you're reading this, you are a human who needs water to survive.

Remember when I said, "Do you know that water can react to words and emotions? That your intention alters it?" This is the book to which I was alluding.

The Healing Power of Water opened my eyes to something larger than life, something that's tangible, yet so intangible. I owe this awakening to a man who somehow crossed my path, *literally and figuratively*. He recommended the book to me along with many kind words, and I'm grateful for his presence in my life.

If I were to tell the average person what I've learned in this book, they would think I'm crazy. There's so much about the earth and ourselves that we don't understand; water is one of them. We think it's simply to bathe in or to drink when we're thirsty, but it has a much higher purpose.

• •

SUPERHUMAN

Close your eyes and go back to a day when you, or someone around you, was in a bad mood. Were they the only person in a bad mood? Probably not! When an emotion grows intense, it becomes charged energy that affects other people. When that magnitude of energy is transferred into water, it changes the structure of it. When any level of energy or frequency is transferred into water, it changes the water in that way.

To show this energetic effect, Dr. Emoto froze droplets of water labeled with different words or phrases. When the frozen droplets were studied, the words or phrases they were labeled with had that effect on them. For example, the one he labeled "this is really beautiful" froze into a beautiful crystal formation. Another that he labeled "demon," came out very...let's just say the image in the book gave me goosebumps. Are you confused? It's not that the water could read what was written. The energy that came from him, from his **feeling** about the word, transferred into the water. Not only does the book include scientific proof but visual proof as well. The images will blow your mind.

> WHEN AN EMOTION GROWS INTENSE, IT BECOMES CHARGED ENERGY THAT AFFECTS OTHER PEOPLE.

• •

Since energy forms structure in water, because we're made up of so much water, it would follow that energy forms structure in us. Words have more of an impact on our health and wellbeing than we know. It makes me think twice about arguing with my parents or ever saying *anything* negative to anyone. Remember the very first agreement in *The Four Agreements*? *BE IMPECCABLE WITH YOUR WORD.*

When someone says something cruel to you, it hurts, right? The negative energy they put out permeates through your mind then travels down to your "gut" where it harbors. It creates a roadblock in your happiness. That energy follows you throughout your day, transferring to other people. It's amazing how much we affect one another, isn't it?

Look at all the young kids who take their own lives because of bullying. Could it be that the words thrown at them are detrimental to more than their emotions? For sure! It destroys their health, their bodies, and their minds. We need to change this world one nice word and one nice deed at a time.

The next time you have something not so nice to say, DON'T SAY IT. Say something positive instead—something that will lighten their day and allow them to pass the positive energy on to others. Watch how it works, affecting you, them, and everyone around!

Doesn't it feel good to be around someone who feels good? I don't mean someone who is noticeably happy or putting on a show, being overly positive, over the top, or sugar-sweet to you. I'm talking about the person who exudes good energy; they **feel** good when you're around them. You know this feeling. Someone can be in pain or have a bad attitude and you may feel it or be affected by it on some level, just as you may be affected by someone who feels great. Energy is contagious! You pick it up from other people whether you realize it or not. I like to call it "speaking energy."

Have you ever had a wild or nervous animal approach you? The possibility of them harming you probably crossed your mind, and the possibility of you harming them may have crossed theirs, but both your vibes said otherwise. You had shared, calm energy. You spoke to each other without talking! Bad energy feels bad and good energy feels good and it's important to learn to speak the language of energy, to protect yourself from the bad, and recognize when the energy is affecting you. How can you protect yourself? Know, through mindful observation, when the energy is not your own and then imagine and believe you have a protective shield around you. Who cares if you can't see it? It's there if you believe it is! You created it with the ENERGY from your thoughts. If it's already affecting you, you can clear it! Switch your mood through positive thinking, take a deep breath, and release what does not and should not belong to you!

If you can't do it already, you can also learn to read character and mood through energy. Every person you meet will tell you about themselves without saying a word. It's damn helpful when deciding if you should welcome or 86 that bad energy out of your life!

• •

We're all affected by one another because we're all connected, and we are ESPECIALLY affected by water, from the infinite oceans to the tiniest drops that live in our cells. WAKE UP! We have an enormous issue with water. Not only do we need it to survive, but it's also killing us! The things we let the people in power do to it is beyond criminal. They only hold power over us because we remain oppressed, conformed, controlled …because we've been a-fucking-sleep to the reality that we are not only destroying our planet but blindly allowing others to destroy it! Do you have kids? Do you want them to inherit this disaster or do you want to stop disconnecting from reality, and contribute to the solution? It all starts with love and respect for energy—your energy and the energy of others. We need to nurture the energy that influences our water; WE NEED TO NURTURE OUR PLANET. Water should be pure because it runs our whole body! Negative energy and pollutants are damaging the earth's water and wiping us out. It's Karma! We're wiping ourselves out! The people in power are looking for the takeover. Their agenda is to let us self-destruct, but I sure have other plans for all of us and I hope you do too.

• •

The Healing Power of Water discusses the sacred waters throughout the earth that were once used to heal people; some still do. The ones that no longer do have been damaged by neglect and disrespect. If any of this seems far-fetched, study, read, and learn about it; you'll discover the shocking truth. Chills ran through my entire body when I learned how powerful water is. It's everywhere! We're surrounded by it, we're made up of it, and everything on this earth needs it to survive. Think about it! Then think about your own footprint. What can you do to improve?

• •

Here are some suggestions:
- Don't dump garbage, waste, or chemicals into the ocean!
- Don't litter …EVER!
- Don't be wasteful.
- Recycle as often as you can.
- Support and buy food created by the earth, not the lab.
- Buy organic produce to support a chemical and pesticide-free earth (and your body!).
- Do a nice deed for a person, an animal or the planet.
- Don't use pesticides, weed killers, or chemicals.
- Smile at someone.
- Compliment someone.
- Be appreciative, giving lots of love and gratitude.
- Put out positive vibes.
- Be kind and understanding with acceptance and love.
- Don't follow the crowd. Do what you know is right.

• •

There are so many damaged people who are taking others along with them. It's like when you're little and you make a whirlpool; the more people you add, the faster and more powerful it becomes. The middle of the whirlpool sinks and spirals downward. When you break the movement, there's a calmness to the water. We need to break our global whirlpool so we can finally have peace.

• •

Please, let's begin to heal for our own survival on this planet. Let's all come to the realization, the FACT, that everything that happens in our lives is for a reason and only meant to empower us. No matter how bad it is right now, **life can be different**. It's how we mentally deal with hardships that will make or break us. Our biggest problem is that we don't understand others or even ourselves enough to block out or release negativity. We harbor the harmful feelings and pass them along to others. To fix this we all need to learn to accept, love, and forgive not only each other but ourselves, so we can let go of emotional baggage. Love negates hate (fear). The more love in the world, the better everything will be. What we put out there, toward others and ourselves, comes back even stronger. So, do we want to give our energy to the "good guy" (love) or the "bad guy" (fear)?

If you do nice things for others every day, like smiling at a stranger or saying a few kind words to a family member, not only will it make *them* feel better, but *you'll* feel better too. The more you do this, the more natural it will become and the easier your life will get, because you'll receive lots of kindness in return. Don't believe me? Give it a try and watch how things go in your favor. The universe will give back to you, threefold.

• •

The Healing Power of Water also discusses self-healing, the main theme throughout this book, *if you haven't noticed*. When you're living the raw lifestyle, your body can heal itself. Did you know that your *mind* can heal your body too? It's true! Illnesses are created from poor health *and* trauma; trauma is memories or stored information from the PAST. It's trapped emotional energy and that energy can be released!

One story in *The Healing Power of Water* was of a woman who developed three ovarian cysts and a fibroid as big as a grapefruit. Instead of complying with the doctor and having surgery, she chose to seek help from Dr. Emoto, who made her revisit her past and dig into the trauma of her father murdering her sister. This enabled her to feel the guilt from that experience, which had created physical calamities in her body from holding onto it into her adult life. After pinpointing that guilt, she was able to let it go and forgive herself. This is what The Sedona Method™ teaches. When we allow ourselves to feel an emotion or thought and then allow ourselves to release it, we set trapped energy free that has been holding us back in life or physically harming us. With Dr. Emoto's therapy and water, in under a year, the woman's masses were all gone, and her health was restored! Just reading this story made my hairs stand on end. It supports the evidence that disease and sickness can occur from trapped or stagnant energy within the human body. It also suggests why a lot of women can't get pregnant. Many times, they're told it's not possible and that belief manifests (it becomes an agreement). Remember what happens when you accept agreements? They become your own.

> DISEASE AND SICKNESS CAN OCCUR FROM TRAPPED OR STAGNANT ENERGY WITHIN THE HUMAN BODY.

Our DNA is encoded with abilities that are accessible when we believe in them. We can physically change the cells in our bodies and heal ourselves, WITH THE POWER OF OUR MINDS!

• •

Do you want to know why cancer returns after people get it surgically removed? While the mass is gone, the energy that created it still lives in the body. When that energy can't find the mass, it creates it elsewhere. This is the reason we must learn to release trapped emotional energy.

The things that have happened to us and the thoughts we hold can create illness. The things we put in our body can too, but if we can mindfully cure ourselves, then why not try it? Why not do it? We can look deeper and believe in something that goes against what everyone else tells us. If you were dealing with something life-threatening, wouldn't you want it to go away without any harmful medicine or invasive surgery? Wouldn't you wish that you could **imagine** it gone and have your life go back to normal? As hard as it is for our resistive minds to believe that this can happen, it can!

Just as the mind can create a disease, it can destroy it. Do you realize how powerful that is? How powerful *you* are? People are afraid of information like this because if anything is possible such as the ability to heal all disease with our minds, then everything we believe in now isn't real. The world as we see it and the ways we approach problems are wrong. Resistance to this information is normal because of the input from the ego, but after everything I've told you, you should now know that it's only doing you an injustice! The truth will overpower your resistance. It will keep nudging you even if you choose to ignore it. Don't fear having an open heart and open mind, because when you accept the truth, you accept healing.

> JUST AS THE MIND CAN CREATE A DISEASE, IT CAN DESTROY IT.

• •

When you open a door, life will open even more for you. I shared my beliefs with a lawyer I had worked with and found he had similar knowledge. He gifted me with some related reading material. In one of the magazines, *Well Being Journal*, I stumbled across an article by Shannon McRae, Ph.D., which explains exactly how this type of healing works.[22] Opening up to the lawyer had led me to this information confirming what I had already learned, and much more. It was the universe once again saying, *You're on track*. Now I can share it with you!

---

22 *Well Being Journal*, Quantum Things and Healing Fields: Cellular Healing and Our Organizational DNA, Shannon McRae, Ph.D. November/December 2011

NATURAL BORN HEALERS

The tiniest energies, or "quanta," are involved in interactions with things such as cells, through human observation. The **intention** or desire that we have makes the quanta influence the tiniest elements in our bodies. How? The intent of healing ourselves by picturing and believing in this healing energy turns possibility into actuality when the energy (intent), which is even smaller than our cells, moves into them, changing their structure. They work the same way as how our attitude influences the physical world, or how by picturing the circuits in our brains changing, we can physically change them. Picture the things you want to see happen, not what's worrying you or bringing you down. See the good, then become the good.

Dr. McRae explains that the unhealthy cells in our bodies are not the original blueprint of our DNA. Stress, beliefs, and negativity have damaged the cells. She states, "The possibility and probability of healing becomes reality when the intent, belief and desire are all in harmony for the healing to occur." It's just like how people become wealthy. They see, feel, and believe in their goal. We can create these healing vibrations or energy fields within ourselves by using our minds! So how do we do this?

Try this exercise: Close your eyes and be aware of nothing but what's going on in your body at a cellular level. Call on your emotions to use pure intention as you picture your cells and picture little fields of energy moving toward them. Now imagine this energy cleansing the unhealthy cells and drawing in new, healthy ones.

• •

We can fight a disease with medicine, but it will fight back, sometimes winning and sometimes losing. YOU CANNOT WIN WITH FEAR OR HATE. Blind the illness with the light of so much love that it can no longer harm you. See it not as something against you but as a part of you that's working *with you*, to change something in your life. Deal with it gracefully by cleansing it with good intentions. When you embrace something negative with the energy of love, the fear that was protecting it disappears, allowing a release to happen; letting go of the illness. Sometimes when people are faced with life threatening diseases or near-death experiences, they realize there's a whole lot more to this life, and it changes them. The reason? When they're presented with their biggest fear and life still goes on, fear no longer holds any weight! Possibilities that were never seen before open new opportunities for healing …in all aspects. The thing that changes is the thought process of the mind—the way it sees life, resulting in the construction of a new reality. It's an awakening that makes them realize they had been sleeping their entire lives.

We all are super humans with the ability to use love as a force to heal everything. To access our healing abilities, we need to make that transition to believing in ourselves and in this universe, by awakening to the truth. Then we can let our pure **intention** and true love guide us. We deserve to be happy and healthy.

• •

While the brain needs the physical body and the physical body needs the brain, if they were hypothetically separated, you would see that the mind is far more important. It holds all the information of who we are and how we act. It processes everything we think and believe and controls how that information is applied physically. The body is merely a vehicle for the brain. So be more aware of the power of your mind. Be aware of the things that are troubling you so you can let them go. After that, focus on what you want because when you can picture something and believe in it, you can create it, without a doubt.

Anything you dream and believe can be achieved. Your mind is capable of powerful things. Keep it open; stay awake. Life is truly amazing and there is so much we don't yet understand.

"Natural forces within us are the true healers of disease."
—Hippocrates

NATURAL BORN HEALERS

The Healing Power of Water has brought on a great amount of awareness that has changed my life in so many ways. It gave me the tools I needed to let go of the anger I had for my brother; to move forward with forgiveness. I had held so strong to the thought that I would never want anything to do with him again, since that Christmas. Six years later, an excerpt from the book completely and immediately changed my perspective, like someone flipped on the light in a pitch-black room. It explained how love and fear are the only two true emotions, and that all others branch off them. When we are fearful, we're lacking love; we can't experience both at the same time. These emotions, along with the others that stem from them, are what determine our levels of happiness. My happiness was put on hold while I harbored unforgiving, unloving, unnecessary energy.

Hale Dwoskin states in *The Sedona Method*,

"By placing a continual emphasis on avoiding what we fear, we call it to mind over and over again, like a perverse mantra, or a focal point for meditation, and it becomes a program limiting our happiness and freedom. Fear can prevent us from doing what we'd like or need to do because we construct elaborate 'what ifs' or expectations around taking action."

This is the reason we need to forgive. If we don't, we're being held captive by the pain that someone else, or even ourselves, has inflicted. It deteriorates our minds and eventually, our bodies. I chose to abandon the happiness that comes from love by allowing fear and hatred to take over. Now, I choose love. What about you, do you choose fear or love? Choose!

"We give thanks to individuals or experiences that we value. However, what about the painful, scary, and challenging people and experiences in our lives? By embracing them with the 'attitude of gratitude' we're acknowledging them as having

worth. Value gives life meaning, and with meaning we're able to transcend victimization and suffering. The most powerful people throughout all of history have endured the most difficult situations. A belief structure that every challenge is an opportunity for growth or a vehicle for spiritual awakening empowers a person to move through life in a heroic fashion."
—Masaru Emoto, *The Healing Power of Water*

• •

For so long, I prevented myself and my family from healing because I treated my brother as if he were nothing. I refused to see him, talk to him, or be around him. I knew it hurt them, but I was too prideful to forgive.

I used to be a *very* prideful person. It's caused a lot of conflict in my life. A little pride is not a bad thing, though. It's when you have too much of it that it ends up defeating your soul. As the character Marsellus Wallace said in the movie *Pulp Fiction*, "The night of the fight, you may feel a slight sting. That's pride fucking with you. *Fuck pride*. Pride only hurts. It never helps. You fight through that shit." Holding onto pride only causes more problems. When you let your pride go, you've already won.

At first, I justified that disregarding my brother wasn't selfish because of all the years I had been hurt by his behavior. In retrospect, it was selfish! While I haven't welcomed him back into my life with open arms, I have forgiven him by showing him love, not hate, by acknowledging his soul, and by being grateful for what he has bestowed upon my life, *as crazy as that may sound*. Honestly, forgiving him was mostly for me; to free myself of the pain and anger that I carried daily. It was like the feeling of going from a pounding, debilitating headache, to complete euphoria in seconds. An amazing, enlightening, comforting feeling took over my body. Is it hard to understand how I let go like that after so long? The lessons I had learned woke me up again. I recognized that the past was once again,

NATURAL BORN HEALERS

weighing on my life. I was hurting myself by letting this grudge take hold of me. I gave his wrongdoings value by understanding that as devastating as they were at the time, in the long run they made me a stronger person. Sal made me grow up "hard;" he contributed to my strength, and for that I *am* grateful. Suffering is the greatest teacher; it helped me to learn, grow, and change for the better. Everyone can do this. It's up to each person to free themselves from their own suffering.

> IT'S UP TO EACH PERSON TO FREE THEMSELVES FROM THEIR OWN SUFFERING.

The most incredible part of letting go and forgiving is that I now want to know my brother better. He's at a different place in his life, and I'm at a different place in mine, and I feel it's time in *our* lives, to finally be friends. That's a big deal! I would never have allowed that thought to cross my mind in the past. Do you see how inviting love in changes everything?

• •

Finally, after all those years, we talked about that Christmas night. He told me how indescribably horrible he felt and still does, and how he was completely out of his mind. I was angry for so long and I honestly didn't want to try to understand it. I wanted to be angry and write him off. I knew he was a good-hearted person inside. I knew he loved his parents. I knew he had issues, but I still didn't get it. Drugs…Drugs fuck people up. Alcohol fucks people up. Unhealed trauma fucks people up. He was psychologically unstable on top of being incorrectly medicated AND on drugs. The result of that combination was unfortunate; it was traumatizing for my family. But now, I have heard and felt his guilt for the first time, for myself, and it healed me. I was finally able to put to rest that last bit of excruciating anger. I was finally able to love my brother unconditionally. Please, take something from this. Never write people off without hearing them out. They may just hold the key that heals you. YOU may just hold the key that heals YOU BOTH.

SUPERHUMAN

• •

We should not only embrace those with similar vibrations but acknowledge everyone who was put in our path, because they're our teachers as well as our students. We learn our lessons for ourselves first, so that we can then help others. We're all here for each other. Forgiving is learning. Forgiving is love. Forgiving is healing the world.

> "...It's important for each individual to work to change their patterns of thought, emotion or habit that keeps their field from being open to the ongoing healing energies of life. One main blockage, if not the central one, is an event that hasn't been forgiven."
> —Shannon McRae, Ph.D.

I've also forgiven both of my parents for the things that have happened, because the way life developed wasn't their fault. The cycle of negativity brings everyone's lives down. No one is at fault for anything they've done if they aren't consciously aware that it's wrong. People are who they are and do what they do because of their upbringing and life experiences. What matters is that we all wake up and choose to live life to the fullest. We can't do that if we're ignoring the truth about ourselves. Make a conscious effort to correct your faults and don't blame others for theirs! Learn to look inside yourself for answers. If more people could understand what I do now, we can change the world. No bullshit.

• •

If you're holding onto something, LET IT GO. Just get over it! We all need to JUST GET OVER IT. The person you're truly hurting by keeping a grudge is yourself. When you've awakened to that fact, you can dig deeper into your mind to see the bigger picture of what that experience *really* did for you.

NATURAL BORN HEALERS

Think about the worst thing someone's done. Is it still affecting you? If so, say out loud that you forgive them; release them and free yourself. How? Use The Sedona Method™. Ask yourself what is your now feeling? Could you welcome that feeling? Could you let it go? Would you let it go? When? Some of that burden, if not all, should be lifted and you should feel lighter. Also, be aware that whatever that person did to you, it was not your fault. As explained in *The Four Agreements*, the actions of others have nothing to do with you and everything to do with them. We each have our own "dream" or vision of the world from the things we've learned and internalized. Life is totally different through each set of eyes. Therefore, when someone does something you can't understand or that you don't like, you can't judge them, and you can't blame yourself! Their actions come from their agreements about themselves and about life. We form a grudge when we take in another person's bad energy, words, or actions, and allow them to affect us. Until you release the emotion that's tied to that grudge, you're unreasonably torturing yourself. Stop it.

• •

No one is perfect and there will always be some people who have more troubles than others. Everyone turns out differently because of their life experiences. Maybe the person who wronged you had terrible things happen to them; if you think about it that way, your feelings will become less of a burden. Think about how you would never do to someone what they did to you and that can show you what kind of person *you* are. Then understand how the situation has brought something into your life besides pain. It may have brought you light and awareness about yourself or others. It might show you the type of person to look out for, or how to get through it if the situation happens again. Don't punish yourself because you can't control others; You can control your own mind! Be happy. Forgiveness is vital to our wellbeing; it's a necessary step to happiness. I forgave my brother because he's just a soul in a body whose life experiences and feelings made him act certain ways. We're not here to judge; we're here to love. I know how hard it is to look past what others have done, but if you do, it will pay off in the end. One act of love will lead to many more in return. Also, DO NOT REGRET. You must let go of your past so you can enjoy your present. There's no time like this very moment, and how you move forward in it will change your future. How do you want to end up?

• •

I'm sad to say that before I published this book, my brother passed away. It was sudden, it was unexpected, it was heartbreaking. We all love and miss him terribly. He was a beautiful soul, yet a tortured human. He's free now, uncovering all the mysteries of the universe for which he so badly wanted the answers. We know he's in an amazing place now and that gives us peace. Of course, it's changed our lives forever. Over the last two years, Sal and I had finally become friends, sharing knowledge, stories, and beautiful insights about life. All those years of not speaking was time we lost in negative feelings. From the beginning, I should have been his friend and he should have been mine. We were both lonely, lost people living in the same house together, sharing the same blood. It made no sense. A grudge is pointless and detrimental. In the end, it's not worth it...it's really not. You expect people to always be here, so when they're not and never will be again, you almost can't grasp their absence. Our human experience causes us to have trouble understanding physical death, but if we are open spiritually, we can have some closure. I can't imagine experiencing this tragedy without knowing there's more out there, without allowing myself to still see my brother's presence here on earth. However, it does hit me at random times, and I can't believe he's gone. I can't believe I didn't just love him unconditionally, always, while he was here. I know there was a greater plan for you, Sal. I love you, and I always have. You will always be my big brother. Love and light to your soul, your life, and your memory.

NATURAL BORN HEALERS

• •

Please remember to love yourself and to love others. We're all here learning, and we can learn a lot faster when we help each other. I've heard that we should stick to people on the same vibrational level as we are. While I agree with that somewhat, I also strongly believe in helping others who have fallen.

Loss of a loved one is the most profound tragedy in our human experience. Don't lose faith in people. Heal yourself, then help heal others. We never know how long we have with each other, so let's make our time together as loving as possible.

• •

There are many wonders of spiritual and emotional healing and you should not only be aware of them, but you should be able to use them. They can drastically improve your life. As much positive influence as we may have on our own thoughts, we're still living in a very negative world. We try to block negativity from entering our mind, but it seeps in anyway, making its way to our subconscious like ants to a crumb. In the hectic world we live in, it's important to have a mental and spiritual practice. I believe wholeheartedly in meditation.

• •

Let's try something: Go sit outside. Sit or lay down comfortably, whichever feels the most relaxing. Sink into the earth. Let every muscle in your body and face melt. Close your eyes. Listen to, feel, and appreciate every noise and sensation around you. Forget your thoughts; tune into your senses. Is the wind caressing your skin? Do you hear birds chirping? Whatever you hear or don't hear, just be. Relax in the appreciation of being alive in this very moment, being able to experience life. Stay in this space for however long you choose. And when you are ready to come back, come back slowly and gracefully by wiggling your fingers, your toes, eventually opening your eyes. How do you feel? I'll bet you feel good right now. Why? You just meditated!

Meditating will put your mind at ease and block stressors. It shoos away the voice of the ego, allowing your jumbled thoughts to rest. When you meditate, find a place where you can relax and let go mentally and physically. You would close your eyes, slow your heart rate by taking long, deep breaths, surrender your body, and allow yourself to be guided from within and from above. You can reach a state where you concentrate on your inner self. When you've practiced this and eventually become skilled, you can access your subconscious mind. You can discover information about yourself from it and even feed it information (i.e., I love myself; I am happy; I am free; I am healthy; I am strong; I am accomplishing my goals.)

> **MEDITATING WILL PUT YOUR MIND AT EASE AND BLOCK STRESSORS.**

Many people believe it's possible to restore the original blueprint of our genes through mediation. In fact, the medical community is starting to recognize its benefits and encouraging patients to meditate. Let's ALL meditate, every day, even if only for a few minutes! It's so healthy, so healing, so peaceful …and *believe me*, we need more peace. Imagine if the whole world stopped what they were doing and meditated at the same time. What if just a crazy-large number of people did? Something unbelievable would happen. It's one of my goals to make that come true. Imagine the healing, restoring, balancing energy field around all those people, around all of us.

Meditation brings an awareness to the soul. It brings love. When you can connect to the "inner you," all the nonsense, hatred, anger, and fear don't exist! Love forms the core of our beings and we forget that when we're not "present" in life.

• •

NATURAL BORN HEALERS

Practicing yoga can contribute to a meditative state. I prefer Hot yoga. I tend to meditate before I practice to prepare myself, and then after, to unwind. Hot yoga is more of a physical healing that brings on spiritual healing, but I believe all types of yoga are beneficial.

In hot yoga, the stretching and pulling of the body into different poses helps release toxins and allows fresh blood to circulate. Some positions are strenuous, but that's why the room temperature is over 100 degrees; the heat helps your muscles to relax so they're not strained.

I would recommend yoga to anyone who wants to challenge their mind and body. While your body can feel like it's going to give out, that's mostly mental. Once you get through your first class, you'll feel you can take on anything, emotionally or physically.

• •

Another form of healing is Reiki. It's a practice that can help you to heal spiritually, physically, and emotionally. Do you remember Mr. Miyagi in *The Karate Kid*, healing Daniel's injuries by doing something with his hands? I watched that movie many times when I was little and I remember thinking during that part, *Why did they put this made up stuff in this movie?* It was cool but it didn't make sense to me. Now it makes perfect sense; I get it.

Children often believe in the magic and mysteries of this world, but I couldn't wrap my programmed little head around what Mr. Miyagi did. I questioned it for a second, thinking, *Maybe this is real?* But I went right back to what I knew—the doctor, the medicine, the surgery—I didn't understand the factual presence of energy and its MAGICAL healing abilities. Do you? Do you know anything about Reiki?

Reiki focuses on healing and balancing our life-force, our bodies, and our minds through **intention**. A treatment can help align the chakras, which are energy centers along the body that make up a life force energy. When a person is willing and open, a practitioner can help clear the chakras and initiate healing. Balance is disrupted by negative energy, life experiences, emotions, and trauma. For instance, the root chakra can become unbalanced from negative sexual experiences. When a chakra is unbalanced, our entire body will be too, because the chakras run vertically through us. Have you ever heard someone say their energy is low? That person was probably not only worn out but imbalanced as well. When the Chi (life energy) is disrupted, it can be from many problems such as fears, worry, stress, or past traumatic events (past or present life)—basically flowing, negative energy that's trapped within, or a blockage of "flow."

• •

The Reiki practitioner will usually call on energy from above and from their inner being. It's categorized as "light work," because spiritual guidance helps the energy move through the conduit (practitioner). As it begins to flow, the practitioner places their hands either on or above the person or animal receiving the treatment. They will move their hands around the body, usually along the chakras unless there are specific areas that need work (if not known, the conduit will usually be guided to them). The energy is charged and transferred by the **intention** of healing.

My cousin, who is certified, did my first treatment. It was astonishing. When she was done, I had an unbelievable feeling of peace flowing through me. It was almost like there was an invisible shield surrounding my body and nothing bad could penetrate. Honestly, I felt high. I remember thinking, *Even if I wanted to pick a fight with someone right now, I absolutely couldn't!*

She told me I had a good session with a lot of healing and mostly concentrated on my head by my third eye chakra (the center of intuition and foresight) because there was an incredible amount of energy coming from it, so much that her hands were "sweating." I felt the heat too, but I thought her hands were just hot!

NATURAL BORN HEALERS

We also discussed the similar, somewhat dark imagery we both saw. It happened while she was working on that same chakra which made perfect sense; there was something there that needed to be released. However, even with all the healing that I've done so far with my body and soul, there are still things buried deep inside me, things that trouble me. That's why I'm working on myself every day to get mentally stronger. Do you see how much we need to do and how important it is? Everyone is a work in progress, and we all need healing.

• •

After experiencing Reiki I'm convinced that everyone on this earth needs to try it. You can find wellness centers that offer it, some doctors do it, and sometimes you can find it at other random places, like spas. I do it and you can learn to do it too. I got certified because there was no turning back after learning, seeing, and EXPERIENCING how amazing "light work" is and how it's changing the world. I wanted to take part in that healing! Everyone has the ability and can become certified by taking courses. It's all about calling energy from a higher power, using pure intentions. If even a small percentage of the population experienced what I did, it would have a tremendous positive effect on everyone else!

> REIKI IS ALL ABOUT CALLING ENERGY FROM A HIGHER POWER, USING PURE INTENTIONS.

I'd also like to add that *combined* with Reiki, "letting go" via The Sedona Method™ is tremendous. Both are ways to release energy and one can be done without the other. However, your healing process will advance more quickly if you use them together.

• •

DNA activation is another form of healing that activates our dormant strands or "junk DNA." It unlocks our healing abilities and allows us to access our full potential, merging our consciousness of the divine and the physical. I had it done and felt amazing during and after. My body was tingling (vibrating) as the activation was taking place.

There is more than one way to activate our dormant DNA. The method I used called upon guidance from the Archangels and it was *so* edifying. My mind and body were energetically communicating with someone from above. I felt it!

As we're being pulled by a force to bring our lives back in tune with the universe, the more people who have this activation done, the more we can speed the process along in others. It opens your mind to a broader consciousness and gives you the ability to energetically share it, just like we share our moods with those around us.

• •

Learning and believing in different healing modalities keeps our mind open and allows our consciousness to expand in many directions. It's like trying to solve a problem and being knowledgeable enough to think there is probably more than one way to tackle it. If I were to tell strangers the things I've experienced and learned, they'd think I was loony! But I know I'm not. Being able to see that you look crazy from another person's perspective tells you that you're *not* because you recognize their side of things; you have "listened to both arguments," but because of the power of your intuition, the truth is undeniable.

> **BELIEVING IN DIFFERENT HEALING MODALITIES KEEPS THE MIND OPEN AND ALLOWS OUR CONSCIOUSNESS TO EXPAND.**

Communication with Archangels is very real to me. I've experienced it. Personal angelic messages that no one else could have known to say or understood have been channeled to me through healers during sessions of acupressure, meditation, Reiki, and intuition classes. Any workshop or meditative healing that calls upon the guidance of Archangels is a mind-expanding, genuine, and touching experience. It has certainly changed my life and can change yours if you're open enough to receive it.

We are all watched over, we are all loved, and the saddest thing is…people don't know it. When you choose to believe, you choose to be loved. You CHOOSE to heal.

• •

Fasts and cleanses are also healing processes. People look at them as torture, but they can be very consciously comforting (spiritual), not to mention good for your health. Yes, good! It's a fact that animals fast when they're sick. Humans need to do it once in a while too, to allow our bodies to heal themselves. It gives our digestive system a break and it also clears the mind. When I do fasts and advanced cleanses, I start to see life differently from anyone else. I see the world in ways that others don't. One of my first 14-day fasts was quite an experience. While it was rough, it was also enlightening.

• •

If you're interested in doing a fast or cleanse, start with something easy. Try juicing for a day. Have freshly squeezed or pressed juices. If that's easy for you and you can take it further, do so. If you're unsure about it because of your current state of health, consult your doctor (or a naturopath) first. Read about the benefits of fasting to understand why a fast is important, as well as how and when to do one.

• •

Detoxification is a key to healthy living. Time is not the death of us, the time disease has to develop is![23] If we keep our bodies healthy at a cellular level, meaning we keep the fluid around our cells flowing efficiently and keep our minds healthy, our time on this earth may be endless. The truth is, there's more evidence that we're supposed to live forever than evidence that we're supposed to die.

---

23 http://www.aboutclay.com/info/uses/detox.htm

SUPERHUMAN

• •

Obviously, there's more to the life I lead than physical health. Living a raw lifestyle means keeping the mind healthy as well as the body. It's actually more important to get your mind right FIRST so everything else can change without too much resistance. While we experience negativity every day, we can control most of what influences us if we're mentally prepared. Remember, focus only on the good and that's what you shall receive. When you master that, you have changed something major within yourself. Things that you once thought never could happen, are the things that begin to happen when you call them into existence. They're called miracles—beautiful synchronicities which are mistakenly regarded as uncommon or unbelievable, but only by those who are lacking faith.

"You see things; and you say 'Why?' But I dream things that never were; and I say 'Why not?'"
—George Bernard Shaw

Faith is one of the most powerful things in this world. It's how miracles occur! It's how *many* miracles can occur in *your* life! When we have positive thoughts or goals and truly believe in them, they transpire into something real. The average thinker might say, "How is that even possible?" It has to do with the fact that this whole world and every being is made up of energy and matter (slowed down energy). Intention (the minds desire) is just energy that influences other energy. Every wave of consciousness you send out is sent back to you! Every person, creature, plant, or thing around you is influenced by your vibrational (physical or emotional) input. The science that explains this in depth is quantum physics. Basically, at the smallest scales of recognizing all particles in nature, we find energy; every object, living or not, is vibrating with a certain frequency.

• •

NATURAL BORN HEALERS

• •

We bring in the moving energy or vibrations that surround us and then put back them out into the world. Whether it's negative or positive, when we use it constructively and to our advantage, we can create anything. Like what I did to spark the change in my life…I realized that I needed to switch up my attitude in order to switch up everything else! That's exactly what I'm doing: CHANGING. I hold all the power. YOU hold all the power in *your* life.

Two books that make this process clear as day are *You're The Best!*, by Frank Nicoletti, and *Think and Grow Rich*, by Napoleon Hill. After reading them, I was dumbfounded by the things I learned. These books have changed my life and my understanding of the power of my mind. They assisted in my transformation into a **Superhuman** by changing my average human thought process. Our brains are more than computers that merely store knowledge; they actively create our fate! If someone had told me this information years ago, I would have thought they were ready to board their UFO. Even if you're not an avid reader, you'll be glad you read these books because you'll finally understand the way life works. The knowledge which comes from their messages is beyond anything we were taught in school.

> YOU HOLD ALL THE POWER IN YOUR LIFE.

School …excuse me while I laugh. If you're still questioning your capabilities at this point, question this: Why do we go through years of schooling only to come out with all this information we can't even use in the real world, information that is so ridiculous, that overcrowds our minds? When our minds are opened through awareness, we realize that kind of information is not what's important. Why are we not taught the most important things—how to love ourselves, how to be happy, and how to eat right? Why aren't we taught how powerful the brain is? Why aren't we taught how to find our passions or encouraged to act on them? Why aren't we taught how to plan and achieve goals? They want us to go out there and get a "good job," but give us no real direction on how to actually obtain it! Could it be the need to control us? That not wanting us to be too powerful, or to even know we are, kind of thing? Think about it. Getting it? Then fuck all the nonsense you learned; that's the past. There's no time like today to learn to stop *only* existing and start living.

• •

It's hard for me to sum up everything I've learned because there's just so much to say. It's probably even harder for someone reading this to believe me, but don't let your ego limit your mind and tell you, *That's impossible.* Be open to new possibilities and they will come. I encourage you to dig deeper and learn new things that will blow your mind and possibly make you rich in all kinds of ways. Read the books I've mentioned because they hold the keys to health, success, peace, and most importantly, happiness. They tie into one another, allowing you to see the true purpose of your existence on this earth. Once you know, you'll be able to truly live.

> "You may control your own mind. You have the power to feed it whatever thought impulses you choose. With this privilege goes also the responsibility of using it constructively. You are the master of your own earthly destiny just as surely as you have the power to control your own thoughts. You may influence, direct, and eventually control your own environment, making your life what you want it to be—or, you may neglect to exercise the privilege which is yours, to make your life to order thus casting yourself upon the broad sea of "circumstance" where you will be tossed hither and yon, like a chip on the waves of the ocean."
> —Napoleon Hill, *Think and Grow Rich*

NATURAL BORN HEALERS

• •

For most of my life I've been unhappy, unhappy with myself and unhappy with my circumstances. I was stubborn. I thought I knew everything. I thought the world was what it was, and the future was unpromising. Yes, I've had some hardships in my life, and by sharing them in this book, I am not looking for pity or reward. I'm aware that there are people who go through a lot worse, so I don't feel bad for myself and I don't expect anyone else to either. My goal has been to show you the big picture. No matter what disgusting, heartbreaking, unimaginable things lie in your past, SUFFERING CONTINUES BECAUSE YOU ALLOW IT TO CONTINUE. When I finally figured this out, I woke the fuck up for the first time in my life. The hard to swallow but honest and totally freeing truth is that…most of my suffering was caused by me! Most of *your* suffering, is caused by you! I wholeheartedly support the fact that each person's life *can* and WILL change according to their active mindset. Do and learn! Learn and do! Learn to find a lesson, a blessing, and an opportunity in everything! You don't have to go through this journey feeling sad and alone. If you keep your head high, take care of yourself, and stay true to your nature YOU WILL OVERCOME ANYTHING.

Faith is a powerful force. If you keep it with you, you'll always be free, free from negative thoughts, free from others' negativity, and free to be happy. Life is what you make of it. No matter how hard it might get, keep yourself strong so nothing and no one can ever knock you down. YOU—yes, you—are capable of anything.

It's important to be the best you that you can be. You are the most powerful in life when you do what's right: being healthy, mentally strong, loving, and undefeatable when it comes to your dreams! Are you ready to do things the right way?

This life is here for us to enjoy, not destroy. It's not until a storm comes and washes everything away that we see the foundation, the earth, and are reminded that it controls *us* right now, not the other way around. So along with our own personal evolution, it's also imperative to change how we treat others—other people and other living things, the earth included. We're so blinded by our fancy technology and comfortable homes that we forget what's real: something bigger than us. These material things and our egotistical ways can't make us happy. There's a deeper reason for us to be here! We need to respect that and appreciate it by expressing love and gratitude for the wind, the sky, the water, the land, and every living thing on the earth. Let's rebuild this planet, along with our minds and bodies, and take control of how we want things to be.

Not everything can change overnight, but the more people who change their lives for the better, the better everything else can be. It forms a ripple effect. When one person switches up their life and attitude, their energy and awareness spreads to others around them. Every good decision, every act of kindness or good deed for the world changes a person's predisposed path, and brings them closer to their soul's completion. If they continue to do bad things or to allow bad things to happen, nothing changes, and they will probably have to work out their karmic debts in another time, in another body. If they continue choosing steps in the direction of love, they won't have to keep living through the pain or let others they affect, live through it either. Those who understand this will be able influence a large amount of people, and this energetic shift will happen more quickly than imagined.

> **THE MORE PEOPLE WHO CHANGE THEIR LIVES FOR THE BETTER, THE BETTER EVERYTHING ELSE CAN BE.**

I've always been able to feel things. I feel strongly that change needs to start now to save this world from what's to come, to fix the wrong things we do to our bodies, our minds, the earth, and everything living on it. The destruction of man is not inevitable. We have the power to stop it, to turn it all around. Start this change by changing yourself for the better RIGHT NOW.

NATURAL BORN HEALERS

"If we don't permit the earth to produce beauty and joy, it will in the end not produce food, either."
—Joseph Wood Krutch

• •

Tips for a successful **personal "Superhuman" transformation**:
1. Discover through self-observation what in your past is holding you back.
2. Let it go (forgiveness, acceptance, love, gratitude, and lots of releasing).
3. Learn to heal your negative mindset.
4. Surrender to the moment.
5. Remain optimistic (re-train your brain if you're pessimistic).
6. Love yourself; know who you are and why you're here.
7. Do what's right for *your* life.
8. Spread love, not fear or hate.
9. Respect animals. Give up meat and dairy.
10. Respect this earth and contribute to its healing.
11. Figure out if you are making the **when, how much**, or **what** mistakes with eating.
12. Correct your eating habits after getting to the root of them through self-observation.
13. Research the benefits of raw food.
14. Detoxify your body.
15. Eat raw (incorporate as much of it as you can into your diet if you're not going 100% raw).
16. Live life with love and be happy!

• •

You are special. You are loved. *You* are the master of your own earthly destiny. When you pursue your dreams, everything comes to you in the most surprising, unexpected ways, and your ability to see life becomes more and more clear. Information and opportunities begin to flow to you in abundance. How? By **believing.** While that may seem like such a vague answer, it's true and there's no way to explain it enough for you to understand, unless you experience it for yourself. Nothing in this book can probably be received in its full nature unless it's experienced, but the truth is, your unlimited potential unfolds when you believe in it and put your plan into action. Resistance is anything or anyone you let hinder you from believing and achieving. Embrace what is special about you, let yourself believe, let yourself finally…be free.

CHAPTER 16

THE END...BUT JUST THE BEGINNING

E ven the most painful wounds heal over time. It's a power within yourself that can ameliorate them faster. All you need is your own inner strength, which is love. Until you return to love-filled thinking and acting, your talents are wasted, your powers are wasted, your happiness is wasted; YOUR TIME ON THIS EARTH IS WASTED. You will be set free at death, but, wouldn't you rather be free now? Have faith in yourself and faith in this world. Believe in the good things that you want to happen, and they will.

• •

I suffered much heartache and dwelled on it for a good portion of my existence. Regretting my past, whether it was a boyfriend, a girlfriend, or a family situation, made me lose hope in life. As a result, I lost myself. When I finally opened my eyes and saw it all as a learning experience instead of a tragedy, I was able to heal. I've learned that people come and go but they all leave an impact. Whether the impact is good or bad, it's what we do with it that counts. I've learned if we keep love with us at all times, everything will unfold beautifully.

SUPERHUMAN

I've learned that headaches, heartaches, and bellyaches don't affect us unless we allow them. I've learned that regret is an unrealistic burden; our pasts don't exist anymore. I've learned there is far more about this world that we don't know, and we should never lose hope; we should always have faith. Using all this constructively, I've rebuilt the person who allowed all these people and experiences to tear down, into a steel machine. I'm now stronger than I ever thought I could be as I create my own future and live with nothing but love in my heart. I want you to have that strength as well. You're entitled to it.

> REGRET IS AN UNREALISTIC BURDEN; OUR PASTS DON'T EXIST ANYMORE.

Sharing my experiences with all of you proves that I am stronger than my fears. It's always been difficult to talk about my life with ANYONE, but I **feel** it's what I need to do. I had a burning desire to help myself and now I have a forest fire sized desire, to help others. Guiding ourselves, then guiding each other …THAT'S WHAT WE'RE HERE FOR. I probably sound a little crazy to some of you, and I've revealed some things about my life, but this is my story and I'm all for sharing it if it can help someone else. I'm not ashamed, and I don't want my family to feel ashamed for the things that happened. When I decided to put that pen to paper, I didn't hold back in fear of judgement. I went all in with faith in change. The past is what it was, and it doesn't matter now. What matters is our self-reinvention in the present. Everyone has problems, and we shouldn't feel bad about them unless we make no effort toward resolution. We overcome our problems through personal empowerment brought on by newfound self-awareness, spirituality, love, and good decisions. Start fresh today and finally end up happy, where you belong. You deserve happiness! Our world deserves peace!

There's a reason I was given the books I've mentioned, and I know there's a reason I'm supposed to share them with you. The fact

THE END ...BUT JUST THE BEGINNING

is, this all works! I'm not telling you this is true because someone else said it was, I've proved it in my own life. But don't take my word... as Sonny in *A Bronx Tale* says, "Believe none of what you hear and only half of what you see." Allow yourself to be the scientist and **experience** the results. Your personal conclusion will be your truth.

• •

I have one last task for you: Dig deep down right now and be real with yourself. Ask for the truth. *Do I believe any of this? Can I do this?* You can feel it, can't you? It's not easy to hide; it always comes to light. Just because we ignore a feeling or shove it way down, it doesn't mean it doesn't exist anymore! The things I've talked about in this book will be the most obvious, easiest things to comprehend once you get it. But you won't *get it* until you GET IT. Get it? Until you do the work! Prove it, find the truth, experience it ...and then shed the light for others. Historic revolutions like the end of slavery or the women's rights movement didn't happen because of ignorance, fear, or people being stuck in their ways. They happened because some people **felt** the truth and were brave enough to step up and do something. They changed everything. They believed in a new life and created it. So if you're with me and the many others who dream of changing this damaged, yet repairable world, then start by changing yourself. Let's march together in this new-world revolution. Let's do things right so that peace, joy, and love can live, and fear can finally perish.

I dream of making my mark on the raw food world one day. I want to do everything in my power to help others and to make a great change in this world. You too, can help make this change. We're all connected and all share energy; we have the power to spiritually guide others by being an example. Don't put your life on hold or in death's grip for another minute. To quote Mahatma Gandhi, "We but mirror the world. All the tendencies present in the outer world are to be found in the world of our body. If we could change ourselves, the tendencies in the world would also change. As a man changes his own nature, so does the attitude of the world change towards him. This is the divine mystery supreme. A wonderful thing it is and the source of our happiness. We need not wait to see what others do." Embody the change!

• •

If you want to make this change, the transformation into a **SUPERHUMAN**, if you want to be healthy, successful, happy, and enjoy life, in **this lifetime**... DO NOT pass up what I'm passing onto you right now. EMBRACE the knowledge. There's a reason you read this book.

With love, light, and gratitude,
Katie G

"When you work simply for yourself or for your own personal gain your mind will seldom rise above the limitations of the undeveloped personal life; but when you are inspired by some great purpose, some extraordinary project, all your thoughts break bounds; your mind transcends limitations; your consciousness expands in every direction; and you find yourself in a new world, a great world, a wonderful world; dormant powers, faculties and talents become alive, and you discover yourself to be a larger man by far than you ever dreamed yourself to be."
—Christian D. Larson, *Business Psychology*, 1912

BOOKS

Fox, Elaine. *Rainy Brain, Sunny Brain: the New Science of Optimism and Pessimism.* Arrow Books, 2013.

Weiss, Brian L. *Many Lives, Many Masters ; Messages from the Masters.* One Spirit, 2002.

Russo PhD, Ruthann. *The Raw Food Lifestyle: The Philosophy and Nutrition behind Raw and Live Foods.* Berkeley: North Atlantic Books, 2009.

Masaru Emoto. *The Healing Power of Water.* Hay House Inc., 2004.

Hill, Napoleon. *Think and Grow Rich.* Tribecca Books, 2010.

Nicoletti, Frank. *You're The Best.* Lincoln: iUniverse, 2001

Dwoskin, Hale. *The Sedona Method.* Sedona Press, 2003.

Ruiz, don Miguel. *The Four Agreements.* Amber-Allen Publishing, Inc., 1997.

Williamson, Marianne. *A Return to Love: Reflections on the Principles of a Course in Miracles.* HarperOne, 2012.

Meyerowitz, Steve. *Juice Fasting & Detoxification: Use the Healing Power of Fresh Juice to Feel Young and Look Great.* Book Publishing Company, 2002.

Billinghurst, Ian. *Give Your Dog a Bone: the Practical Commonsense Way to Feed Dogs for a Long Healthy Life.* Ian Billinghurst, 1993.

MacDonald, Carina Beth. *Raw Dog Food: Make It Easy for You and Your Dog.* Dogwise Pub., 2004.

Lonsdale, Tom. *Work Wonders: Feed Your Dog Raw Meaty Bones.* Rivetco, 2005.

THE KEY TO LIFE:

LET GO OF EVERYTHING THAT'S EVER HAPPENED TO YOU AND LIVE LIKE YOU WERE RE-BORN IN THIS VERY MOMENT. KEEP YOUR MIND OPEN TO THE IMPOSSIBLE AND IT WILL BECOME POSSIBLE. CREATE YOUR OWN DESTINY. LOVE YOURSELF UNCONDITIONALLY AND LOVE ALL MISTAKES. LOVE OTHERS AND FORGIVE THEM. BE IMMPECABLE WITH EVERY SINGLE WORD THAT COMES OUT OF YOUR MOUTH. TAKE CARE OF YOURSELF ON EVERY LEVEL, IN EVERY WAY, MIND, BODY, AND SOUL. TAKE CARE OF OTHERS, TAKE CARE OF ANIMALS, AND TAKE CARE OF THE EARTH. LIVE PEACEFULLY, LIVE ABUNDANTLY, AND LIVE FREE. BE HAPPY.

A LITTLE ABOUT ME...

...AND A LOT ABOUT YOU

Since I was little, I've always had a strong desire to do what I wanted, and no one could tell me anything. Constantly running barefoot, taking my shirt off when the boys did, refusing to wear sunscreen, climbing furniture to get what I wanted, making up my own words, and picking out my own outfits, *even if that meant a wool skirt in the summer,* I felt free when life was in my control. Anything unnatural or against my free will felt agonizing. That's still the case.

In high school, I had no clue where I was going to college or what I would be studying, when everyone else seemed to have it all figured out. I didn't know what I wanted be for the *rest of my life.* Everyone would say, "Just be a teacher," but that never sat well with me. Could I really be a teacher forever? I didn't want to settle; there was always something burning inside me, telling me, *You're meant to do something big.* I didn't know what that was, but for some reason, I just knew it was going to be something that had nothing to do with anything I learned in school.

When college came, I "spun the wheel" to pick classes. I thought, *Why am I here? This is a waste of time and money* ...until I took a creative writing class. A flame ignited in me—that familiar burning desire. It was a desire to be heard in a way that would not only exorcise my demons, but clear someone else's house too! I wanted to be a writer; I *always* wanted to be a writer. The class gave me the push I needed to put my dreams into action by showing me that it's ok to be open, because my story *can* help someone.

Years earlier, I started a book, but never thought I could get it out there without a million and one fears attached to it. During the class, everyone would share their deepest, darkest stories, but I sat there quietly, looking like I didn't have any of my own. How could I put my experiences and feelings out there for the world to see when I had been programmed my entire life to be terrified of that? How could I tell my family's story without them resenting me? How could I do this? How could I do that? That's when the desire took over my *whole* being, and my fears fell away. I didn't know how I was going to accomplish my goal, but I knew I would accomplish it. I started writing more, experiencing more, and learning more, until I had what I have now: a message of hope for anyone who needs it.

I dream that my message will travel far beyond this book to wherever it needs to go. I dream of making unconventional moves in our stagnant world. I dream of health and happiness for all, and not to sound like a beauty queen, but world peace. We're all entitled and capable of happiness. Coming from someone who thought happiness was impossible, I hope it says something to you. Wishing you love and light and sending you lots of gratitude for reading my book, I hope you awaken to the truth so that all your dreams can come to fruition. Everything that happened to me, happened *for* me, to help you.

www.ingramcontent.com/pod-product-compliance
Lightning Source LLC
Chambersburg PA
CBHW071342290426
44108CB00014B/1416